The Forex Trading Course

A Self-Study Guide to Becoming A Successful Currency Trader

ABE COFNAS

John Wiley & Sons, Inc.

Published by John Wiley & Sons, Inc., Hoboken, New Jersey.
Published simultaneously in Canada.

Wiley Bicentennial Logo: Richard J. Pacifico

Library of Congress Cataloging-in-Publication Data:
Cofnas, Abe, 1950–
The Forex trading course : a self-study guide to becoming a successful currency trader / Abe Cofnas.
p. cm. — (Wiley trading series)
Includes index.
ISBN 978-0-470-13764-2 (pbk.)
1. Foreign exchange futures. 2. Foreign exchange market. 3. Speculation.
I. Title.
HG3853.C64 2008
332.4′5–dc22 2007019251

Printed in the United States of America

10 9 8 7 6 5 4 3

The Forex Trading Course

Founded in 1807, John Wiley & Sons is the oldest independent publishing company in the United States. With offices in North America, Europe, Australia, and Asia, Wiley is globally committed to developing and marketing print and electronic products and services for our customers' professional and personal knowledge and understanding.

The Wiley Trading series features books by traders who have survived the market's ever-changing temperament and have prospered—some by reinventing systems, others by getting back to basics. Whether a novice trader, professional, or somewhere in between, these books will provide the advice and strategies needed to prosper today and well into the future.

For a list of available titles, visit our Web site at www.WileyFinance.com.

This book is dedicated to my students throughout the world, who have the courage to take on the challenge of forex trading. I have learned much from them about trading and about the human condition.

Contents

Foreword

Over 30 years ago, Abe Cofnas was a student of mine at the University of California at Berkeley. At the time, I am certain to have delivered a long-held admonition: 95 percent of what you read in economics will be either wrong or irrelevant. I am pleased to report that *The Forex Trading Course* falls into the 5 percent residual category of materials that are worth reading.

In addition to satisfying those with a healthy obsession to work on improving their professional skills, *The Forex Trading Course* will force readers to think outside the box and to develop an appetite for the pursuit of knowledge about trading. This, of course, is the most important aspect of the book and reminds me of an observation made by Sir Hugh Rigby, surgeon to King George V. Sir Hugh was once asked, "What makes a great surgeon?" He replied, "There isn't much to choose between surgeons in manual dexterity. What distinguishes a great surgeon is who *knows* more than other surgeons." The same can be said for traders.

In the interest of putting the reader a leg up, an understanding of the structure of exchange-rate regimes is essential. There are three distinct types of exchange-rate regimes—floating, fixed, and pegged—each with different characteristics and different results.

Hanke's FX Trichotomy

Type of Regime	Exchange-Rate Policy	Monetary Policy	Source of Monetary Base	Conflicts between Exchange-Rate and Monetary Policy	Balance-of-Payments Crisis	Exchange Controls
Floating	No	Yes	Domestic	No	No	No
Fixed	Yes	No	Foreign	No	No	No
Pegged	Yes	Yes	Domestic and Foreign	Yes	Yes	Maybe

Although floating and fixed rates appear dissimilar, they are members of the same free-market family. Both operate without exchange controls and are free-market mechanisms for balance-of-payments adjustments. With a floating rate, a central bank sets a monetary policy but has no exchange-rate policy—the exchange rate is on autopilot. In consequence, the monetary base is determined domestically by a central bank. With a fixed rate, there are two possibilities: either a currency board sets the exchange rate but has no monetary policy—the money supply is on autopilot—or a country is "dollarized" and uses a foreign currency as its own. In consequence, under a fixed-rate regime, a country's monetary base is determined by the balance of payments, moving in a one-to-one correspondence with changes in its foreign reserves. With both of these free-market, exchange-rate mechanisms, there cannot be conflicts between monetary and exchange-rate policies, and balance-of-payments crises cannot rear their ugly heads. Indeed, under floating- and fixed-rate regimes, market forces act to automatically rebalance financial flows and avert balance-of-payments crises.

Fixed and pegged rates appear to be the same. However, they are fundamentally different: pegged-rate systems often employ exchange controls and are not free-market mechanisms for international balance-of-payments adjustments. Pegged rates require a central bank to manage both the exchange rate and monetary policy. With a pegged rate, the monetary base contains both domestic and foreign components. Unlike floating and fixed rates, pegged rates invariably result in conflicts between monetary and exchange-rate policies. For example, when capital inflows become "excessive" under a pegged system, a central bank often attempts to sterilize the ensuing increase in the foreign component of the monetary base by selling bonds, reducing the domestic component of the base. And when outflows become "excessive," a central bank attempts to offset the decrease in the foreign component of the base by buying bonds, increasing the domestic component of the monetary base. Balance-of-payments crises erupt as a central bank begins to offset more and more of the reduction in the foreign component of the monetary base with domestically created base money. When this occurs, it is only a matter of time before currency speculators spot the contradictions between exchange-rate and monetary policies (as they did in the Asian financial crisis of 1997–1998) and force a devaluation or the imposition of exchange controls.

Steve H. Hanke
Professor of Applied Economics
Johns Hopkins University
Baltimore
July 2007

Preface

As forex's popularity increases to unprecedented levels, people around the world are considering its potential. There are many reasons for its popularity. First, we are truly in an online revolution, powered by the globalization of the Internet. From your desktop—whether at home, an airport, or at an Internet café—you can actually trade any of the world's currencies. The implications are profound. People can be liberated from the confines of one's economy and engage in a new profession—forex trading. Additionally, globalization of the world's economies has created great uncertainty regarding individual career paths. Individuals can no longer expect to work for one employer. Baby Boomers are facing the opportunity and challenge of post-retirement careers.

In response to forex's popularity, many new trading firms and training firms have arisen to supply services to this new group of aspiring forex traders. The result has been a cacophony of information overload, instant gurus, and instant trading solutions that appeal to those looking for shortcuts to success. These programs essentially confuse people and divert them from a realistic approach to training in forex trading.

This book is written for the purpose of providing a *getting started guide* in forex trading. It, however, is not only for the person new to forex, but for those who have tried to trade forex but received mixed results through trial and error. It is also for those who have experience in trading other markets and seek to apply that experience to forex. They will be able to build upon their experience and gain new insights into how to approach forex. Those who have achieved a level of initial success but seek to optimize their performance will find training strategies and tactics particularly useful.

The underlying premise of this book is that traders are not born—they evolve. Our goal is to sharpen the insights and the skills of the reader by providing both fundamental and technical knowledge that are common to successful traders. An underlying philosophy of this book is that successful forex trading requires a total approach that integrates fundamentals, technical analysis, and psychology.

The book is organized as a self-paced sourcebook. Each chapter topic is in essence a module of knowledge, which can be read individually or sequentially.

- Part I (Chapters 1–9) focuses on the forces that move prices, also known as fundamentals. The topics included in the fundamentals show the reader how to use fundamental knowledge to arrive at trading decisions. The chapters provide insight on how currency price movements are affected by things like interest rates, interest rate differentials, trade-weighted indexes, commodities, housing data, China, and more.
- Part II (Chapters 10–15) focus on technical knowledge—how to read and analyze charts. The reader will build specific knowledge about the components of technical analysis and how to evaluate price action in terms of classical and advanced tools including: support and resistance, retracement concepts, trend analysis, and volatility and momentum indicators. Nontraditional charting using renko and three-line break are featured.
- Part III (Chapters 16–19) provides strategies for testing one's knowledge and skills in the real world of trading. The final chapter includes 100 questions that the reader should be able to answer at that point.

Learning about trading must be interactive, so throughout the book you will find "assignments" that test your skills. They are designed to help you assess how well you understand the material and guide you in finding and using valuable information for scanning currency conditions.

Ultimately, all knowledge needs to be actionable. It is my hope that experience of trying forex trading is enhanced by this book and that forex trading becomes a journey which is enjoyable for its enormous challenges and more profitable than it otherwise would be.

Acknowledgments

This book is dedicated to the students I have encountered and had the privilege of mentoring throughout the years. I applaud them for their courage to pursue the challenges of forex trading and I have learned much from them about how to teach forex with improved effectiveness. I must acknowledge the late Professor Aaron Wildavsky, at the Graduate School of Public Policy, who shaped my thinking skills more than 30 years ago into the tools of inquiry that allowed this book to emerge.

About the Author

Abe Cofnas has been the forex trading columnist of *Futures* magazine since 2001 and has been a leader in designing and delivering forex training courses. He has conducted seminars in the United States, London, and Dubai as well as online training in all time zones. Mr. Cofnas founded www.learn4x.com in 2001 as the desktop forex trading industry started to provide education and training in this field. He recently founded www.currencygames.com, a company providing forex education and global forex competitions. He has been in the financial service industry as an equity broker, futures, and forex trader since 1990.

Mr. Cofnas holds two master's degrees, in political science from the Graduate School of Political Science, University of California, and in public policy from the University of California, Graduate School of Public Policy. He currently lives in Longwood, Florida, with his wife, Paula, where he conducts research on artificial intelligence programs using cellular automata and enjoys digital photography. He has a daughter Paige, 25, and a son Paul, 22.

The Forex Trading Course

PART I

What Drives the Forex Market?

Part I of this book offers a look at the "big picture" in foreign exchange (forex) trading, that is, what forces influence currency price movements. These forces are accepted by economists around the world as responsible for changes in the value of currencies. The person learning to trade forex or trying to improve his or her trading will benefit from a gain of knowledge of these fundamentals. In fact, as you will see, fundamental forces act as leading indicators of currency movement.

U.S. and global interest rates, economic growth, and market sentiment toward the dollar are the key ingredients that shape trading opportunities. Part I provides basic knowledge on how these factors impact forex prices and how they can be used in selecting trading opportunities.

CHAPTER 1

The Fundamentals of Forex

We begin in this chapter with an exploration of the forces that move the prices: the fundamentals. The reader will learn why fundamentals are important to foreign exchange (forex) traders as well as what kind of economic activity are most important in affecting price movements. These include interest rates, interest rate differentials, economic growth, and sentiment regarding the U.S. dollar.

WHY FUNDAMENTALS ARE IMPORTANT

In many ways, forex trading is similar to playing a game. You have an opponent (the market). In game of chance the key feature is that everyone faces the same odds and therefore the same level of information. In these games, no player can change the odds.

Playing forex, however, is not a game of odds. Participants in forex trading do not share the same amount of information. In forex, this asymmetry of information results in advantages and disadvantages to trades. Some players have more information than the others. In forex, information about fundamental aspects of economies does not arrive simultaneously to all participants. The real important question is what kind of knowledge and information can improve trading performance. The search for an edge starts with a fundamental understanding of the nature of the forex market. Having a foundation of knowledge in fundamentals is a first step in evolving into a winning trader.

In getting acquainted with the forex market, most people start by looking only at price charts and price patterns. This is called technical analysis. But the study of what moves those charts is called fundamental analysis. The goal of Part I is to identify the components of fundamental analysis in regard to forex and then provide a recipe for developing your own fundamental analysis of a currency pair.

Why take time to look at forex fundamentals? Why should fundamentals matter if a trade is done off a short-term time interval such as the 5-minute chart? The short answer is that one cannot separate the fundamentals from the technical analysis without exposing oneself to great distortions in understanding the forex market. Foreign exchange is by its nature *both* fundamental and technical and reflect the increased globalization of the world economy.

It is worthwhile to note the comments of the late, great Milton Friedman in a 2005 conversation with Dallas Fed president Richard Fisher:

> *The really remarkable thing about the world is how people cooperate together. How somebody in China makes a little bit of your television set. Or somebody in Malaysia produces some rubber. And that rubber is used by somebody in the United States to put on the tip of a pencil, or in some other way. What has happened has been an enormous expansion in the opportunities for cooperation. (http://dallasfed.org/research/swe/2006/swe0606e.html)*

Consider the following: every transaction in the world settles in a currency. Whether it is a consumer purchase, an imported or exported item, an investment in an equity, or even cash under the mattress, the world's economic activity is essentially a flow of money. What makes forex fascinating as a market and as a trading vehicle is the fact that currencies provide an intimate linkage to the world economy. The currency trader by putting on a currency trade becomes a participant the world economy. The trader is participating as a speculator looking for a very short-term profit. The forex trader is riding on a global wave. Some will surf the waves, jumping on and off; others will stay in much longer and face the volatility. Forex trading becomes possible because the world is constantly assessing and reassessing the value of one currency against another. The forex currency trader is looking to tap into this stream of changing values.

The challenge is to find the right combination of tools that can assist the trader in finding high-probability profitable trades. In meeting this challenge, the first step is understanding what moves currencies over time. In putting together a recipe for successful forex trading, knowing the fundamental chemistry of forex is highly recommended. Anyone who doubts this should simply look at daily headlines that evoke names and places that are part of the daily consciousness of a trader. These names should be familiar to all traders: Bernanke, Fukui, Trichet, Xiaochuan. The words and decisions of these central bankers of the United States, the Bank of Japan, the European Central Bank, and the Bank of China alert the trader to interest rate policy and news that affect sentiment about the direction of the dollar. Mention the capitals Pyongdong, Baghdad, Tehran, and they evoke emotions of fear and crises. Detect news about retail giant Wal-Mart's sales, and one starts anticipating a potential reaction in the currency markets. These and other factors mix together and form the chemistry of forex, which results in shifts of sentiment regarding the U.S. dollar. These shifts in sentiment cause price reactions and shift the balance between buyers and sellers. Let's look in more detail at these fundamental factors.

THE MAIN INGREDIENT: INTEREST RATES AND INTEREST RATE DIFFERENTIALS

Interest rates are the "dough" of the fundamental forex pie. They are one of the most important factors that affect forex prices, as interest rates are the modern tool that central banks use as a throttle on their economies. The central banks of the world do not hesitate to use this important tool. In recent years almost all of the central banks increased interest rates. The European Central Bank raised interest rates eight times from December 6, 2005, to June 13, 2007, to a level of 4.0 percent to guide a booming European economy to slow down and avoid too high inflation. The United States' central bank—the Federal Reserve—increased interest rates 17 times between June 30, 2004, and August 2006, and then paused when it decided the economy no longer needed the brake of interest rate increases.

Interest rate increases do much more than slow down an economy; they also act as a magnet to attract capital to bonds and other interest-bearing instruments. This has been called an "appetite for yield," and when applied globally the flow of capital in and out of a country can be substantially affected by the difference in interest rates between one country and another. In recent years the outflow of capital from Japan to New Zealand, Australia, and Great Britain has reflected money chasing more yield and has been a major multibillion-dollar feature called the "carry trade." The carry trade was driven by the interest rate differential that has existed, for example, between Japan (0.50) and New Zealand (8.0), causing low-cost borrowing in yen to invest in higher-yielding kiwis.

There can be no doubt of the critical role interest rates play in forex price movements. Some forex traders learned this lesson when the U.S. stock market sold off on February 27, 2007. It was precipitated by traders getting out of their carry trade positions. Since billions of dollars were sold to be converted back into yen, equity markets were also affected because equity positions had to be sold to buy back the yen positions. In Figure 1.1 we see how the Dow Jones Industrial Index correlated directly with the U.S. dollar–Japanese yen (USDJPY) pair that day.

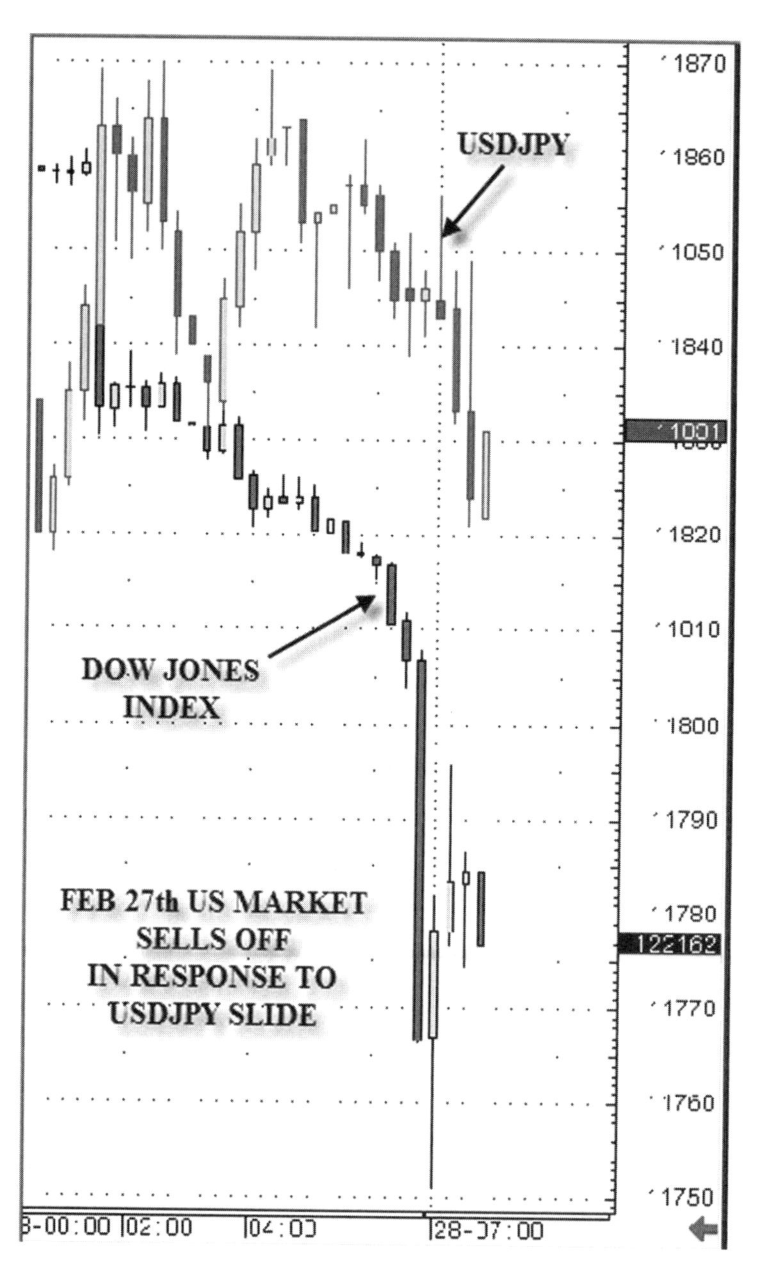

FIGURE 1.1 Dollar Yen Slide Causes Dow Sell-Off.
Source: CQG Inc.

THE ROLE OF HOUSING IN FOREX PRICE MOVEMENTS

Fundamentally, however, one of the most important categories of economic data around the world, which is sensitive to interest rate changes, is housing data. The housing sector in the United States, as well as other nations, provides a major share of wealth, consumer spending, and job creation. Recent years have seen an international housing boom, with prices growing at more than 10 percent per year in many countries. For example, Ireland grew at 15 percent in 2006; Spain's growth actually slowed down to 13 percent. Canada, Norway, and Sweden shared more than 10 percent growth. The United States, in the face of a slowdown, saw prices up 7 percent. This means that the value of homes around the world has doubled in the past 10 years, and as a result the increased wealth has fueled economic growth and consumer purchase.

Closely watched are data releases that relate to housing activity. Some of the main data releases track:

- The level of unsold homes
- Mortgage loan applications
- New and existing home sales
- Single-family housing permits
- Housing prices

Forex traders' expectations of the future direction of interest rates are significantly affected by housing data because, for example, weak housing leads to expectations of a slowdown on consumption. The economic reasoning is that consumers start seeing a decline in housing values and restrain their consumer spending. One of the most important factors related to housing market strength in recent years has been mortgage equity withdrawals (MEWs). As home prices have increased around the world, consumers take out loans against their mortgages, which stimulates consumption. During periods of housing booms, MEWs rise. MEWs have been, in fact, calculated to contribute to the growth of gross domestic product (GDP). Figure 1.2 shows that MEWs have reached nearly 6 percent of U.S. GDP. However, if MEWs slow down, this can portend a decline in consumption and a slowdown in the economy. If and when a slowdown in MEWs occurs, central bankers view it as lessening the likelihood of an interest rate increase. Damon Darlin wrote in the *New York Times* ("YOUR MONEY; Mortgage Lesson No. 1: Home Is Not a Piggy Bank," November 4, 2006):

> *Economists argue over what effect the access to money, which mortgage equity withdrawals allow, has had on consumer spending. Homeowners cash out to pay off more expensive credit card debt, remodel the house to build more equity, or just*

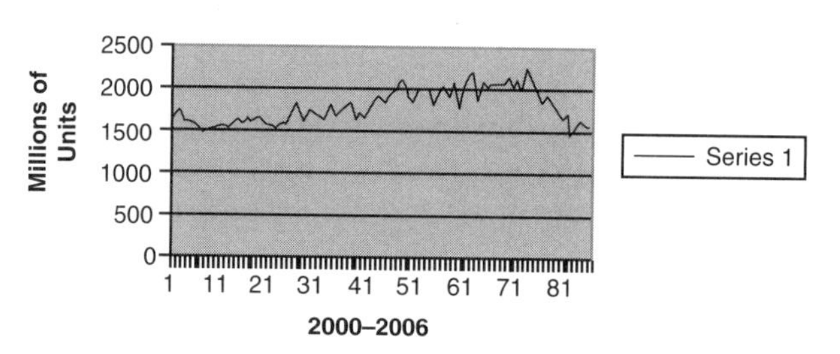

FIGURE 1.2 Home Building Has Slumped.
Source: Census Bureau, Bureau of Economic Analysis.

have fun. They may very well have used it to buy another house or not spent it at all, but added it to savings. Economists really are not certain.

"I guess it is one of those mysteries," said Christopher D. Carroll, an economics professor at Johns Hopkins University. "I don't think anyone knows what the answer is."

Nevertheless, mortgage equity withdrawal is closely watched as an indicator of the general economy because, Mr. Carroll said, "there is a lot of concern that a cooling housing market could result in a sharp fallback in consumer spending."

A recent paper that Mr. Carroll helped write contends that for every $1,000 change in housing wealth there is an immediate propensity to consume about $20 more. The wealth effect, as the phenomenon is called, is twice as high for housing wealth as it is for stock wealth, Mr. Carroll and his associates said.

At the end of 2006, the data on MEWs showed a large decline from the year before in the United States. This was an early indicator of a slowdown in the U.S. economy because it is estimated that two-thirds of the money from MEWs goes for consumption. So the forex trader seeing signs of an MEW slowdown can get ready for its effect to take place months in advance.

The importance of housing data as a factor in shaping currency moves has been highlighted further by the events relating to subprime mortgages in the United States. These mortgages were issued during the housing boom/bubble, without the traditional credit requirements. Economic forces ultimately worked to create mortgage delinquencies and a collapse in this market. For the forex trader it is a clear case where fundamentals affect the dollar. More housing weakness translates to weaker consumer demand and that translates to lowering the probability of interest rate increases. It's difficult to be bullish on the dollar in this environment. However, if the housing market starts recovering, the pressures to increase interest rates (or not decrease them) will help attract dollar buyers.

ASSIGNMENT

Find the MEW Rates in Canada, Australia, and the United Kingdom

This will take some exploration on the Internet, but it is worth tracking.

HOUSING DATA AS A LEADING INDICATOR

What is important to realize about fundamental analysis of housing sector data is that the trader can identify pending changes in trends and direction of the economy. Of course, it is true that forex prices move all the time in reaction to news and the like, but economies don't change direction overnight. By understanding housing data, one can develop a fundamental viewpoint that leads to trading strategies before technical price patterns reflect the change.

For example, in Table 1.1 we see data on U.S. new housing starts. The year 2005 was a year of a high level of housing starts peaking in February at 2.2 million units and then testing that peak in January 2006 (see Figure 1.2). After January 2006, the data showed a decline, and by August 2006, the decline in housing starts reached levels of 2003. The forex trader may not have picked the start of the slump by looking at this kind of data, but clearly would have seen that right after the start of 2006 new home starts were in a period of weakening. When housing starts reached a peak and then started declining, it was difficult to be pro-dollar. Although housing data showed a slump, the Federal Reserve didn't stop the increase in rates until August 2006. In this case the new housing start data was a very reliable leading indicator that interest rates would not increase.

HOUSING SENTIMENT INDICATORS

One can argue that economic data on housing activity is lagging and that a trader needs to find indicators that are more coincident with activity or even leading. A valuable source for assessing housing activity in the United States is the survey releases of the National Association of Housing Builders (NAHB). According to the NAHB, "The Housing Market Index (HMI) is based on a monthly survey of NAHB members designed to take the pulse

TABLE 1.1 Number of New Privately Owned Housing Units Started (Seasonally Adjusted)

Year	New Privately Owned Housing Starts (Unit = Thousands)	Year	New Privately Owned Housing Starts (Unit = Thousands)	Year	New Privately Owned Housing Starts (Unit = Thousands)
Jan-00	1636	Jun-02	1717	Nov-04	1782
Feb-00	1737	Jul-02	1655	Dec-04	2042
Mar-00	1604	Aug-02	1633	Jan-05	2137
Apr-00	1626	Sep-02	1804	Feb-05	2213
May-00	1575	Oct-02	1648	Mar-05	1856
Jun-00	1559	Nov-02	1753	Apr-05	2079
Jul-00	1463	Dec-02	1788	May-05	2034
Aug-00	1541	Jan-03	1853	Jun-05	2078
Sep-00	1507	Feb-03	1629	Jul-05	2070
Oct-00	1549	Mar-03	1726	Aug-05	2075
Nov-00	1551	Apr-03	1643	Sep-05	2158
Dec-00	1532	May-03	1751	Oct-05	2046
Jan-01	1600	Jun-03	1867	Nov-05	2131
Feb-01	1625	Jul-03	1897	Dec-05	2002
Mar-01	1590	Aug-03	1833	Jan-06	2265
Apr-01	1649	Sep-03	1939	Feb-06	2132
May-01	1605	Oct-03	1967	Mar-06	1972
Jun-01	1636	Nov-03	2083	Apr-06	1832
Jul-01	1670	Dec-03	2057	May-06	1953
Aug-01	1567	Jan-04	1911	Jun-06	1833
Sep-01	1562	Feb-04	1846	Jul-06	1760
Oct-01	1540	Mar-04	1998	Aug-06	1659
Nov-01	1602	Apr-04	2003	Sep-06	1724
Dec-01	1568	May-04	1981	Oct-06	1478
Jan-02	1698	Jun-04	1828	Nov-06	1565
Feb-02	1829	Jul-04	2002	Dec-06	1633
Mar-02	1642	Aug-04	2024	Jan-07	1565
Apr-02	1592	Sep-04	1905	Feb-07	1525
May-02	1764	Oct-04	2072		

of the housing industry, especially the single-family industry. The survey asks respondents to rate general economic and housing market conditions."

By looking at the HMI data for 2005 and 2006 we can discern an increasing pessimism on the health of the housing market (see Tables 1.2 and 1.3). The survey results in the summer of 2005 were at a peak on all HMI component measures. The Federal Reserve stopped increasing rates in August 2006, reflecting their judgment that the economy didn't require more rate increases. Using the HMI index, the forex trader saw a

TABLE 1.2 Housing Market Index (Seasonally Adjusted)

2005									
May	Jun	Jul	Aug	Sep	Oct	Nov	Dec	Jan	Feb
70	72	70	67	65	68	61	57	57	56
2006									
Mar	Apr	May	Jun	Jul	Aug	Sep	Oct	Nov	Dec
54	51	46	42	39	33	30	31	33	32

Source: National Association of Housing Builders.

significant weakening in the housing market, which was an omen that increases in rates were increasingly not likely. At the end of 2006, the HMI survey shows that the previous rate of decline in housing starts was slowing down. This can be interpreted as possible bottoming out of the housing market. Using this data, those traders expecting an interest rate decrease would have to reconsider their confidence in a rate cut.

The importance of housing data as an indicator for traders is reflected in the fact that new sources of data on housing are being developed for investors. One of the more recent sources is the Standard & Poor's (S&P)/Case-Shiller home price index. It is a benchmark measure for housing prices. It tracks the value of single-family homes in the United States. Twenty metropolitan areas are tracked, and the index is measured monthly. The

TABLE 1.3 Housing Market Index Components (Seasonally Adjusted)

2005									
May	Jun	Jul	Aug	Sep	Oct	Nov	Dec	Jan	Feb
Single-Family Sales: Present									
76	77	76	73	72	74	67	64	62	61
Single-Family Sales: Next 6 Months									
77	80	77	77	70	73	65	65	66	64
Traffic of Prospective Buyers									
53	55	55	50	49	51	46	40	41	40
2006									
May	Jun	Jul	Aug	Sep	Oct	Nov	Dec	Jan	Feb
Single-Family Sales: Present									
59	55	50	47	43	37	32	32	33	33
Single-Family Sales: Next 6 Months									
62	59	55	51	46	41	37	42	45	48
Traffic of Prospective Buyers									
40	39	33	29	27	22	22	23	26	23

Source: National Association of Housing Builders.

last Tuesday of each month at 9 A.M. is the release time of the announcement. Traders looking for leading indicators of a housing recovery will likely see it in increases in housing prices tracked by this monthly index, posted at www.indices.standardandpoors.com. Detailed housing data can also be found at www.macromarkets.com.

ALSO WATCH HOUSING EQUITY SECTOR STOCKS

Another way for the forex trader to get a grip on housing data is to watch equities that are housing related. For example, Lennar Homes is a leading home builder. Its stock price and earning forecasts offer good clues regarding the direction of the housing market and by inference interest rate policies (Figure 1.3). In April 2006, Lennar homes broke down below its support at $55 per share. Lennar Homes' weakness was an omen about the end of interest rate increases. Interestingly, when the forex market begins to conjecture whether the Federal Reserve will raise rates in the future, the trader following Lennar Homes's stock price or another housing equity leader will be helpful in shaping an opinion about the likelihood of an interest rate increase.

FIGURE 1.3 Lennar Homes Trying To Recover.
Chart courtesy of Aspen Graphics, www.aspenres.com.

Here is what the Lennar chief executive officer (CEO) said as 2007 started (*Wall Street Journal*, March 1, 2007):

> *Lennar Corp. (LEN) Chief Executive Stuart Miller is seeing no signs that the deteriorating home-building market has bottomed, and Lennar expects to take land-related write downs of between $400 million and $500 million in its fiscal fourth quarter to reflect the weak conditions.*
>
> *"Market conditions continued to weaken throughout the fourth quarter, and we have not yet seen tangible evidence of a market recovery," said Miller, in a statement.*

ASSIGNMENT

Find Other Equities that Provide Insight into the Housing Market

In this assignment, the trader should select the top equities that represent aspects of the housing sector and start watching their weekly performance. When these housing equity stocks start probing their weekly support, resistance, and trend lines, the trader will have clues as to a potential change in the housing market.

HOUSING DATA AND GREAT BRITAIN

As discussed earlier, housing provides a strong indicator regarding interest rates throughout the world. For example, as 2006 ended, the situation in Great Britain regarding housing indicated a very strong housing market and therefore supported sentiment of interest rate increases by the Bank of England. In 2006, housing prices inflated by nearly 10 percent in Great Britain. Economist Diana Choyleva believed prices could rise by as much as 15 percent in 2007. But she warned that if the Bank of England did not prevent people's taking on excessive debt by raising interest rates, it risked laying the foundations of another major collapse. In January 2007, she said, "The Bank could risk finally spawning a house price bubble in 2008" (Edmund Conway, economics editor, "House Prices at Their Most Overvalued for 15 Years," *Telegraph*, January 2, 2007).

In other words, expectations of an interest rate cut in Britain would require evidence of a slowdown in housing price increases. The trader trading the British pound should watch British housing data very carefully and gain an edge in shaping trading strategy. A useful web site for staying on top of British housing data is www.hometrack.co.uk/.

SUMMARY

Tracking changes in how an economy is growing is clearly an important part of gaining a sense of whether a currency will be strengthening or weakening. The relationship of growth and currencies applies throughout the world. While there are many aspects to economic growth, the forex trader's main focus should be on interest rates. An increase in interest rates tends to strengthen the currency. The trader needs to go further than just knowing what the rate levels are. They trader needs to assess whether the economy is strengthening or weakening. Housing data is one of the most important areas that affect the decision to increase rates, keep rates the same, or decrease rates. The forex trader should keep track of housing data when trading a currency.

CHAPTER 2

The Role of Inflation

Inflation is in many ways the elusive enemy of central banks throughout the world. Much progress has been made over the decades. In the period of 1973 through 1987, inflation levels in industrialized countries were near the 7.5 percent range. A decade later, in 1989, inflation levels ranged at the much lower level of 3 percent. Today, all you have to do is read the central banks' public documents to realize that their major mission is to contain inflation. Many central banks, in fact, announce inflation targets. In fact, Bernard Bernanke, the successor to Alan Greenspan, has favored formal inflation targeting for the U.S. Federal Reserve, and this is a significant change from Greenspan's famous verbal ambiguity in his communications strategy.

Central banks around the world monitor inflation and raise interest rates to try to slow down inflation. Central banks often include in their statements accompanying interest rate decisions that they will be vigilant over potential risks of inflation. This is commonly known as being an inflation "hawk." Whenever inflation is feared to be lingering in the economy, traders interpret this fear as raising the probability that interest rates will increase.

A fear of lingering inflation tends to generate in the market the anticipation of higher rates, and therefore works to support the buying of a currency. That is also why strong retail prices tend to undermine bond prices. Bondholders fear increased rates because they reduce the attractiveness of the bonds they hold, and the market lowers the prices of the bonds in order to equalize the yield of the old bonds with the new interest rates.

Inflation is the ever-present yet stealthy ghost that spooks the forex market and challenges central banks. It is particularly difficult to track. There is ongoing controversy even among the best economists on how to measure and detect inflation, and as a result there are many data sets relating to inflation. Central banks all over the world are trying to get an accurate answer to the question of what is true core inflation?

This level of complexity in measuring inflation sets up the forex market for surprises when data comes along that inflation has not been contained. If central banks can't be accurate in measuring inflation, why should an individual trader? Surprises can be expected. For example, in December 2006, when inflation data rose the highest in 30 years, it provided a boost in the dollar value as more traders were betting that the Fed would not decrease rates, or might even increase rates.

Speaking of the challenge in interpreting monthly inflation numbers during his tenure on the Federal Reserve Board, former vice chairman Alan Blinder said, "The name of the game then was distinguishing the signal from the noise, which was often difficult. The key question on my mind was typically: What part of each month's observation on inflation is durable and what part is fleeting?" (Commentary on "Measuring Short-Run Inflation for Central Bankers," *Federal Reserve Bank of St. Louis Review*, May/June 1997).

The challenge to getting a true measure of inflation has also been a focus of recent activity in Britain. The Office of National Statistics is introducing a new inflation calculator that allows persons to calculate their own inflation measure! In other words, the other measures [such as the Retail Price Index (RPI), the Retail Price Index excluding Mortgage Payments (RPIX), and the Harmonized Index of Consumer Prices (HCIP)] are still in force, but there is recognition that inflation needs more measures for an accurate assessment. This confusion and debate over how to detect inflation in Great Britain underscores the issue is an international one. The Monetary Policy Committee of the Bank of England (www.parliament.the-stationery-office.co.uk/pa/ld199899/ldselect/ldmon/96/9615.htm) offers more details on this subject.

The good news is that the forex trader doesn't have to become a Ph.D in economics to follow inflation data. There are many key measures of inflation that are tracked. But you have to check the central bank web sites.

ASSIGNMENT

Find Out the Target Inflation Rates of Central Banks

Traders need to keep track of inflation rates and targets in each country. The best way to do this is to first check the web site of the central bank. They contain a great deal of information on inflation and inflation policy.

INFLATION MEASURES IN THE UNITED STATES

The Federal Reserve Bank of the United States measures inflation using something called the Core Personal Consumption Expenditure Index, or Core PCE Index. Core inflation refers to the components of inflation that are more durable and not a result of temporary events, such as a hurricane. Core inflation excludes food and energy prices, which vary temporarily.

The PCE is now the favorite measure used by the Federal Reserve. However, in an attempt to be even more accurate, economists have gone further and developed a trimmed PCE, which is designed to give a truer view of inflation. Table 2.1 shows three measures of PCE, but what is really important is to realize that any rate above 2 percent is considered to be a signal of too much inflation in the economy by most central banks, and these kind of levels lead to expectations of central banks' increasing interest rates or at least not decreasing rates.

The Producer Price Index (PPI) is another key measure that is reported and tracked. The PPI measures what businesses charge one another for everything from iron ore and diesel fuel to cases of soda pop. The U.S. Bureau of Labor Statistics generates PPI data for over 8000 different product categories, reflecting price pressures among different industries. A net PPI figure, of course, is more general in nature (www.bls.gov/). In November 2006, the PPI surprisingly rose 2 percent higher than the month before. The index had not risen by that much in a single month in more than 32 years, since the energy and stagflation crises of the mid-1970s. The fact that the PPI and the core inflation may differ adds to the uncertainty of the true condition of the economy regarding inflation.

The Consumer Price Index (CPI) tracks consumer price changes given a fixed basket of goods and is part of the data set watched by traders in all countries. The U.S. Bureau of Labor Statistics provides comprehensive data on inflation and, in fact, tracks the various inflation rates. It conducts extensive sampling of 87 urban areas, 50,000 homes, and 23,000 retail establishments. Persons interested in getting deeper into their methodology for generating inflation data will be rewarded by going to the Bureau of Labor Statistics' web site. From time to time, the CPI basket changes to more accurately reflect new items

TABLE 2.1 12-month PCE Inflation

	Jun 06	Jul 06	Aug 06	Sep 06	Oct 06	Nov 06
PCE	3.5	3.4	3.2	1.9	1.5	1.9
PCE excluding food and energy	2.3	2.3	2.4	2.4	2.4	2.2
Trimmed mean PCE	2.6	2.7	2.7	2.5	2.5	2.4

available in the economy. The problem with CPI is that it doesn't reflect housing prices and therefore may underreport inflationary pressures.

Tracking gold, the Commodity Research Bureau, and other commodity indexes and patterns will also help you get a handle on inflation. We look at the commodity-currency connection in Chapter 5. The main point here is that the forex trader needs to pay serious attention to inflation rates and expectations of inflation rates, because they are a key to discerning what the central banks fear, and a clue to whether they will raise interest rates.

ASSIGNMENT

Find the Latest CPI per Country and Compare It against Their Target Rate. Which Countries Have Inflation above the Target Rate?

Take the indicators or economic data releases coming out and group them. Which are leading? Which are lagging? Which are coincident?

Which countries have inflation rates over 2 percent?

Which country has a central bank policy to *increase* inflation?

CHAPTER 3

Exploiting Information About Economic Growth

Interest rate and inflation levels are the main ingredients of forex price movements, and economic growth data follows closely in shaping the currency flows. Countries that are experiencing economic growth generate more jobs in their economy. Consumer spending therefore increases. In turn, the demand for housing increases as people have more disposable income and can better afford housing. Other sectors, such as the auto sector, also experience changes in demand as consumers' propensity to spend reflects greater confidence regarding their economic conditions. The transactions of a modern economy intimately involve global flows of capital as exports and imports are part and parcel of the vitality of an economy. The term *economic growth* is really a wide category. How is economic growth measured and tracked by the forex trader?

The rate of economic growth or development of a country is mainly measured essentially by its gross domestic product (GDP), so news about GDP becomes an essential ingredient in shaping trader sentiment about the value of a currency. A slowdown or expected slowdown in GDP translates into anticipation that interest rates will not go higher or may even decrease. This anticipation results in pressures to lower a currency's value. The importance of economic development statistics in currency trading is evidenced by the fact that whenever an economic data release is scheduled, the currency market hesitates in its price movements and then often moves vigorously when the news surprises the market. In fact, one of the best times to trade is after a news release. Technical strategies for trading the news will be thoroughly explored in a later chapter.

Traders can gain insight into economic growth and development data by following several sources that track global economic growth, such as the Organisation for Economic Co-operation and Development (www.oecd.org), the International Monetary Fund (www.imf.org), the Group of Seven, (www.g7.utoronto.ca), and the World Trade Organization (www.wto.org).

IMPORTANCE OF JOB DATA

Employment data is used to determine how fast the economy is growing. A growing economy has new job creation and lower levels of employment. An economy that is slowing down (or showing signs of slowing down) has increased jobless claims, a declining rate of job creation, and higher unemployment levels.

Whenever job data is released by governments, the forex markets react. The forex markets look at whether the data is positive or negative for expectations of whether that country's central bank will increase rates, keep rates the same, or decrease rates. There are many layers of information regarding employment data. The following list illustrates what's trackable in the United States:

Aggregate Weekly Hours Index: private nonfarm payrolls
Aggregate Weekly Hours: private nonagricultural establishments
Civilian Employment: 16 years and older
Civilian Participation Rate
Civilian Labor Force: 16 years and older
Employment Ratio—Civilian Employ/Civilian Index of Help Wanted Advertising in Newspapers
U.S. Manufacturing Employment
Payroll Employment of Wage and Salary Workers
Total Population of the United States
U.S. Employment in Service-Producing Industries
Civilian Unemployed for 15 Weeks and Over
Civilian Unemployed for Less Than 5 Weeks
Median Duration of Unemployment
Unemployed: all civilian workers
Unemployment Rate
U.S. Employment in Construction
U.S. Employment in Finance, Insurance, and Real Estate
U.S. Employment in Goods-Producing Sectors
U.S. Employment in Government

U.S. Employment in Mining

U.S. Employment in Services

U.S. Employment in Transportation and Public Utilities

U.S. Employment in Retail Trade Industry

U.S. Employment in Wholesale Trade Industry

For more information on job data, visit the following web sites:

www.economagic.com
www.globalfinancialdata.com

THE ROLE OF CRUDE OIL AND PETRODOLLARS

Crude oil and its derivative products fuel the engine of economic growth. As long as the world is dependent on hydrocarbon-based energy, oil prices become a factor in stimulating or delaying economic growth. Economic studies demonstrate that for every $10 per barrel rise in oil prices, real GDP in the United States is reduced by about 0.4 percent economic growth (*Federal Reserve Bank of St. Louis Review*, November/December 2006, http://research.stlouisfed.org/publications/review/06/11/NovDec2006Review.pdf).

In the near term, higher oil prices result in reducing economic growth expectations as well. Higher hydrocarbon prices portend increases in transportation costs and the per-unit cost of outputs in the economy, and therefore become an inflationary factor in the costs of goods. More importantly, crude oil prices' moving quickly higher disrupts anticipated prices and further encourages fears of slowdowns. One of the most important aspects of oil prices is that the market reaction to oil price increases often tends to overemphasize its importance, particularly for the U.S. economy. Recent studies by the Federal Reserve show that an oil price shock can be easily absorbed in the $14 trillion U.S. economy. Recent research shows that "a 100 percent increase in the price of crude oil... translates into only a 3.2 percent price increase in the typical basket of consumption goods. Since unrefined oil is not a consumer good, the oil price shock is passed through indirectly in the prices of many other goods and services" (Federal Reserve Bank of Cleveland, November 2006, www.clevelandfed.org/research/commentary/2006/Nov.pdf).

A quick rise in oil prices, or even just the fear of a rise, offers trading opportunities. Hurricane Katrina is a good example, as we saw some countries benefit from high crude oil prices, while others did not. The result impacts currency prices as well. Closely tracking oil is important in shaping currency-trading strategies. See Figure 3.1.

Oil has another impact. Oil-producing countries have amassed huge sums of money, and what they do with their increasing petrodollars impacts currency values. The International Monetary Fund (IMF) reported that the surplus of dollars to oil producers

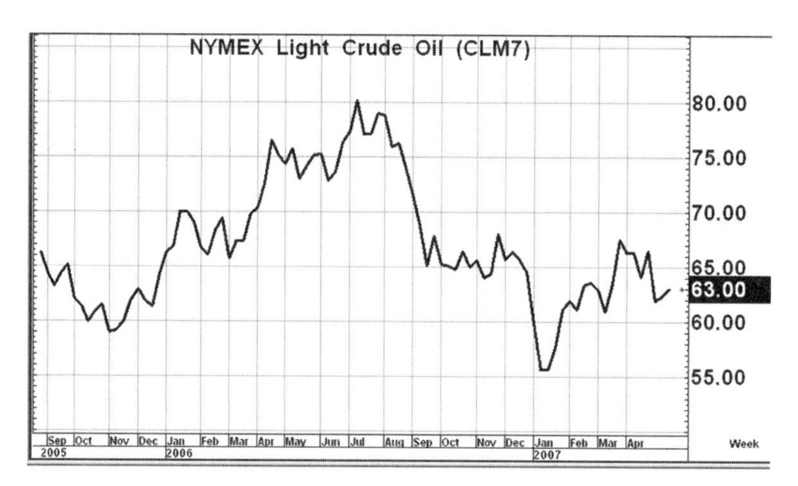

FIGURE 3.1 Crude Oil Weekly Patterns.
Source: CQG, Inc. Copyright © 2006. All rights reserved worldwide.

amounts to $500 billion! The economies of Organization of Petroleum Exporting Countries (OPEC) nations are accumulating current account surplus due to petrodollars that are nearing 30 percent of their GDP! If oil producers start to shift into nondollar assets such as the euro and pound sterling, the dollar fundamentally weakens. This has already begun. The *Financial Times* reported on December 11, 2006, in a story titled "Oil Producers Shun the Dollar," that the Bank of International Settlement data showed a shift into euro, yen, and sterling. OPEC and Russia data showed that the dollar holdings were cut from 67 percent to 65 percent. Also, the report indicated a cut by Iran of US$4 billion holdings and by Qatar of US$2.4 billion.

It was not a coincidence that the 2003 highs of the euro coincided with the last known shift of oil producers from dollars to euros. It is also not a coincidence that the Canadian dollar strengthens when oil prices increase and weakens when oil prices decline. We can see that crude oil patterns have had wide ranges and are likely to continue to have such swings. This will benefit the forex trader.

YIELD CURVE AND ECONOMIC GROWTH

As Arturo Estrella and Frederic S. Mishkin said, "The yield curve—specifically, the spread between the interest rates on the ten-year Treasury note and the three-month Treasury bill—is a valuable forecasting tool. It is simple to use and significantly outperforms other financial and macroeconomic indicators in predicting recessions two to six

TABLE 3.1 Estimated Recession Probabilities for Using the Yield Curve Spread (Four Quarters Ahead)

Recession Probability (Percent)	Value of Spread (Percentage Points)
5	1.21
10	0.76
15	0.46
20	0.22
25	0.02
30	−0.17
40	−0.50
50	−0.82
60	−1.13
70	−1.46
80	−1.85
90	−2.40

Note: The yield curve spread is defined as the spread between the interest rates on the 10-year Treasury note and the 3-month Treasury bill.

Source: Federal Reserve Bank of New York.

quarters ahead" ("The Yield Curve as a Predictor of U.S. Recessions," *Current Issues in Economics and Finance*, Federal Reserve Bank of New York, June 1996).

Guessing what phase of the business cycle an economy is in is a great game. Is the economy going into a recession? Since economic data mostly is lagging, we don't know we have begun a recession until it actually has begun and been confirmed. However, sentiment about an expected recession is not stopped by lack of data. One of the most important measures that traders track is the shape of the yield curve. *The yield curve is defined as the difference between the 10-year Treasury note and the 3-month Treasury bill.* We see here the key role that interest rates play in reflecting expectations in the market. The Federal Reserve Bank of New York published an important study of the yield curve and recessions, which included a table relating probability of recession to the yield curve (Table 3.1). A separate study (see Figure 3.2) shows the strong correlation of the yield curve as a precursor of a recession 4 months in advance.

We can see that the yield curve provides an important barometer for the future GDP growth. With regard to the yield curve, what is particularly important to track for the forex trader is the shape of the yield curve. Is it flat? Is it upward sloping? Is it inverted? These are the key patterns to observe. In normal times, people are willing to pay more for longer-term maturities and bonds. This is a natural reaction to the fact that there is more risk over a longer period of time. But a slowdown or fear of a recession causes the market to demand higher interest rates for short-term borrowing. The yield curve becomes inverted. Short-term interest rates become greater than longer-term rates! A

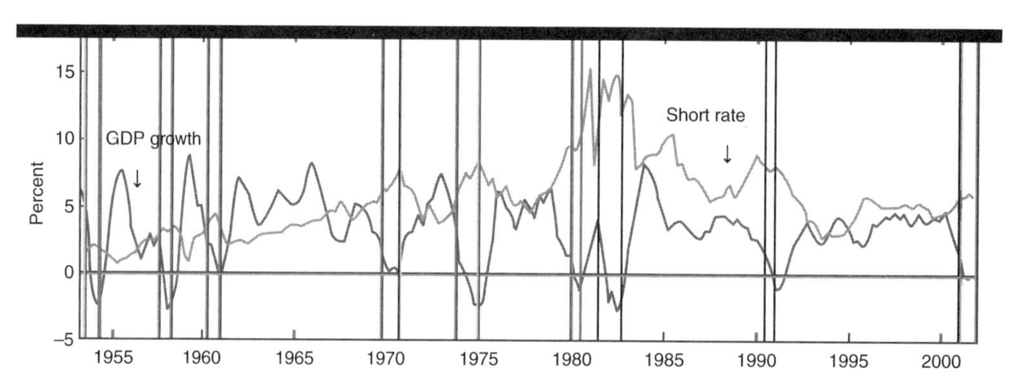

FIGURE 3.2 Four-Quarter GDP Growth.
Note: The figure plots 4-quarter GDP growth together with the 20-quarter term spread (upper panel) and the 1-quarter short rate (lower panel) lagged 4 quarters.

common interpretation is that when the yield curve inverts, a recession is coming. An inverted yield curve situation makes it difficult for the central banks to increase rates and more likely, in fact, that rates may decrease. Such a situation becomes negative for the dollar or any currency involved. A flat yield curve indicates uncertainty about the economy. On December 27, 2005, the yield curve inverted for a few days for the first time in five years. Also, there is no guarantee that an inverted yield curve will always predict a recession, but when the yield curve inverts, the forex trader should be very vigilant. Strategies favoring a weaker dollar or currency pair should be considered.

CALCULATING PROBABILITY OF A RECESSION

A quick way to discern if the United States is nearing a recession is to generate an estimate of the probability of a recession based on the Federal Reserve hypothetical model. The formula (for those who want to set up an Excel spreadsheet) is (www.federalreserve.gov/releases/h15/update/):

> NORMSDIST(−2.17 – 0.76*(10Year – 3Month) + 0.35*FederalFundsRate)
> Where:
> 10Year = 1-quarter Average of Daily 10-Year Constant Maturity Treasury Yields
> 3Month = 1-quarter Average of Daily 3-Month Constant Maturity Treasury Yields
> Federal Funds Rate = 1-quarter Average of Daily Federal Funds Rates

The easiest way to do the calculations is to link to the following web site and input the data required in the formula. You can easily get the value of the 10-year Treasury

TABLE 3.2 Bond Yield and Federal Funds Rate Data

Input Data	March 21/07	April 23/07
10-Year Treasury Bond Yield (%)	4.56	4.68
3-Month Treasuy Bond Yield (%)	5.06	4.99
Federal Funds Rate (%)	5.26	5.23
Probability of a Recession in Next 12 Months (%)	52	49.5

Source: www.politicalcalculations.com.

bond, the 3-month yield, and the federal funds rate at www.federalreserve.gov/releases/h15/update/. Once you get the value of the 10-year Treasury bond and the 3-month yield, simply input their values into the inversion calculator, available at http://politicalcalculations.blogspot.com/2006/04/reckoning-odds-of-recession.html.

On March 21, according to the current model, the probability of a recession due to the relationship between the 10-year and 3-month bond yield curve was 52 percent. Table 3.2 shows the data inputs giving this result. One month later, on April 21, the data showed that the probability of a recession was even lower, at 45.9 percent. These probabilities are the results of models. They are not guarantees but do give insights into what the professional economists are thinking.

A further visualization of the relationship between a recession and the yield curve as developed by the Federal Reserve researchers is shown in Figure 3.3. Obviously, a great

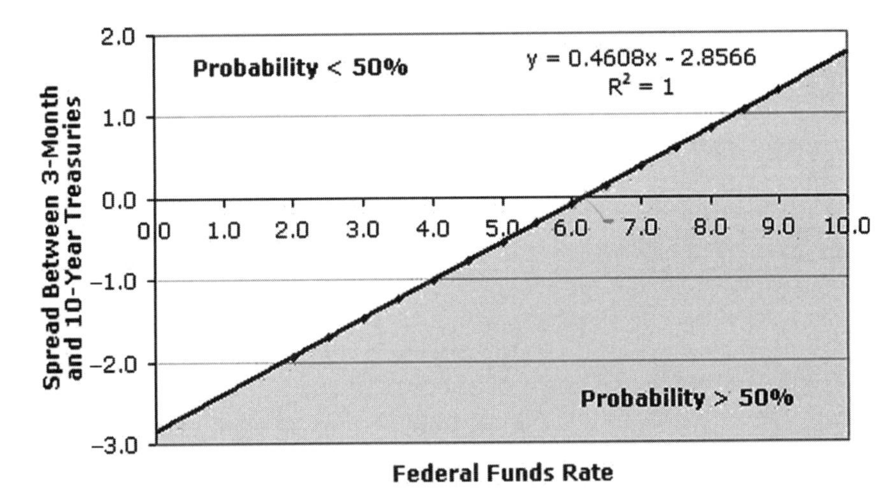

FIGURE 3.3 Spread Required between 3-Month and 10-Year Treasuries vs. Federal Funds Rate for 50 Percent Probability of Recession Occurring in Next 12 Months.
Source: www.politicalcalculations.com.

deal of work is being constantly done by economists to try to pinpoint the probability of a recession.

ASSIGNMENT

Using the Formula in this Section, Calculate the Probability of a Recession on a Weekly Basis

Check whether the probability is rising or falling as you are monitoring the results. At the same time, ask yourself the question: Is the dollar getting stronger or weaker? Doing this assignment will help you sharpen your understanding of sentiment toward the dollar and whether that sentiment reflects economic fundamentals.

CHAPTER 4

The China Factor

China is becoming increasingly important to forex traders in evaluating trading opportunities. This chapter provides a review of key China developments that every trader should know about.

Watching Chinese economic developments is likely to become a daily pastime for many traders all over the world. Since the 1970s, China's growth rate has been approaching over 10 percent per year. In 2006, the Chinese reported that China's gross domestic product (GDP) reached 20.94 trillion yuan, up 10.7 percent from the year before (*Financial Times* Information). Almost every day there is news on China's economic performance. China is impacting every region of the world and every industry. For example, the Chinese Ministry of Information Industry reported that China has the world's second largest population of Internet users after the United States, with 137 million people online.

In March 2007, China replaced the United States as Europe's second biggest source of imports after Britain. This occurred after a 21 percent increase in imports from China to the 25 countries forming the European Union (*Financial Times*, March 23, 2007, p. 2). China's trade with Russia is another example. The trade between China and Russia is reported to exceed the 30 percent per year growth from 1999 to 2005 and is now over $7 billion per year (China economic net). Over half of China's trade is within Asia, between Japan and South Korea. Regarding China and the United States, it has been reported that "from 2000 to 2005, U.S. exports to China grew almost 160 percent, while U.S. exports to the rest of the world rose by only 16 percent. During that period, China accounted for roughly 25 percent of total U.S. export growth" (C. Fred Bergsten, Bates Gill, Nicholas R. Lardy, and Derek Mitchell, *China: The Balance Sheet: What the World Needs to Know Now about the Emerging Superpower.* New York: PublicAffairs, 2006).

It will certainly benefit all to become familiar with China's economic events and how they may impact currency moves. Let's explore some key factors.

CHINA REVALUES YUAN: A TURNING POINT?

On July 21, 2005, after more than a decade of strictly pegging the renminbi to the U.S. dollar at an exchange rate of 8.28, the People's Bank of China (PBOC) announced a revaluation of the currency and a reform of the exchange rate regime. This was the beginning of a long-term strategy to integrate China into the world economy by easing the ability of capital to flow into and out of the country. The ability to exchange currency is a key factor in this process of integration. The revaluation signaled that China was beginning to allow the strengthening of its currency. As of March 2007, the renminbi value was at approximately 7.74. This means that it takes fewer renminbi (6 percent) to convert to one dollar since revaluation. Many economic studies believe that a free-floating Chinese currency would appreciate by 20 percent. Under the foreign exchange reform, the PBOC incorporates a "reference basket" of currencies when choosing its target for the renminbi. The five currencies are the U.S. dollar, the yuan, the yen, the Korean won, and the pound. However, the exact weighting of these currencies in the basket is not being disclosed and there may be other currencies included.

Even though the Chinese currency known as the renminbi does not float on the market, and it is tied to the dollar within a narrow price, the influence of China on global currency flows is profound. This limited managed float in effect is a subsidy for China's manufacturers and lowers the cost of Chinese goods, making competitor firms in the United States and the rest of the world very upset with China. There is increasing pressure on China to allow the renminbi to increase in value, either through a wider managed envelope or through a full float. A full float is highly unlikely because the Chinese government is not interested in giving up control of its economy, which would occur in a full float. Any increase in the value of the renminbi could result in a significant benefit to exporters in the United States and Japan. In recent years, even speculation that the Chinese were about to allow the renminbi to increase in value led to price moves that strengthened the Australian dollar and the yen.

China is becoming a global economic power that impacts the economic development of the world. It is the processing plant of the world, wherein many product components are imported and then put together. According to the Bank of New York, China's top 10 trade partners (in dollars) are:

European Union (18.5 percent)

Japan (18 percent)

United States (17.5 percent)

Hong Kong (11 percent)

Association of Southeast Asian Nations (ASEAN) (11 percent)

South Korea (9.5 percent)

Taiwan (8.5 percent)

Russia (2 percent)

Australia (2 percent)

Canada (1.5 percent)

In looking at China's top trading partners, we can see that China trade is spread out among the world, with Europe, Japan, and the United States almost equally weighted. But just over 40 percent of its trade is with Asia.

The importance of watching China's economic conditions is highlighted by the following remarks of U.S. Federal Reserve chairman Bernard Bernanke at the Chinese Academy of Social Sciences (Beijing, China, December 15, 2006):

The emergence of China as a global economic power is one of the most important developments of recent decades. For the past twenty years, the Chinese economy has achieved a growth rate averaging nearly 10 percent per year, resulting in a quintupling of output per person [see Figure 4.1]. In overall size, China's economy today ranks as the fourth largest in the world in terms of gross domestic product (GDP) at current exchange rates, and the second largest when adjustments are made for the differences in the domestic purchasing power of national currencies.

IMPORTANCE OF CHINESE DOLLAR RESERVES

China imports resources for its growth from many countries and exports manufactured goods. Currently, however, this process is not balanced. The Chinese export more than they import, and therefore accumulate a great deal of cash. China also possesses over $1 trillion of reserve currencies, and how it uses and invests this reserve of U.S. dollars will have a major impact on the direction of the U.S. dollar. The Chinese State Administration of Foreign Exchange (SAFE) is the key agency on the future of these dollar reserves. For the forex trader, following Chinese developments and intentions on global trade and currency policies can be rewarding because it can point the way for new trading opportunities. One big effect could result from a possible slowdown in the China economy. The U.S.-China Economic and Security Review Commission concluded that:

A financial crisis in China would harm its economy, decrease China's purchase of U.S. exports, and reduce China's ability to fund U.S. borrowing, particularly to

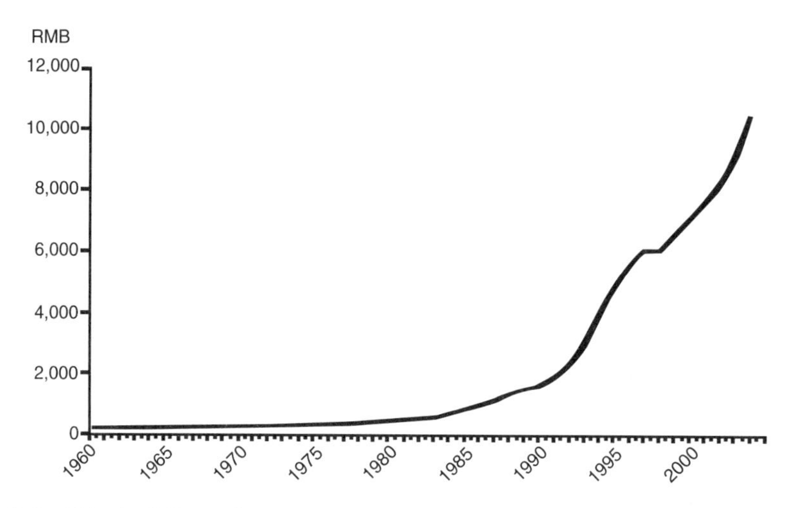

FIGURE 4.1 China's GDP per Capita.
Sources: National Bureau of Statistics, China Statistical Yearbook 2004; National Bureau of Statistics Plan Report.

cover the U.S. budget deficit. An economic crisis in China has the potential to raise the U.S. interest rates, thereby placing major additional costs on U.S. businesses and individual consumers and producing dislocation in the U.S. economy. It could also exacerbate Chinese domestic political tensions in an unpredictable fashion. This is why the condition of China's financial system is of concern to the United States. (October 30, 2006)

If a possible slowdown in China worries U.S. traders, possible changes in China's investment in U.S. assets worries them even more. The influence of China was most recently demonstrated when during the 2006 Thanksgiving holiday, a statement by the Chinese minister alluding to China's potential for investing in nondollar assets started a major slide in the U.S. dollar around the world. Here is an excerpt from recent Congressional testimony:

The United States will run a current account deficit of over $800 billion, or approximately 7 percent of the GDP, in 2006. This is historically an extremely high level that no other country has been able to sustain for any significant period. The danger is that the U.S. economy could suffer a precipitous decline if the ability of the United States to borrow ever-greater amounts should end abruptly. Interest rates and inflation might suddenly soar as the dollar fell and the stock market crashed. ("China's Exchange Rate and the Effect on the U.S. Economy," Committee on Financial Services, October 1, 2003)

Other currencies do not escape the impact of Chinese economic developments. Since the Chinese growth rate of over 10 percent per year GDP generates a voracious appetite for resources such as oil, copper, steel, iron ore, cement, and Ag complex, the countries that provide these resources experience a demand for their dollars. When China buys copper from Australia, renminbi must be converted into Australian dollars. This provides support for the Australian dollar and the Australian economy. Since China imports major resources such as copper from Australia, the aussie would be affected by a potential Chinese slowdown. Also, Japan, a significant trading partner of China, and its currency will often weaken or strengthen on expectations of a Chinese slowdown or sustained growth.

Chinese influence has begun to extend also to Africa. For example, Chinese exports are beginning to shift to the Suez Canal, rather than going around Africa. This is causing Turkey, Italy, and other nations to invest in Egypt to tap into Chinese export to Europe.

In the coming years, the trading world will focus on whether China can control its growth rate, avoid inflation, and increase its currency float. Therefore, China's economic and monetary policy will be valuable to watch. Traders need to keep track of key performance parameters such as Chinese GDP and inflation projections, as well as Chinese interest rate decisions. Between 2006 and July 2007, China increased its interest rates to reach a level of 6.84 percent for one-year notes to try to slow down the economy. Whether this will work is unknown. But as China, which is now the seventh largest economy in the world and the second largest in purchasing power parity, becomes more of a consumer economy, the status of the Chinese economy will become easier to monitor. Companies such as Home Depot, Wal-Mart, Kingfisher (British), and Best Buy are entering the Chinese market, and many other firms are acquiring Chinese companies. As a result, the coming years will provide more reliable data on Chinese consumer spending and growth.

Watching China's currency policies can also pinpoint new trading opportunities in the China market. The Shanghai Composite Index is very sensitive to whether the renminbi will strengthen. When the Bank of China's governor, Zhou Xiachuan, commented that China wasn't interested in increasing its foreign reserves further, the Shanghai index soared because Chinese company land and property is denominated in Chinese currency. Their value would increase (*Wall Street Journal*, March 22, 2007, p. C8).

To monitor activities in China on an ongoing basis, I recommend the following web sites:

http://research.stlouisfed.org/publications/review/06/11/Poole

www.chinadaily.com

http://english.people.com.cn/

http://en.ce.cn/main/index.shtml

Track the Current Value of the Yuan

Go to www.xe.com and find the latest value of the renminbi in the quote table that is supplied. It is listed as the symbol CNY (as shown in Figure 4.2). Is it getting stronger or weaker?

HF	RUB	CNY	ZAR
57	25.9860	7.73350	7.25611
69	0.03848	0.12931	0.13781
83	34.7137	10.3309	9.69347
35	0.02881	0.09680	0.10317
20	51.1161	15.2123	14.2732
25	0.01956	0.06574	0.07006

FIGURE 4.2 Finding the Value of the Renminbi.

CHAPTER 5

The Commodities Connection

Gold, Copper, CRB Index, Equities, and Forex

The value of a currency and how it moves is related to events in the commodity markets. Commodities are key resources in world growth, and they impact global inflation. This chapter focuses on what the forex trader should know about the commodity connection to currencies.

GOLD

Gold price movements are important for currency traders to understand. Gold acts in many ways as a surrogate currency and a "safe haven" when money moves out of the dollar in response to geopolitical crises. But gold is also a commodity on its own, adding strength or weakness to currencies of countries that produce gold. South Africa, of course, is the leading producer of gold, but its currency, the rand, is not floating, so traders can look to the Australian dollar and the Canadian dollar for trading those currencies when gold patterns provide trading opportunities.

Gold price action can also be a misleading guide to the currency trader. In recent years, Gold has attracted a great deal of investment demand from exchange-traded funds (ETFs). In 2003, ETFs were buying 20 tons of gold, and this rose to 500 tons in 2005. The trader who looks at gold prices rising may interpret it as a reaction to the dollar, when it actually can be reacting as a function of investment demand. Figure 5.1 shows gold versus the U.S. Dollar Index (USDX).

Central banks have an important role regarding gold. They hold gold as part of their reserves (see Figure 5.2). The world's central banks have about 3.5 trillion dollars in

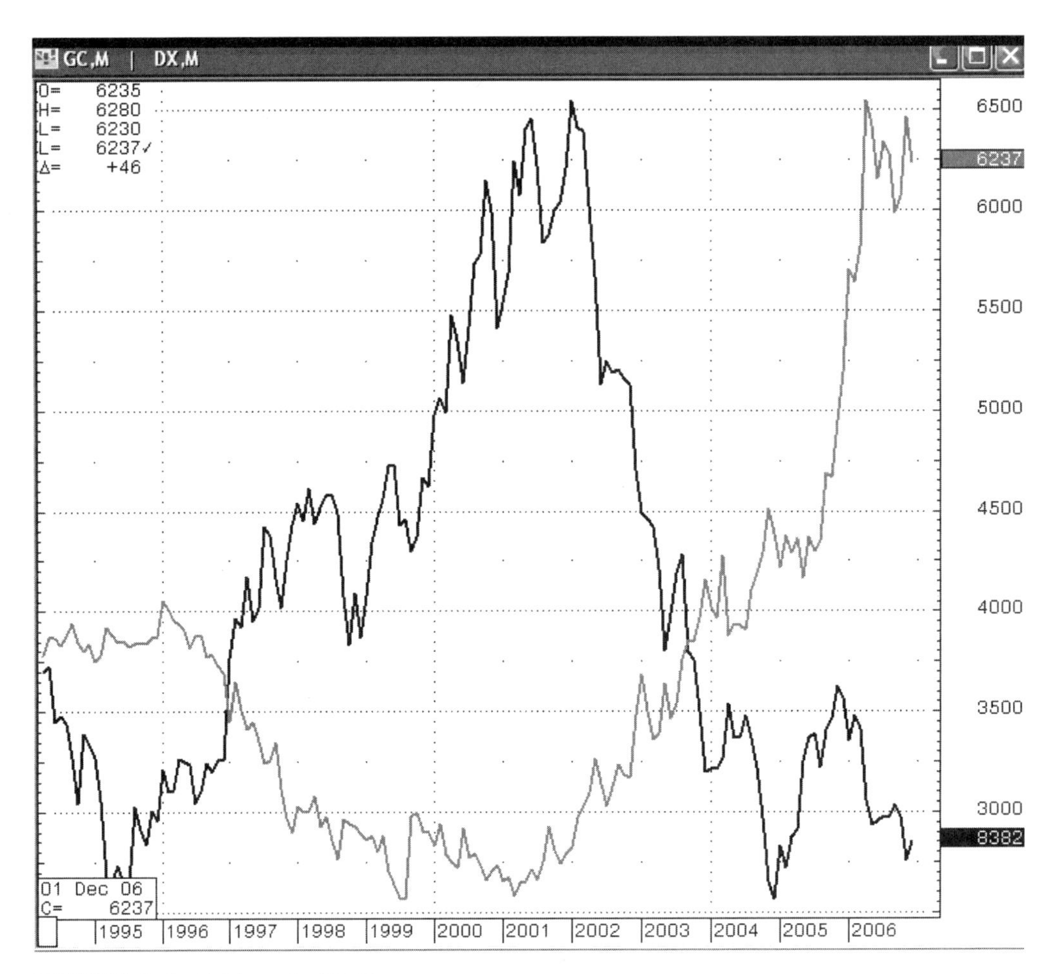

FIGURE 5.1 Gold vs. the USDX.

reserves, and 15 percent is in gold. The key variable that can affect currency prices is whether a central bank will increase its gold reserves and thereby decrease its reserves of dollars or another currency. As a result, rumors of central banks increasing gold reserves can disrupt currency prices.

The idea that gold is important to currency moves is sound, but needs to be qualified and put in the context of world events. Sometimes gold acts as a store of value in times of crises. But the correlations between gold moves and currency moves provide a great deal of variation. The trader needs to be vigilant regarding what factors are moving gold. At the end of the day, in the words of Phillip M. Hildebrand (member of the Governing

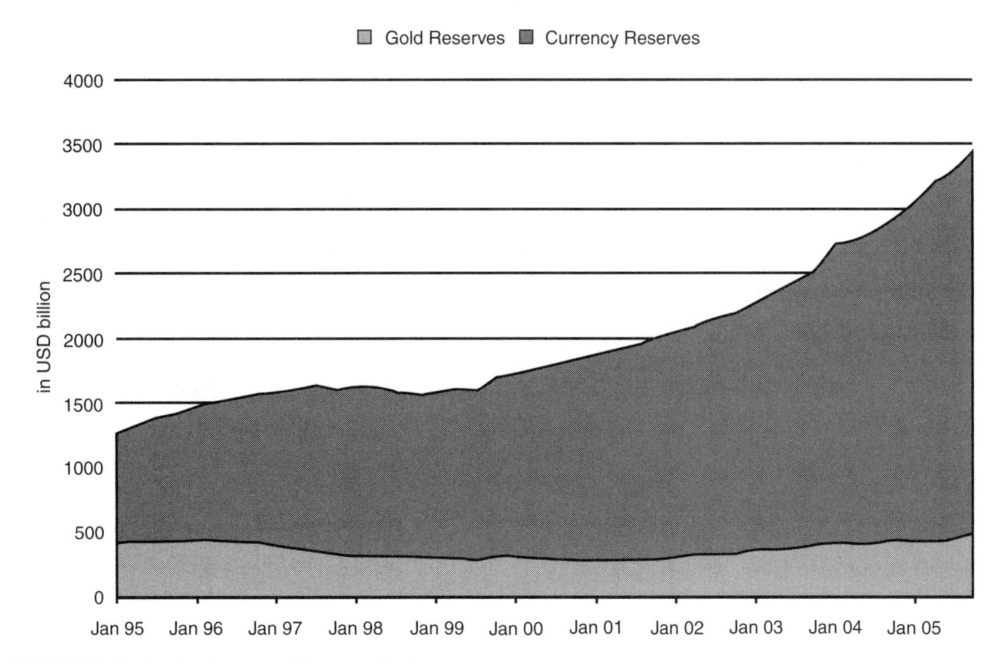

FIGURE 5.2 Evolution of World Official Reserves.
Source: Phillip M. Hildebrand, member of the Governing Board, Swiss National Bank.

Board, Swiss National Bank), "the yellow metal continues to have a special significance for central banks."

COPPER

Copper is one of the world's commodities that is strongly related to economic growth because it is a key material for global infrastructure in the building and telecommunications industry. For example, copper plays an important part in the industrial development of China. As the world grows, more copper is in demand. The forex trader has to ask the question: Who benefits from copper demand?

To answer this question, we should look at who produces copper. The world's leading producer of copper is Chile; however, the Chilean peso does not float. Australia is the second largest producer of copper, and since its currency is freely floating, the Australian dollar can be traded. The commodity connection with currencies is particularly strong for the Australian dollar, the New Zealand dollar, and the Canadian dollar. A closer look is presented in our section on currency personalities. Figure 5.3 shows the synchronicity of the commodities to each other.

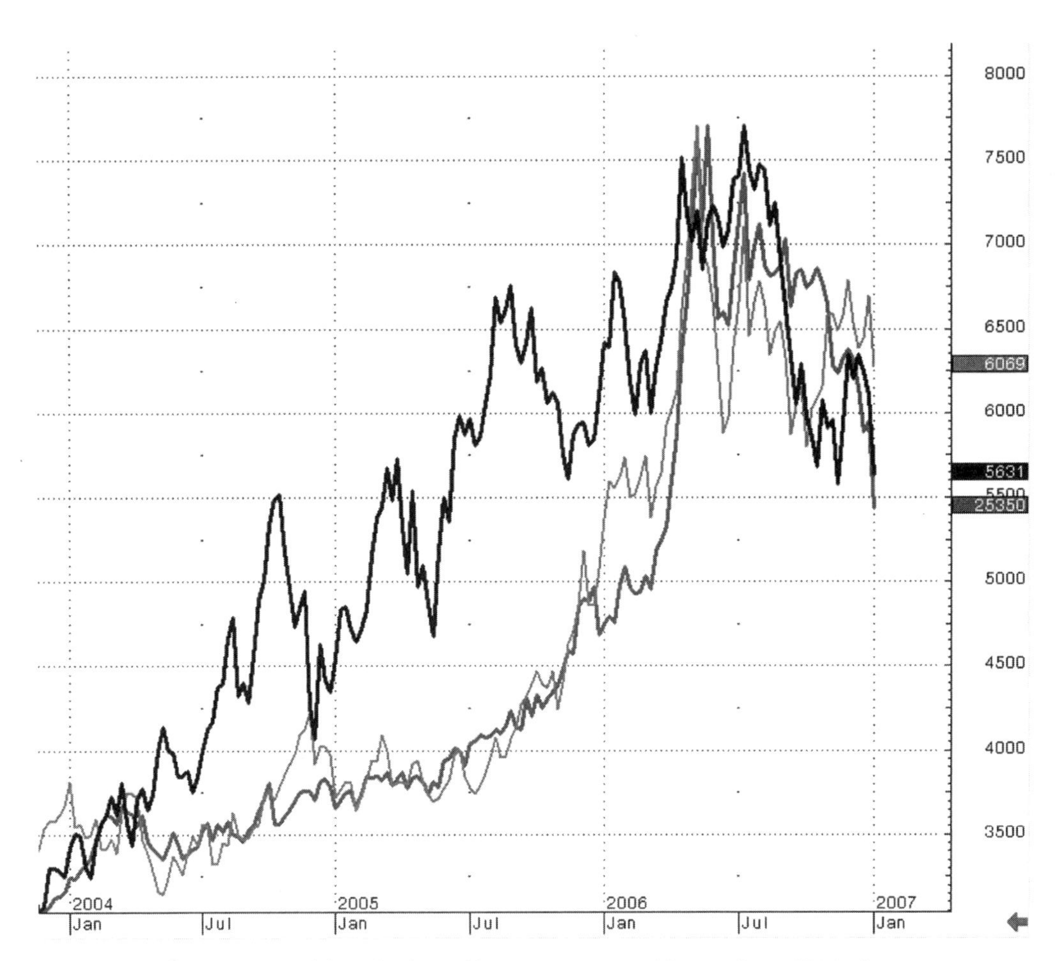

FIGURE 5.3 Copper, Gold, and Oil Weekly Movement Are Often in Sync CRB Index.

CRB INDEX

Traders looking to track the commodity and currency relationships should follow the Commodity Research Bureau (CRB) Index. The CRB Index consists of a basket of commodities and provides a useful measure of potential inflationary pressure. When commodity prices rise, this price increase can spread into the economy by increasing the costs of production and goods. This inflationary tendency is closely watched by central banks. We can see in Figure 5.4 that at the end of 2006, the CRB Index showed a decreasing price trend due to a collapse in the energy price sector.

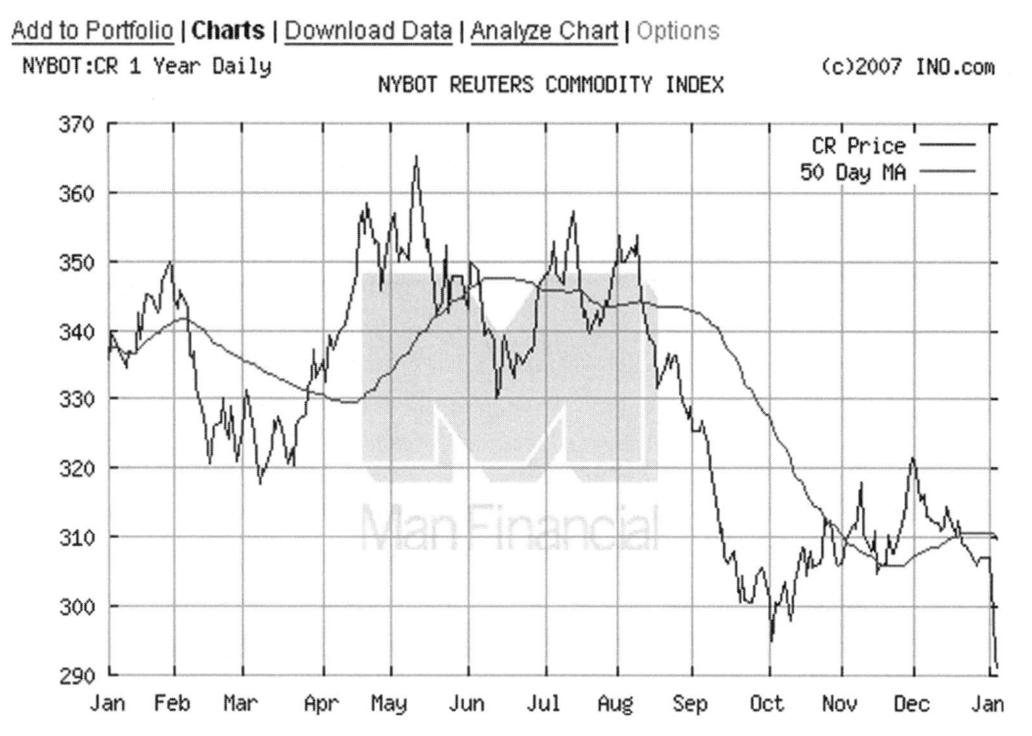

FIGURE 5.4 Reuters Commodity Index.
Source: www.ino.com.

EQUITIES AND FOREX

The relationship between currencies and equities is an area of interest that is becoming increasingly evident and important for traders to become knowledgeable about. For example, when the yen is weak, Sony's and Canon's share values become more attractive because they are exporters and, in effect, dollar earners. In all equity markets around the world, exporting sectors benefit from a weaker home currency or the expectation of one. DaimlerChrysler, Renault, and Peugot suffer share declines when the euro surges beyond expectations. As we noted in our section on China (Chapter 4), when there is speculation that the renminbi will increase, many Chinese equities increase in stock value due to expectations that their assets will increase in value.

U.S. housing sector equities have a direct link to forex. For example, in December 2006, Black and Decker warned its shareholders that it faced "significant challenges" due to a slump in the housing market. The equity market sell-off on February 27, when the

Dow Jones Industrial Index suffered its worst day in four years, was a direct example of the link between equities and forex. The sell-off was precipitated by a sudden fall in the dollar against the yen. This decline caused a liquidity crisis as hedge funds needed to sell equities to release funds to buy back their positions in the yen. (See Chapter 1 for a discussion of this event.) As globalization increases, strong currency moves will impact equity markets as it did on February 27. In a real sense, tracking equities where their dollar earnings are important can benefit a trader in providing leading indicators of forex price moves.

The relationship between the dollar and the equity markets is further underscored by the Dow Jones Industrial Index reaching historic highs. This occurred as the USDX entered into an extended downtrend (see Figure 5.5). Why has the relationship been inverse between the equity market and the value of the dollar? A deeper look reveals the answer. As the dollar value declines versus other currencies, the companies that export to the rest of the world benefit from increased sales, as exports become more attractive to foreign buyers. Additionally, multinational corporations having assets abroad experience an increase in the dollar value of those assets.

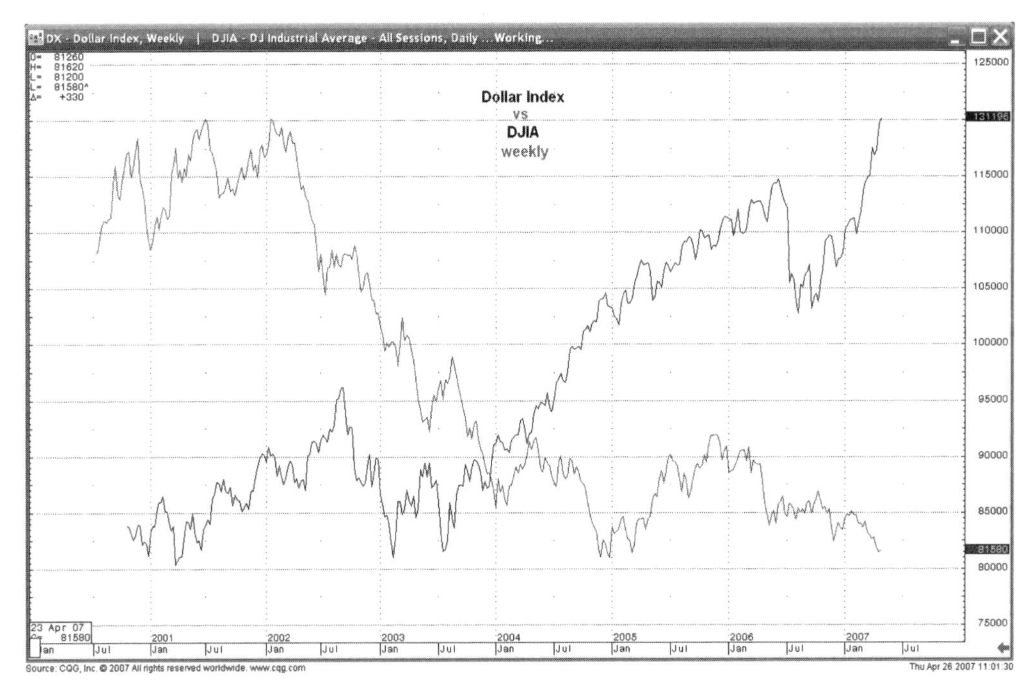

FIGURE 5.5 Dollar Index vs. the Dow.
Source: CQG, Inc. Copyright © 2006. All rights reserved worldwide.

Check the Weekly Crude Oil, Copper, and Gold Charts

Which commodities are probing support or resistance? Are any of these commodities in a channel pattern?

CHAPTER 6

How Business Confidence and Consumer Sentiment Affect the Market

A powerful response force that moves forex prices, as well as other markets, is business and consumer confidence data. These reports are results of extensive professionally designed surveys that are conducted on a regular basis in many countries. When these survey results are released, they provide important information on expectations regarding the economy of a country. This information is seriously assessed by central banks in determining their next moves in controlling inflation. Growth in business or consumer confidence has inflationary potential, while a decline in business or consumer confidence portends economic slowdown. When these releases come out, they move the market, especially if the results are surprising.

Beyond having an impact upon their release, confidence indicators can also provide a leading indicator for the forex trader. If business confidence is at its highest in years, the market will interpret it as positive for the currency because greater confidence indicates expansion and growth of an economy. Where there is expectation of expansion and growth, there is the concomitant expectation of interest rates *not* going lower and possibly going higher. These confidence surveys are not perfect predictors of resulting currency moves. They are one of the most important ingredients in the mix of fundamental forex factors.

Some of the important confidence indicators are listed on page 42 and should be followed. Their release times are tracked in the numerous economic calendars available, and strategies for trading these economic data releases should be learned by traders. It is interesting to note that every major country has its version of investor and business confidence indicators. These form in effect a leading indicator about currency directions.

Investor/Business Confidence Indicators

- Zew Economic Sentiment Indicator (www.zew.de)
- IFO Business Climate Survey (www.cesifo-group.de)
- Institute of Supply Managers (www.ism.ws/)
- Tankan Report (www.boj.or.jp/en/)
- National Australian Bank Business Survey (www.nabmarkets.com/research/flagshippublications/nationalmonthlybusinesssurvey.aspx)

U.S. Sentiment Indicators

- Consumer Confidence (www.conference-board.org)
- University of Michigan Sentiment (http://about.reuters.com/productinfo/universitymichigan)
- ABC Consumer Comfort Index (www.washingtonpost.com/wp-srv/business/articles/consumerindexdata.htm)
- Fed Beige Book (released two weeks prior to Federal Open Market Committee meetings, eight times a year)
- ISM Nonmanufacturing (www.ism.ws/ISMReport/index.cfm)
- Empire State Manufacturing Survey (monthly report, www.ny.frb.org/research/regional_economy/empiresurvey_overview.html)
- Chicago PMI ISM Nonmanufacturing (released on the third business day of the month, can be found at www.ism.ws/)
- Richmond Fed Manufacturing Survey (www.richmondfed.org/research/regional_conditions/manufacturing_conditions/index.cfm)
- Philadelphia Business Outlook Survey (monthly, www.phil.frb.org/econ/bos/index.html)

Go to an Economic Calendar (www.econoday.com) and Find the Next Business or Consumer Confidence Report Release Time

Watch what happens upon the release to the currency pairs.

CHAPTER 7

Fundamental Personalities of Currencies

If each currency's value is a reflection of the underlying economy of its country or region, we can begin to think of them as having a fundamental personality that can guide our strategies for trading. This chapter focuses on how a trader can gain an understanding about the strength and weakness of a currency. The concept of a trade-weighted currency basket is introduced as well as how to obtain the latest trade-weighted information and data that can be directly used in trading.

TRACKING CURRENCY STRENGTH: HOW STRONG IS A CURRENCY?

In reviewing the "big" fundamental picture for a currency, we have reviewed what moves forex prices from an economic point of view. We can be convinced that currencies reflect world opinion about how well an economy is doing or expected to do. The next step in fundamental analysis is to be able to make a judgment about a particular currency itself. Ultimately, the question arises for the trade: How strong is the currency? In spot forex trading, the trade itself is always a paired event of one currency against another. But when a trader makes a judgment about the strength or weakness of a currency by only comparing one currency against another (usually the U.S. dollar), the conclusion can be misleading as to the global strength or weakness of the currency. When trading majors where the U.S. dollar is part of the pair, the comparative question becomes: How strong is the U.S. dollar against that currency? It's important to get an insight on how strong a currency is with respect to its total global trade position. To enable an answer to the question of how strong a particular currency is on its own terms without reference to another pair, the trade-weighted index (TWI) is used by economists and should also be used by currency traders.

The TWI represents how well the currency of a country is doing against a basket of other currencies. The currencies included in the TWI are those that reflect the major trading relationships with the index currency. Each currency receives a weight in the index that reflects its importance. For example, in Table 7.1, we can see that Japan is Australia's major trading partner and has the greatest weight in the Australian TWI. We can also see that Canada and many other nations have a very small percentage component of the TWI.

Each year the central bank and economists adjust the weights to reflect changing realities of international trade. As China increases its trading relationships around the world, it will receive more weight in TWIs. The point is that the TWI represents a way

TABLE 7.1 Weights in the Australian TWI (2002 versus 2005)

	Trade Weight (%)	
Currency	**2002**	**2005**
Japanese yen	17.2058	16.3596
U.S. dollar	15.0681	11.9388
European euro	12.3981	13.0819
Chinese renminbi	8.5754	12.7491
Sourth Korean won	6.5588	5.7178
New Zealand dollar	5.5689	5.6381
U.K. pound sterling	5.1365	4.1785
Singapore dollar	4.0090	4.1299
New Taiwan dollar	3.5877	3.3041
Indonesian rupiah	3.2399	2.6159
Malaysian ringgit	2.8733	3.3057
Hong Kong dollar	2.4360	1.5237
Thai baht	2.3356	3.1509
Saudi Arabian riyal	1.6315	1.2539
Canadian dollar	1.5743	1.4786
Indian rupee	1.5280	2.8263
Vietnamese dong	1.0583	1.4794
South African rand	0.9971	1.1587
Papau New Guinea kina	0.9588	1.1396
UAE dirham	0.8940	0.8146
Phillippine peso	0.8454	0.6089
Swedish krona	0.8310	0.8737
Swiss franc	0.6875	0.6723

Source: Reserve Bank of Australia.

of gauging the change in value of a currency in terms of its global trading position. By knowing the TWIs of each currency, the forex trader can detect a strengthening and weakening of a currency and also get a sense of how a currency can be impacted by events in countries of their trading partners.

Many traders often ask the question: What do you think of the U.S. dollar (or yen, pound, or euro)? One important way of answering is from the perspective of the TWI. Each currency gains a trading personality, and knowing the TWI for each currency is very useful, because it will reflect the big picture much more accurately.

Most recently, the International Index Company issued a new product line called iBoxxFX®, which are indices that are, in fact, trade weighted. They allow an average forex trader to take a snapshot of the strength of a currency without the noise of the forex market. Table 7.2 shows the iBoxxFX® currency baskets for each currency. Notice how each currency index reflects the varying importance of its different trading partners. We will see shortly that these trade weights are a clue to defining the fundamental personality of a currency.

AUSTRALIAN DOLLAR (AUSSIE)

The Australian dollar, also known as the "aussie," as a floating currency started in 1983. Before that time, it was pegged to the dollar, and before that it was pegged to the British pound. By floating its currency, the market sets the value of the currency and the central bank can avoid the necessity of intervening by buying and selling dollars to keep the currency value. But a floating currency also permits capital to float out of a country. The fear of floating is great among totalitarian regimes and emerging countries that want to maintain control of their economy. By looking at the aussie TWI (see Table 7.2b), we can see that the aussie is affected by economic growth in all parts of the world and has its trading relationships almost evenly distributed among Asia, Europe, and North America. The role of Australia as a global trading country makes it an attractive currency to trade.

The recent years of economic expansion have created strength in this currency. The currency in 2006 had a strong upward trend, which, from a world trade perspective, remains intact. The Australian dollar is almost as equally sensitive to the Japanese economy as it is to the euro or the U.S. economy. We can even see that its neighbor New Zealand can impact the value of the aussie because it generates 11 percent of Australia's trading volume (see Figure 7.1).

Important also to consider are commodity-related events such as movements in copper and gold. Australia is a major producer of both of these commodities and is affected by price patterns. Figure 7.2 shows the Australian dollar–U.S. dollar (AUDUSD) pair

TABLE 7.2 Trade-Weighted Indexes of Eight Currencies

(A) Iboxx® Trade-Weighted Basket For European Euro	Weights (%)
U.S. dollar	38.74
British pound	28.37
Japanese yen	16.84
Swiss franc	9.33
Swedish krona	6.62

(B) Iboxx® Trade-Weighted Basket for Australian Dollar	Weights (%)
Japanese yen	31.95
European euro	25.55
U.S. dollar	23.32
New Zealand dollar	11.01
British pound	8.17

(C) Iboxx® Trade-Weighted Basket for British Pound	Weights (%)
European euro	66.59
U.S. dollar	21.47
Japanese yen	5.91
Swiss franc	3.14
Swedish krona	2.89

(D) Iboxx® Trade-Weighted Basket for Canadian Dollar	Weights (%)
U.S. dollar	86.14
European euro	5.96
Japanese yen	5.29
British pound	2.18
Swiss franc	0.43

(E) Iboxx® Trade-Weighted Basket for New Zealand Dollar	Weights (%)
U.S. dollar	30.94
European euro	26.02
Australian dollar	18.74
Japanese yen	17.30
British pound	7.00

(F) Iboxx® Trade-Weighted Basket for U.S. Dollar	Weights (%)
European euro	35.70
Canadian dollar	32.17
Japanese yen	19.82
British pound	9.52
Swiss franc	2.79

(*continues*)

TABLE 7.2 *(Continued)*

(G) Iboxx® Trade-Weighted Basket for Swiss Franc	Weights (%)
European euro	70.43
U.S. dollar	15.04
British pound	7.40
Japanese yen	5.15
Australian dollar	1.98

(H) Iboxx® Trade-Weighted Basket for Japanese Yen	Weights (%)
U.S. dollar	60.91
European euro	25.89
British pound	6.33
Australian dollar	3.67
Canadian dollar	3.20

versus using the Goldman Sachs Commodity Index. We can see how the movements are in sync, visualizing a strong correlation between commodity moves and the aussie-dollar pair.

Figure 7.3 takes a closer look at how the aussie-dollar pair calibrated against copper. It shows that in 2006, these commodities began to diverge down while the aussie

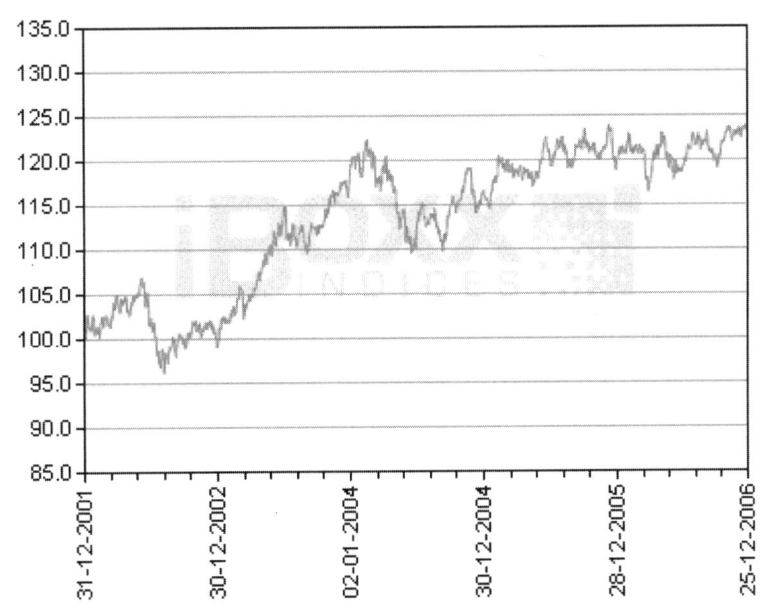

FIGURE 7.1 Trade-Weighted Australian Dollar.
iBoxx® is a registered trademark of International Index Company Limited.

FIGURE 7.2 Australian Dollar versus Goldman Sachs Commodity Index.

continued strengthening. When a trader sees divergence from the traditional relationship, questions arise. Why would the aussie continue to be strong if copper is weak? The answer was that there was great strength in other sectors of the Australian economy, making copper less important.

The fundamental personality of the aussie is that of a commodity- and trade-dependent currency. The aussie will be affected by global economic growth and, in particular, Chinese growth. China is now the second largest buyer of Australian exports, making the aussie more sensitive then ever before to the direction of the Chinese economy.

A special feature of the aussie is that it has a multiple fundamental personality. It can be considered an Asian currency, reflecting Asian growth, and it can be considered a currency that also is impacted by the United States and Europe. This means that the forex trader should seriously look to trade the aussie pairs such as the Australian dollar–Japanese yen (AUDJPY) and Australian dollar–euro (AUDEUR), as well as the traditional Australian dollar–U.S. dollar (AUDUSD) pair. The Organisation for Economic

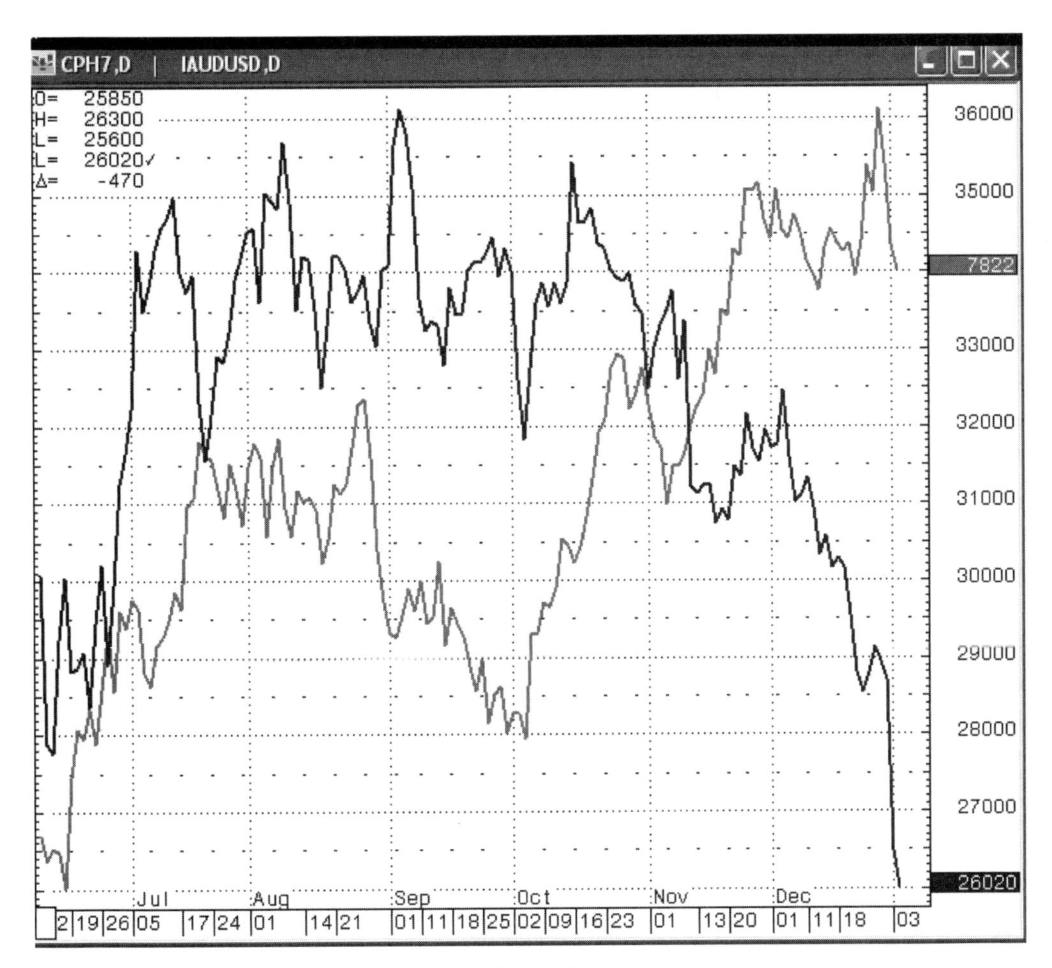

FIGURE 7.3 Copper Futures versus Australian Dollar.

Co-operation and Development's (OECD's) Economic Outlook report summarized the fundamental Australian picture as:

> *A pick-up in export volumes is likely to bring output growth gradually back up above the trend rate of over 3% by 2008, despite a decline in the terms of trade and a cooling of the business investment boom. Growth will, however, be held back in 2007 by the effect of a drought on the agricultural sector.*

The cycle of growth that the aussie is in will be certainly tested. Events in China and the commodity markets will be important factors to watch. Also, perhaps more

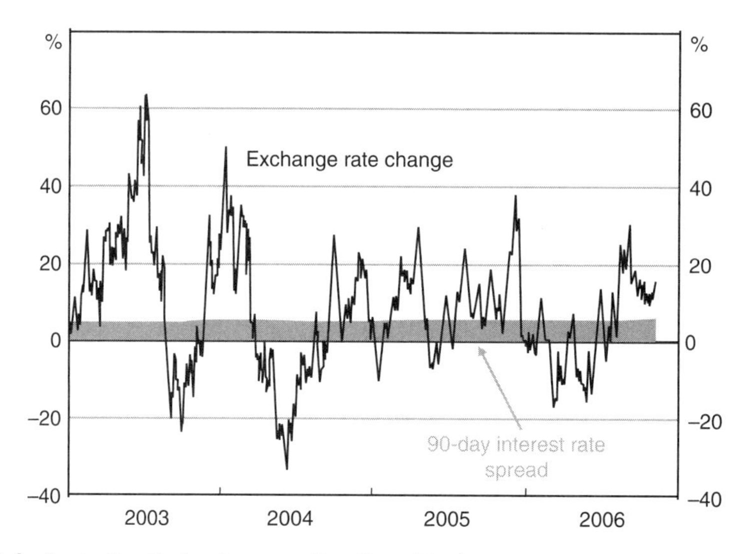

FIGURE 7.4 Australian Dollar-Japanese Yen Carry Trade.
Source: Guy Debelle, head of the International Department, Australian Foreign Exchange Market, November 2006.

significant over the coming year are events in Japan. If Japan raises its interest rates, the aussie will suffer because the conditions for the carry trade will decline. The Japanese rate of 0.50 percent and the aussie rate of 6.25 percent has encouraged a great deal of investment flow out of Japan and into Australia. If this spread changes, so will the conditions encouraging a stronger aussie.

Figure 7.4 shows why the carry trade has been persuasive. In recent years, it has been very rare for the aussie to depreciate against the yen. This made the risks of an unhedged carry trade very low. But the risk of carry trades providing a big decline remains very real.

Domestically, the Australian economy entered 2007 with 30-year lows in unemployment at 4.6 percent. The Reserve Bank of Australia increased rates to 6.25 percent to help slow down the economy. At the end of 2006, inflation rates were at 3.9 percent, still high for global standards and above the central bank's target rate of between 2 percent and 3 percent. The combination of domestic growth and global growth makes trading the aussie in the coming years a lot of action.

CANADIAN DOLLAR (LOONIE)

Canada has experienced significant economic growth, surpassing $1 trillion of gross domestic product (GDP). Its robust expansion led the Central Bank of Canada to increase interest rates to 4.50 percent as of July 2007. This currency's fundamental personality reflects its big sister, the United States. The United States is Canada's major trading partner, reflecting the fact that the U.S. dollar receives a weight of 86 percent in the trade-weighted basket. Refer to Table 7.2d.

Therefore, when the U.S. economy slows, the Canadian economy also suffers. The other major factor influencing the direction of the Canadian dollar, also known as the "loonie," is crude oil. Canada's tar sands are an important magnet for capital, and Canada is a net exporter of oil. When oil prices increase, the Canadian currency benefits. Figure 7.5 demonstrates the strong relationship between crude oil and the Canadian dollar.

FIGURE 7.5 Crude Oil and the Loonie.

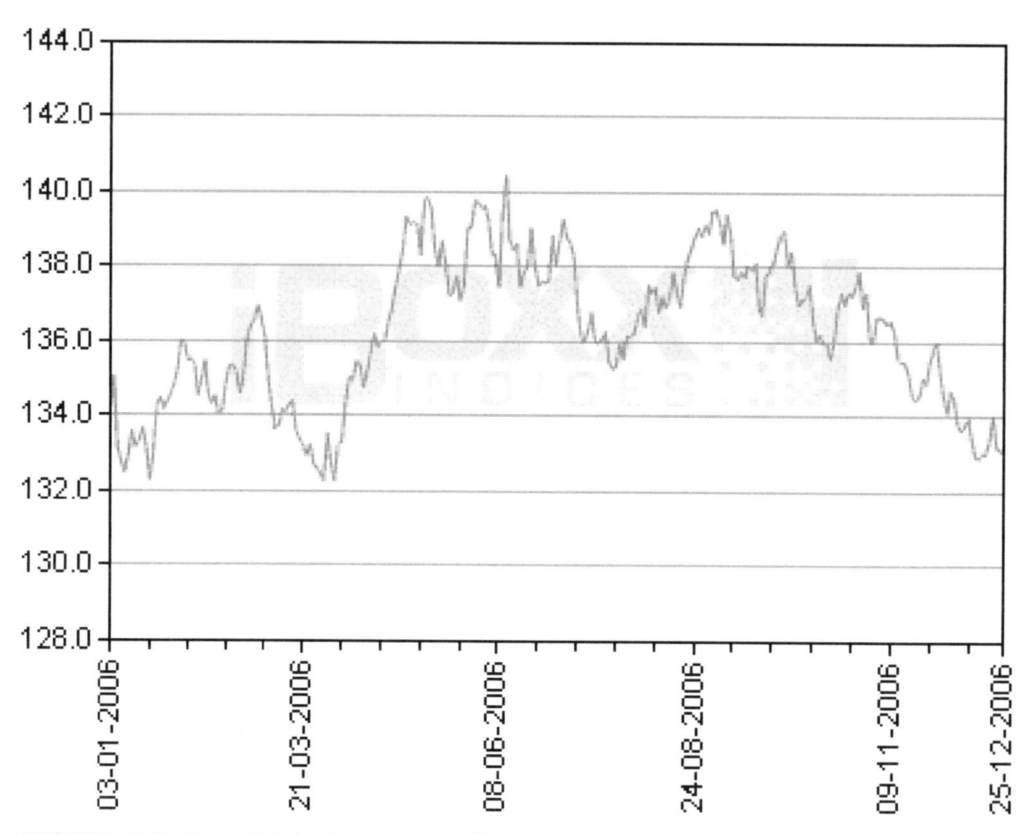

FIGURE 7.6 Trade-Weighted Canadian Dollar.
iBoxx® is a registered trademark of International Index Company Limited.

The Canadian currency's performance against a trade-weighted basket in 2006 shows a broader range than most currencies due to the decline in the price of oil (see Figure 7.6).

From a fundamental point of view, trading the Canadian dollar against the U.S. pair is the most effective way to play this currency. A useful web site for tracking the Canadian economy is www.canadianeconomy.gc.ca/.

NEW ZEALAND DOLLAR (KIWI)

The New Zealand dollar, also known as the "kiwi," should get more of the attention of forex traders. New Zealand is almost a classic example of how fundamentals can drive currency movements. The New Zealand economy is small. It exports about $2.8 billion and imports $3.4 billion. Since its consumer economy is small, the fundamental characteristic that affects its economy is whether its exports can grow. Therefore, interest rates and the resulting currency valuation are key to its future economic vitality. The fact is that 151 companies generate 78 percent of New Zealand's exports. Data show only 4 percent of the New Zealand firms do any exporting.

New Zealand's interest rates are now at 8.0 percent and, as a result, the currency has risen substantially in strength. New Zealand's unemployment rate has been at a low level of 4.6 percent; however, its inflation rate is high, at 3.6 percent. New Zealand's central bank is in a difficult position. At current interest rate levels, New Zealand's rates are the highest of all the major currency pairs. But this level was recognized as having risks of slowing the New Zealand economy. In fact, the New Zealand Central bank intervened for the first time since 1990 and sold the New Zealand dollar on June 11. If it tries to raise rates further to slow down inflation, it can choke off exports and cause a major contraction. If it doesn't, inflation may rise to unacceptable levels. The fundamentals point to a mixed situation that can go either way. As a result of this uncertainty, the kiwi offers potentially very many trading strategies, as the currency will be extremely sensitive to central bank actions as well as surprises in economic data.

New Zealand's major trading partners are balanced between the United States, Europe, and its neighbors Australia and Japan (refer back to Table 7.2e). China's influence is also growing and will soon be reflected in its official trade-weighted indexes (see Figure 7.7).

The forex trader looking to trade the kiwi can explore trading the dollar pair U.S. dollar–New Zealand dollar (USDNZD), as well as the kiwi against the aussie (NZDAUD), the yen (NZDJPY), or the euro (NZDEUR).

MEXICAN PESO

The peso is a currency that offers potential for trading more than ever. Mexico's economic profile reflects a growing potential. Its GDP is now nearly $900 billion, and Mexico may overtake Canada in GDP. Mexico is the world's fifth largest oil producer and ninth largest oil exporter. Pemex, Mexico's monopolistic oil company, generates an estimated 35 percent of federal government revenues. The OECD projects a GDP growth in Mexico of 3.5 percent in 2007 and 4 percent in 2008. Importantly, inflation is projected to be just above 3 percent (www.oecd.com).

Also important in understanding the dynamics of Mexico's economic growth is the impact of China. China is a competitive threat to Mexico, and as it grows, Mexico's manufacturing and export business have suffered because of China's advantage in its low cost of manufacturing and assembly due to the lack of a float of its currency.

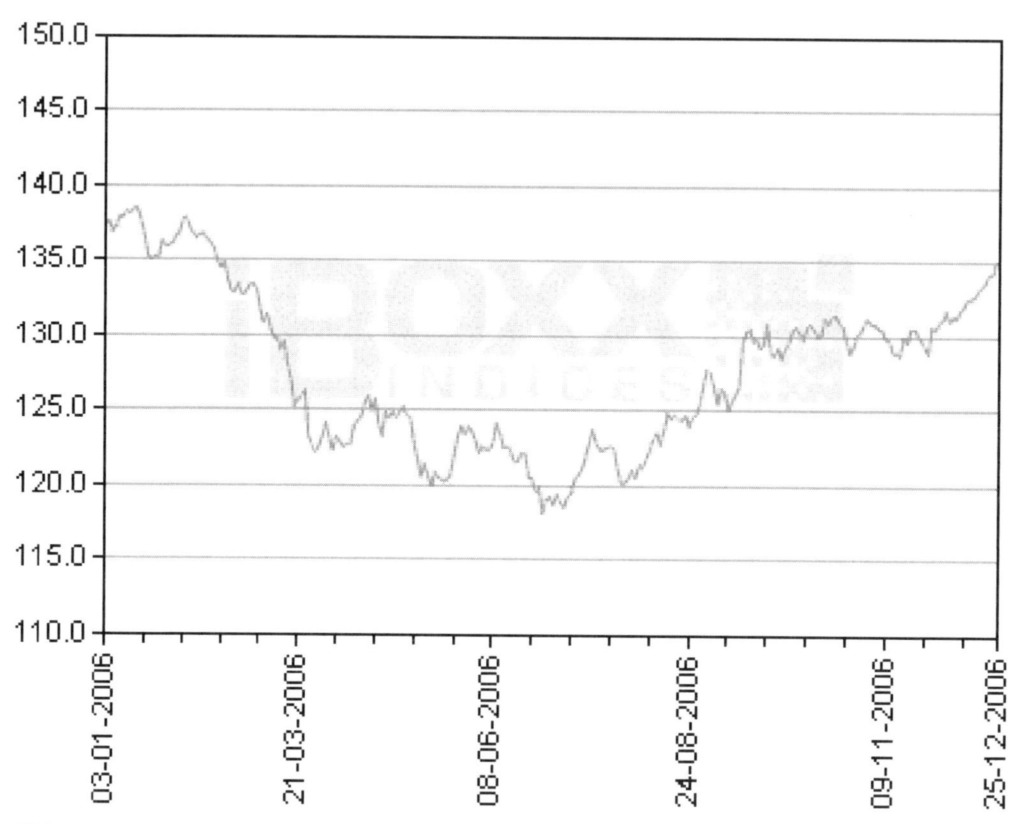

FIGURE 7.7 Trade-Weighted New Zealand Dollar.
iBoxx® is a registered trademark of International Index Company Limited.

The peso's value will also tend to be supported by its relatively high interest rates, which are now at a level of 7.2 percent, but lower than previous highs of 8 percent. Additionally, the peso is strengthened by its ability to attract capital flows. It is useful to note that those traders who sell the U.S. dollar and buy the Mexican new peso (MXN) in the USDMXN pair, receive interest rate payments. So the peso can be used as a carry trade currency pair. The second major factor is the U.S. economy. Mexican exports are at a level of over 80 percent to the United States, and there is a high inflow of capital coming from Mexicans living in the United States.

Oil also needs to be considered. Like Canada, Mexico is a net exporter of oil and attracts petrodollars. A major negative factor is business confidence. The Mexican business climate is often marred by inefficiencies, and the political economy generates a great deal of negative sentiment. Another factor emerging is Asian competitiveness. As countries such as Vietnam and others in East Asia are emerging as low cost manufacturers, Mexico's comparative advantages in world trade suffer.

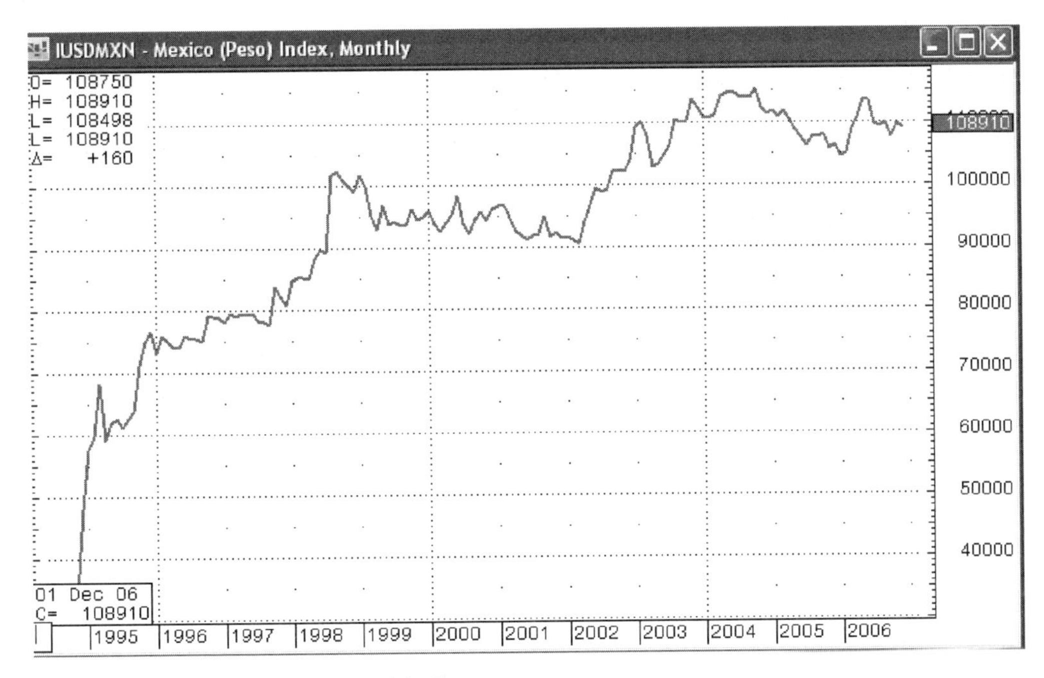

FIGURE 7.8 Mexican Peso Monthly Chart.
iBoxx® is a registered trademark of International Index Company Limited.

From a fundamental point of view, there are many risk factors impacting the peso's direction. If Mexican interest rates fall, the peso could weaken substantially; if the U.S. economy slows, Mexican growth will suffer. Based on this fundamental picture, trading the Mexican peso should be considered mainly against the dollar, and trading this pair using longer-duration charts is more advisable (see Figure 7.8).

JAPANESE YEN

Japan is the second largest developed economy in the world. Yet its size doesn't guarantee a successful economy. To understand Japan today, one has to have a sense of where the Japanese economy has come from.

In 1989, the Nikkei 225 Index, which is a price-weighted index of the top 225 stocks on the Tokyo exchange, peaked around 39,000. In 1990, the Nikkei Index fell by 39 percent, and in March 2007, it was at the 17,400 mark, still quite a way from the highs of the previous era. The "bubble" (1987–1991) in Japan had broken. The "bubble" was characterized by extremes in consumption of luxury cars, expensive food, outlandish art auction prices, and surges in sales of luxury brand bags and jewelry. The Nikkei had tripled in price in the 45 months prior to its peak. Also, metropolitan land prices tripled between 1985 and 1989. Finally, there was a significant increase in borrowing to finance home purchases (Atsushi Maki, "Changes in Japanese Household Consumption and Saving Behavior before, during, and after the Bubble Era: Empirical Analysis Using NSFIE Micro-data Sets," *Japan and the World Economy*, January 2006).

Then Japan experienced what has been called "The Lost Decade." Between 1995 and 2002, the average annual GDP growth rate was an anemic 1.2 percent. Compare this to the same period growth rate of other nations, shown in Table 7.3.

The Japanese stagnation had many causes, but a major contributor was the Japanese consumer. Studies (e.g., Charles Horioka, "The Causes of Japan's Lost Decade: The Role of Household Consumption, *Japan and the World Economy*, Vol. 18, 2006) have shown that in Japan, what could go wrong in consumption did. Household disposable income declined, household wealth declined, and, coupled with uncertainty about the future, the result was low confidence in prospects of strong growth. Once the forex trader appreciates what the era of stagnation was like in Japan, he or she will have a greater understanding of why Japan today is still not on firm footing of renewed growth.

For example, household disposable income had a growth rate of only 0.98 percent for 1991 through 2003 compared to 3.32 percent for 1980 through 1991. Household wealth declined by an average 0.39 percent. Interestingly enough, there is data showing that the proportion of people saving for old age rose from 50.5 percent in 1991 to 60.4 percent in 1995, demonstrating great fear of the future and lack of confidence in the economy. The data from Japan underscores the importance of consumer confidence. When confidence is low regarding one's country, consumers tend to save much more. This makes it difficult to stimulate growth through traditional monetary measures such as lowering interest rates. Another important characteristic was that prices were actually in deflationary mode, and when prices keep falling there is little incentive for consumers to purchase since they expect cheaper prices.

TABLE 7.3 Growth Rates, 1995–2002

Country	GDP Growth Rate
Canada	3.4
United States	3.2
United Kingdom	2.7
Eurozone	2.2
Australia	3.8
Mexico	2.6
Japan	1.2

Few of today's forex traders remember this period of time in Japan, even though it was less than a decade ago. It was before the emergence of the retail forex market. But the era of stagnation also holds clues as to whether Japan will experience robust, uncertain growth or retreat again into stagnation. Much will depend on the interest rate decisions of the Bank of Japan and business and consumer confidence surveys because the core cause of stagnation was lack of consumer confidence and spending. Therefore, the core of recovery will be a recovery in consumer spending.

But it is not easy to stimulate the Japanese consumer. This means that the forex trader should carefully watch consumer confidence and inflation data coming out of Japan for clues as to whether Japan is overcoming deflationary fears. One such clue occurred in March 2007 when, for the first time in 16 years, Japanese land prices showed an increase. Other clues will be necessary before the Japanese inflation rate moves beyond its current 0.0 percent rate. Also important is export data on Japan. Stimulating exports becomes a critical factor in determining the ability of the Japanese economy to grow. Any significant strengthening of the Japanese yen, particularly against the dollar or the euro, could threaten Japan's export growth. However, any extreme level of weakening of the yen would help exports. But remember that too weak a yen against, for example, the euro may help Japanese exports but would undermine European exports. The forex trader should note that where there are beneficiaries to a currency direction, there are also losers. The Japanese finally increased interest rates to 0.50 percent as part of its central bank's policy of encouraging inflation. But the interest rate differential between Japan and other nations is still quite steep. Even if the Bank of Japan increases rates to 0.75, if other central banks also increase their rates (the central bank of New Zealand increased rates to 8.0 in June 2007), the effect of this differential may encourage continued outflows of capital from borrowing yen to invest in kiwi and other currencies (see the next section on the carry trade).

This uncertainty in the Japanese economy creates a great deal of increased ranging behavior in the currency. Traders of the yen should almost always expect the unexpected because economic news from Japan has a built-in greater potential to surprise us. Also important to consider is the growing impact of China on the Japanese prospects for growth. China has now surpassed the United States as Japan's largest trading partner. As a result, if the yen were to move toward a strengthening, Japan's exports could be hurt. A weak yen, in contrast, stimulates Japanese export growth. Export growth data therefore becomes very important in affecting sentiment toward the yen.

With regard to Japan, perhaps the best word to describe current conditions is *uncertain*. The uncertainty whether the Japanese consumer economy is strong enough to grow, combined with the uncertainty of whether Japanese interest rates will rise, dominates trading of the yen. The complexities facing the Japanese economy also involve aging workforce and potential shortages in labor. All these factors make trading the yen more challenging than the other currency pairs.

CARRY TRADE

The Japanese big picture implications are profound. With interest rates at 0.50 percent, the difference between Japan's rates and those of other countries may continue to result in huge outflows of capital in the form of carry trades. This is where Japanese investors can borrow at extremely low rates and place the capital in bonds of other nations and receive a net gain in interest rates. New Zealand and Australia have been major beneficiaries of the carry trade. For example, New Zealand interest rates are almost the highest in the world, at 8.0 percent. It therefore is a major attraction for the low-interest-rate costs of borrowing yen. A popular way to do this is called the Uridashi bond. The World Bank is a major issuer of these bonds, issuing over 2 billion yen's worth. The total flow of such bonds is in billions more. These bonds are of short duration, most being two to three years. If the market perceived that Japanese rates will increase, the huge amount of carry trade money outflow could suddenly decline. On February 27, 2007, this is exactly what happened, with a sudden sell-off of the dollar against the yen. This caused simultaneously a sell-off of the Dow Jones Industrial Index as big funds got out of equity positions to cover losses in their previous selling of yen. Even gold sold off during this crisis. Refer back to Figure 1.1, which shows the yen and the Dow on February 27. But the sell-off didn't last, as the interest rate differential between the Japanese rates and other countries continued to attract carry trade investors.

The big picture on Japan is one that focuses on uncertain growth and relatively low interest rates. Here is what the *OECD Economic Outlook* report stated at the end of 2006:

> *The current economic recovery, the longest in Japan's post-war history, has matured into a self-sustained expansion driven by private domestic demand. The expansion is projected to continue, with growth of about 2% in 2007–08, thanks to buoyant business investment underpinned by record corporate profits and private consumption. Inflation is expected to increase only gradually ("Developments in Individual OECD Countries and Selected Non-OECD Economies: Japan,"* OECD Economic Outlook, *No 80. Preliminary edition, November 2006).*

During 2007, the yen had a wide range between its index lows and highs and ended near its lows (see Figure 7.9). Its value largely depends on what happens in the economies and the currencies of the United States and Europe. Refer back to Table 7.2g.

Let's summarize several fundamental strategies that emerge from the conditions of the Japanese economy. The first is the bet that the interest rate differences between Japan and the rest of the world will continue. For the forex trader believing this and looking to trade the yen, imitating the "big" money and putting on carry trades as a strategy in a small retail account is one strategy that can be pursued.

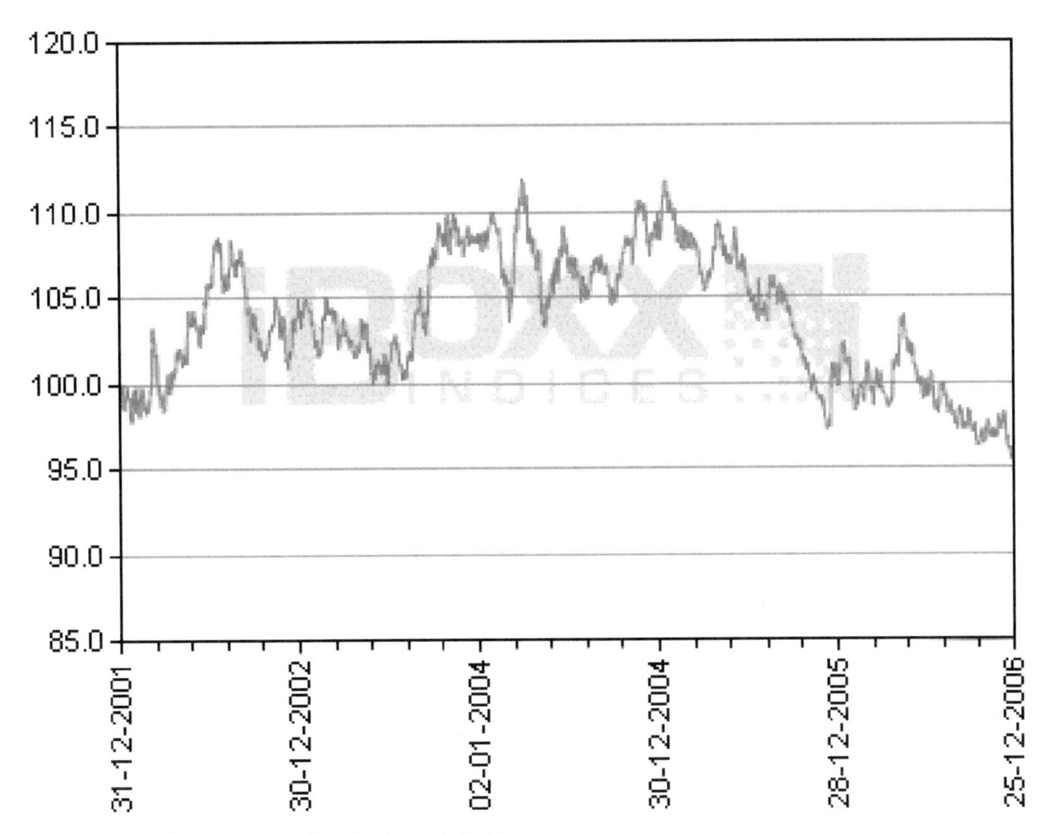

FIGURE 7.9 Trade-Weighted Index of the Yen.
iBoxx® is a registered trademark of International Index Company Limited.

An additional strategy is simply to be selling yen until the key fundamentals change and the trade-weighted index reverses toward the mean of 100. The fact that the trader may observe that the yen is weakening, even in the face of good economic news, should not be a surprise. Instead, the trader looking to buy yen would wait for the period of technical strengthening to run its path and then look to go long the yen. Any surprise news that is positive for the yen can just mean to be prepared for a reversal toward strengthening. The USDJPY pair and the EURJPY pairs are the best trading instruments for the yen.

A third strategy is to buy into the longer view that the Japanese economic recovery will continue and that interest rate increases are inevitable. The trading strategy is to buy the yen (sell USDJPY)—of course, at the right technical locations, which we discuss in Part II.

EURO

The euro as a currency is the most complex in the world. The creation of the euro was a tectonic event in world economic news. Other currencies reflect one unified economy, whereas the euro reflects 13 economies comprising the Eurozone:

- Belgium
- Germany
- Greece
- Spain
- France
- Ireland
- Italy
- Luxembourg
- The Netherlands
- Austria
- Portugal
- Slovenia
- Finland

When combined, the Eurozone economy presents a powerful part of world trade. Table 7.4 snapshots the key measures of the regions, such as population, GDP, sectors of production, and unemployment rate.

This increased level of complexity introduces more uncertainty on the currency's behavior. Managing to control the multiple economies of the Eurozone makes the mission of the European Central Bank (ECB) one of the most challenging of all central banks. To succeed, the policies of the ECB need to succeed in all of the member countries. Keep in mind that this is not easy. Each country has its own domestic policies, and its own

TABLE 7.4 Economic Profile of the Eurozone

	Euro Area	United States	Japan
Population (millions)	313.2	296.7	127.6
GDP (share of world GDP) (%)	14.8	20.1	6.4
GDP per capita (thousands in euro)	25.5	35.6	25.9
Sectors of production:			
Agriculture, fishing, forestry (% GDP)	2.2	0.7	1.2
Industry (% GDP)	26.6	21.1	20.2
Services (% GDP)	71.3	78.2	69.6
Unemployment rate	8.6	5.1	4.4

Source: European Central Bank.

TABLE 7.5 iBoxx® Euro Trade-Weighted Index

Basket Currencies	Weights (%)
U.S. dollar	38.7426
British pound	28.3728
Japanese yen	16.9379
Swiss franc	9.3343
Swedish krona	6.6124

inflation rates. Events in any country can undermine, achieving the average inflation rate that the ECB sets. The forex trader has to expect the unexpected in regard to the euro.

The personality of the Euro as a currency is based on which countries are the Eurozone's trading partners. We can observe these trading relationships in the Trade-Weighted Index for the euro (refer to Table 7.5). The U.S. dollar has the greatest weight, with the British pound and then the yen following. There is more than one trade-weighted index that the trader should be aware of. For example, we also have a fairly new trade-weighted index for the euro called the Dow Jones Euro Currency 5 Index (Table 7.6). The DJEC5 places a greater weight on Japan and less weight on the United Kingdom. It also includes Australia, which is ignored by the TWI. For those traders interested in the mathematics behind this new index, the following equation is used to calculate it:

$$\text{Index} = \frac{\sum_{i=1}^{n}(p_{it} \times q_{it})}{D_t} = \frac{M_t}{D_t}$$

where D_t = divisor at time t
M_t = the sum of component midprices multiplied by their respective weight factors at time t
n = the number of currencies in the index
p_{it} = the midprice of currency i at time t
q_{it} = the weight factor of currency i at time t

Source: Dow Jones Indexes.com.

TABLE 7.6 Dow Jones Euro Currency 5 Index

Currency	Weight (%)
U.S. dollar to euro	44.28
Japanese yen to euro	24.91
British pound to euro	21.55
Swiss franc to euro	6.29
Australian dollar to euro	2.98

In any case, trading the euro in the absence of knowledge about which countries the euro trades with will undoubtedly lead to misjudgments about the performance of that currency. The importance of the euro as a currency reflects the fact that its trading partners are global, and as a result the euro as a currency may become less dependent on U.S. economic prospects. Traders have many choices of pairs to shape the trade. The EURUSD pair is the most popular, followed by the EURJPY pair and the EURGBP pair.

The fundamental picture of euro performance at this point in time is that of sustained strength. It has been probing trade-weighted highs, which reflects strong economic performance in its member countries. The economic growth of the Eurozone has led to interest rate increases by the European Central Bank to contain inflation near a 2 percent level. This increase in rates has served to further strengthen the demand for the currency. The ECB raised its benchmark interest rate seven consecutive times, from 2 percent in December 2005 to 4.0 percent now, and is in a position where it can order up more rate increases in 2007 without squeezing growth. The issue for the Eurozone's future direction will significantly depend on whether its high interest rates will contain inflation or fear of inflation and lead to market expectations of no further rate increases. However, the Eurozone also faces a relatively high unemployment rate of nearly 8 percent.

If the currency continues to have strength against a weakening yen, the Eurozone may face a slowdown on exports, of which Japan is an important trading partner (Figure 7.10), which would result in a slowdown in its economic performance. The trader should carefully watch the EURJPY pair (Figure 7.11) if it presses on to new weekly and monthly highs. Fundamental forces will kick in and provide the impetus for a sell-off.

BRITISH POUND (CABLE)

Great Britain remains a vigorous part of the global economy. Consider the fact that over half of the profits coming from the *Financial Times* and London Stock Exchange (FTSE) 100 are profits from overseas activity. The British economy is intimately linked to global trading patterns. The TWI of the pound as tracked by iBoxx® (see Table 7.7) shows that the major trading partner is the Eurozone, followed by the United States.

This immediately suggests that in trading the pound, the EURGBP and the USDGBP pairs would be the main pairs to trade. The British pound's fundamental personality is that it is more oriented to European economic events than the United States.

We can see in Figure 7.12 that 2006 was a key year showing increasing strength of the pound as a currency that has underlying strength. In 2006, it broke the index number of 100. We can also see that the pound is getting close to topping out in global strength, and traders need to watch for a possible probing or trend break in its TWI, as we can see in Figure 7.13.

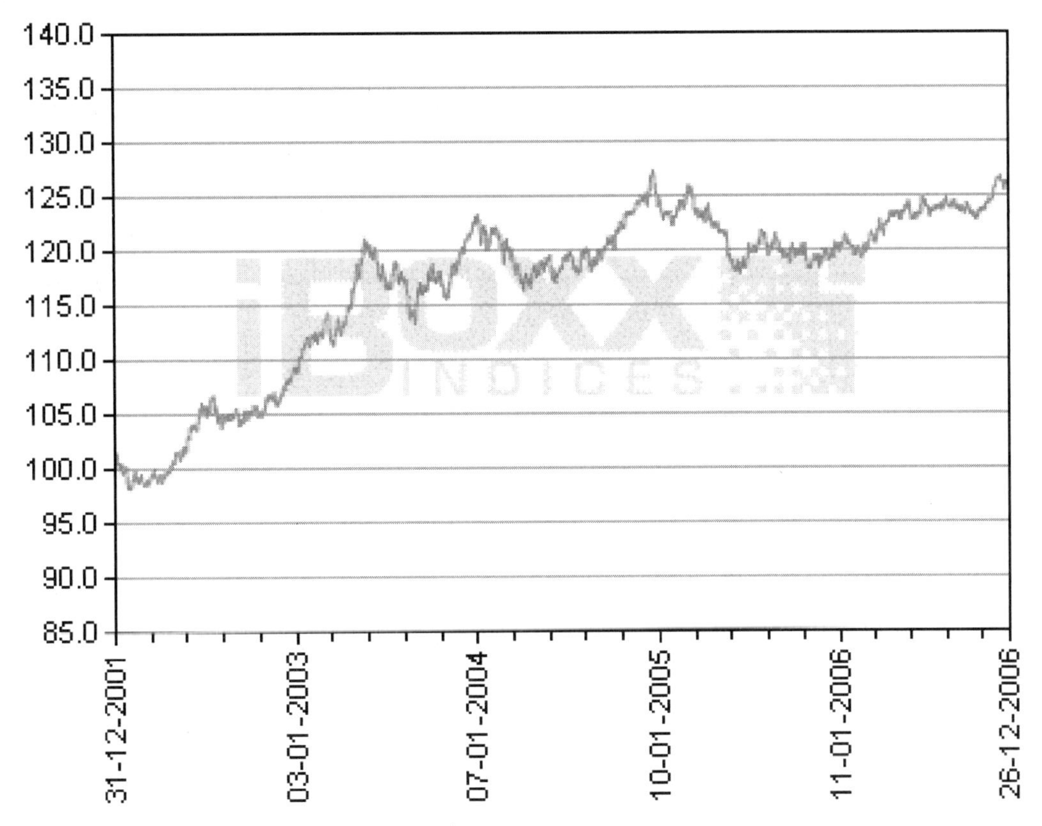

FIGURE 7.10 Trade-Weighted Euro Index.

Series Level Information

Title complement	**ECB Real effective exch. rate CPI deflated, EER-23 group of currencies against Euro**
Series key	EXR.M.Z30.EUR.ERC0.A
Unit	Points
Last update	2006-12-23 07:45:33.0
Decimals	Two(2)
Collection indicator	Average of observations through period(A)
Publications	Monthly Bulletin: Overview table, section 01 Monthly Bulletin: Table in chapter 08, section 01 Statistics Pocket Book: Table in chapter 04, section 10
Frequency	Monthly

Data Chart

112.5
110
107.5
105
102.5
100
97.5
95
92.5
90
87.5
85
82.5
1994 1996 1998 2000 2002 2004 2006

FIGURE 7.11 Trade-Weighted Euro Chart.

TABLE 7.7 iBoxx® Trade-Weighted GBP

Basket Currencies	Weight (%)
European euro	66.5900
U.S. dollar	21.4700
Japanese yen	5.9100
Swiss franc	3.1400
Swedish krona	2.8900

The British economy at the end of 2006 was growing at its fastest rate over the previous two years nearing $^2/_9$ percent annualized GDP growth. The Bank of England (BOE), in response to the hot British economy, raised rates in a surprise move in August 2006, and raised rates again to 5.75 percent as of July 2007. These actions of the BOE show that its policy on raising rates is very sensitive to data and that the central bank is not ideological about it.

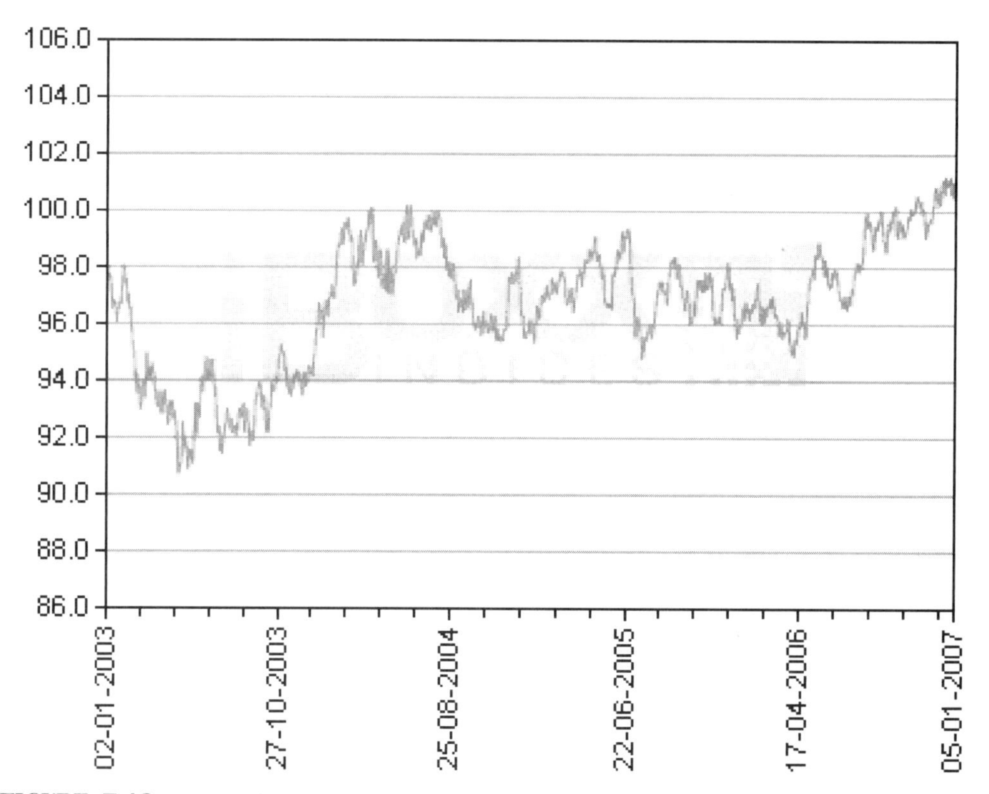

FIGURE 7.12 GBP Trade-Weighted Weekly Chart.
iBoxx® is a registered trademark of International Index Company Limited.

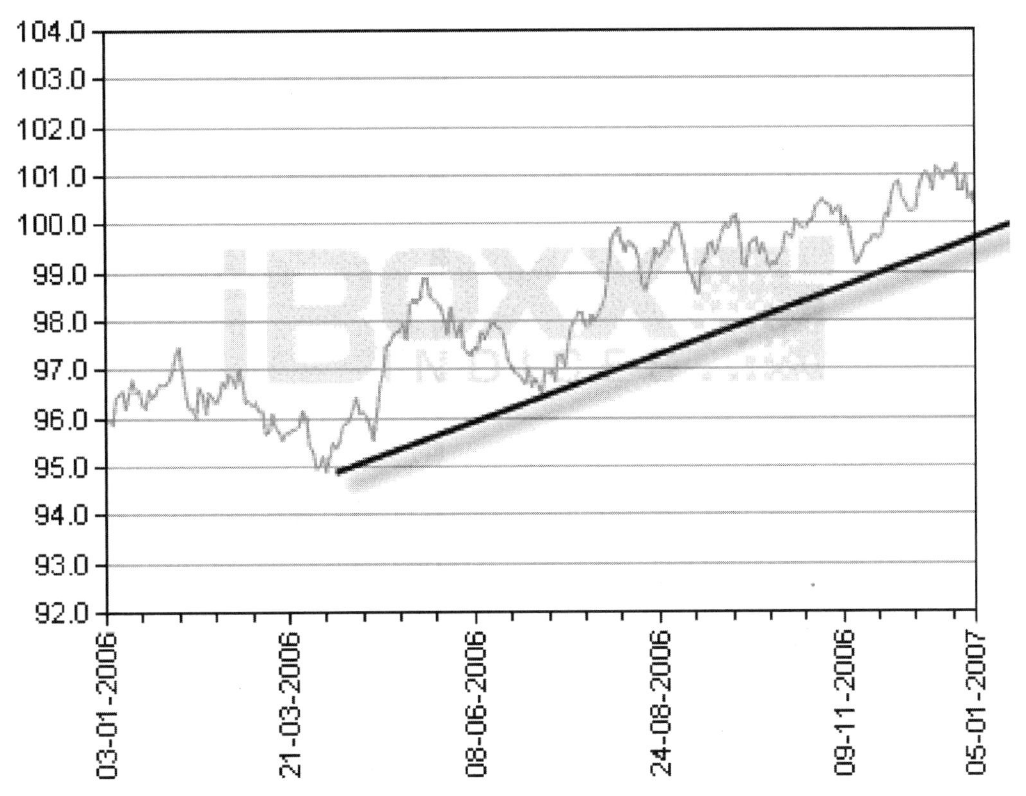

FIGURE 7.13 GBP Trade Weighted Daily Chart.
iBoxx® is a registered trademark of International Index Company Limited.

The key factor for traders to watch will be what the BOE does on interest rates. As indicated in the section on fundamentals, housing continues to be a major component of decisions of central banks. Figure 7.14 shows that the hot housing market of Great Britain has not, as of this writing, experienced a downturn like the United States.

With regard to inflation, the BOE's target is 2 percent, and it is now at 2.7 percent, which leads to significant pressure and expectations that interest rates will not go down. But any data that shows a slowing of inflation would translate into a selling of the pound. Beyond the critical components of interest rates and GDP, Great Britain has unique economic challenges due to an increase in migration levels. The surge in migration can affect inflation and employment levels in a variety of ways, and those who watch and trade the pound must not ignore these aspects of fundamentals and Great Britain.

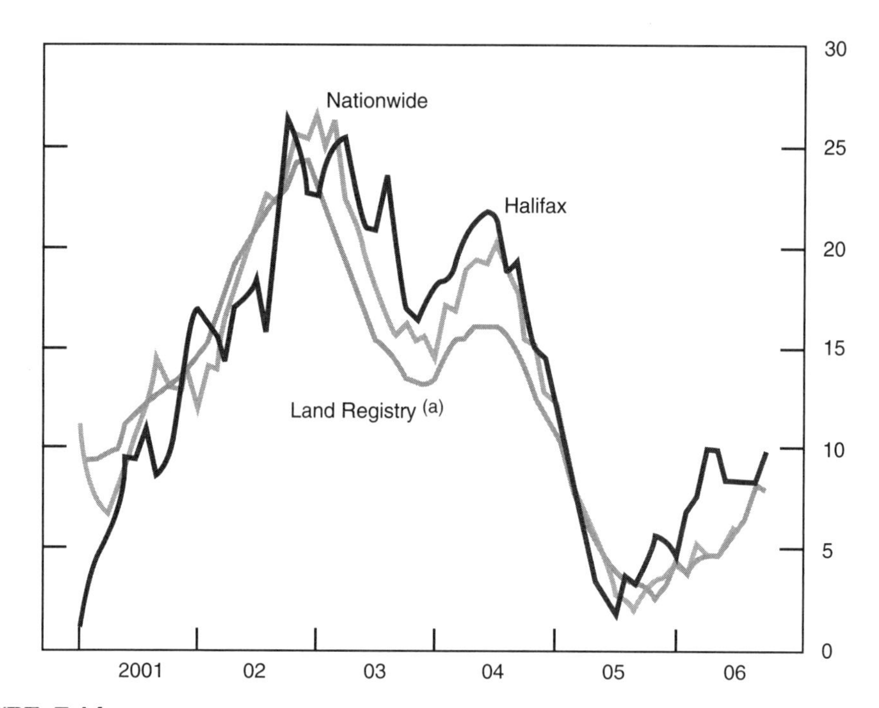

FIGURE 7.14 House Prices (Percentage Changes from a Year Earlier).
(a) Lagged by two months to reflect the fact that the index is based on completions whereas the lenders' indices are based on mortgage approvals.
Sources: Reproduced with kind permission of Land Registry. The house prices data being used is Crown copyright and is reproduced with the permission of Land Registry under delegated authority from the Controller of HMSO.

SWISS FRANC

The Swiss franc represents an interesting niche among the global floating currencies. Over the years, it has been used as a safe-haven currency because it had a link of convertibility. This link was abandoned in 2000, but the Swiss National Bank (SNB), the central bank, still holds 30 percent of its assets, about 1200 tons in gold. Even though it is more than 70 years after the global collapse of the gold standard in 1936, there is still an association of gold and the Swiss franc.

In a speech commemorating this anniversary, John Pierre Roth, chairman of the governing board of the SNB, said the following:

> *As I said at the outset, the role of gold has faded over the years. But gold had an afterlife long after it ceased to be relevant in any form for the conduct of monetary policy. First and foremost, the legal link between the Swiss franc and gold*

continued to exist until very recently. The constitutional changes that severed this link took effect in 2000, followed, within the same year, by the corresponding changes in the relevant law. The new law no longer includes an obligation on the part of the SNB to redeem banknotes for gold—an obligation which—in practice—had been suspended for decades. Moreover, it has abolished the minimum gold coverage of the banknotes in circulation and the gold parity of the Swiss franc. With these changes, gold finally became a normal and marketable asset for the SNB. In May 2000, the SNB began to sell part of its gold stock. About 50 percent of the gold once owned by the SNB has now been sold. I should emphasise that the SNB will continue to hold gold as a monetary reserve, but the legal relics of the gold standard era no longer immobilize the gold stock as they did for decades (Opening remarks, conference, "Seventy Years After: The Final Collapse of the Gold Standard in September 1936," University of Zurich).

The Swiss franc's personality is not limited to an orientation to gold. It reflects the fact that it is embedded in the European economy. From a trade-weighted point of view the most important currency impacting the franc is the euro followed by the U.S. dollar (see Table 7.8).

Trading this currency offers several alternative strategies. It can be used as a hedge against the EURUSD trade; it can also be used as a method for buying dollars. In fact, in trading the news, the hedge effect of the USDCHF against the EURUSD is employed to implement a trading the news strategy. The Swiss franc also can be used as an alternative to the yen for those traders looking to construct a carry trade. They would be selling the Swiss franc, which has an associated low interest rate of 2.5 percent, and then buying currencies that have higher interest rates such as the New Zealand dollar, the Australian dollar, and even the British pound. Finally, by understanding the state of the Swiss economy and evaluating the trade-weighted index charts (Figure 7.15), the trader can decide whether to buy or sell the Swiss franc ("Export Accessibility in Switzerland," Switzerland Economic Studies, 2000, p. 21 [AN 5847930]).

TABLE 7.8 iBoxx® Trade-Weighted Index CHF

Basket Currencies	Weight (%)
European euro	70.4304
U.S. dollar	15.0363
British pound	7.4008
Japanese yen	5.1537
Australian dollar	1.9788

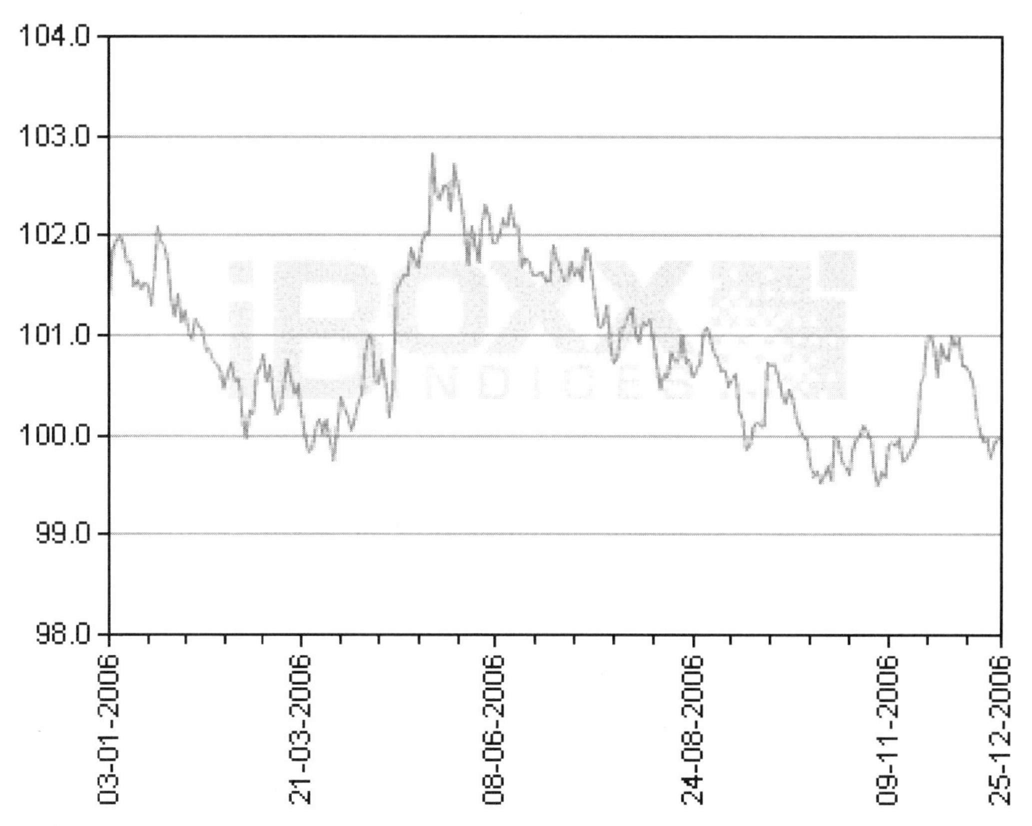

FIGURE 7.15 CHF Trade-Weighted Index Daily Chart.
iBoxx® is a registered trademark of International Index Company Limited.

Track the Trade-Weighted Indexes of the Currencies

Go to www.iboxx.com and register. You will then be able to generate the latest TWI charts in a few simple steps.

CHAPTER 8

The Personality and Performance of the U.S. Dollar

Gaining a fundamental understanding of the U.S. economy is a critical part of being prepared fundamentally for forex trading. The U.S. economy is still the largest developed economy in the world, and therefore the U.S. dollar reflects this importance. Much of the world's trade is denominated in dollars, and global reserves of central banks hold over US$4 trillion, which is about 60 percent of all reserves, according to latest data. It is true that we are in a period when the world economy is growing, particularly with the growth of Asia. This growth may mean that in the coming years, the preeminence of the U.S. economy will diminish. However, as the U.S. economy remains the critical pivot point of the world economy, forex trading will continue to pay close attention to U.S.-based economic events. In particular, the forex trader, in trading a currency pair involving the dollar, is actually making a judgment or a bet about the direction of the U.S. dollar with regard to the other pair. This can be a five-minute bet or one that goes substantially longer in duration. But the fundamental question the trader has to answer is whether to be bullish or bearish on the dollar for his next trade.

A first approach to getting a picture of the global position of the U.S. dollar and gauging whether it is strong or weak is by looking at the Trade-Weighted Index (TWI). In Figure 8.1 we can see that the "health" of the U.S. dollar has declined significantly. It is probing the lows of this index, and if it breaks below 80, the world, through global trading forces, will demonstrate an unprecedented decline in dollar values.

This 30-year chart certainly provides a perspective missing from day-to-day trading, but a forex trader can zoom in on the U.S. dollar performance by generating a nearer-term chart. For example, in Figure 8.2, we see the U.S. Dollar Index–TWI recent patterns. The trader can use this chart and generate strategies to prepare for future moves if they occur. The next time you are asked the question, "What do you think of the U.S. dollar?,"

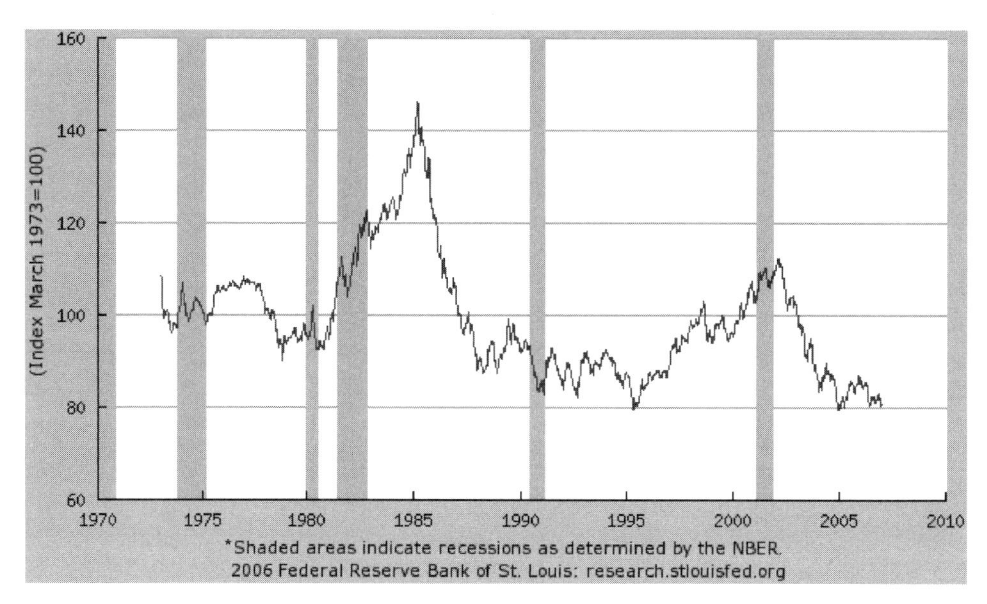

FIGURE 8.1 Trade-Weighted Exchange Index: Major Currencies (TWEXM).
Source: Board of Governors of the Federal Reserve System.

FIGURE 8.2 USDX Day Chart.
Source: www.ino.com.

based on a review of Figure 8.2, you can answer that the U.S. dollar is in a compressed triangle and that it is testing historic support near 80 on the TWI. One can also go further and develop a trading strategy and state: "If it breaks below 80, I will be a seller of dollars, but if it stays above it, I will be a buyer." This kind of strategy, which comes from a fundamental perspective but also reflects good technical strategy, is a recipe for success.

Gaining insight into the strength of the U.S. dollar can also be done by looking at the New York Board of Trade's (NYBOT's) U.S. Dollar Index (USDX). This index is traded at the NYBOT and is a weighted index. It is not trade weighted and therefore does not reflect the dollar's strength or weakness in the context of global trading patterns. But the USDX is traded by major funds and is considered an important barometer of sentiment regarding the dollar. It can easily be tracked at www.ino.com. Let's take a closer look.

STRUCTURE OF THE USDX

The USDX has its own basket of currencies, just like the TWIs. But notice the differences in the weights between the USDX's basket and the Federal Reserve's in Table 8.1.

The question arises of which is better? The answer really depends on how you use it. The USDX is more popular and provides a trader an accepted way to track dollar sentiment, though it is less accurate from an economic point of view. When the USDX is showing a dollar decline, it may be exaggerating the real decline from a global trading point of view. In Figure 8.2, we can see that as 2006 ended, the dollar had retraced somewhat on better housing news and was testing a key 50-day moving average. The USDX chart provides a good way of checking dollar sentiment.

It should be clear that there are many ways to evaluate the dollar. In fact, new measures are always being introduced. Citigroup recently introduced its own dollar index called the Citigroup Flow-Weighted Index. This index scrutinizes international capital flows, which have become an important influence on forex. Additionally, there is the

TABLE 8.1 New York Board of Trade's U.S. Dollar Index

Currency	Weight
European euro	0.576
Japanese yen	0.136
British pound	0.119
Canadian dollar	0.091
Swedish krona	0.042
Swiss franc	0.036

J. P. Morgan Dollar Index, which looks at the dollar in terms of a basket of 18 currencies. The bottom line is that the forex trader has now an improved ability to answer the question of how well the dollar is doing in terms of its fundamentals by looking at the different TWIs of the dollar.

U.S. FOREIGN DEBT AND WHO BUYS U.S. ASSETS

One of the fundamental variables that affect sentiment regarding the U.S. dollar is the fact that as a nation the United States has huge foreign debt. For example, economist David Levy said recently:

> *The current account deficit measures the difference between what U.S. residents spend abroad and what they earn abroad in a year. It now stands at almost six percent of GDP; total net foreign liabilities are approaching a quarter of GDP. Sudden unwillingness by investors abroad to continue adding to their already large dollar assets, in this scenario, would set off a panic, causing the dollar to tank, interest rates to skyrocket, and the U.S. economy to descend into crisis, dragging the rest of the world down with it (www.foreignaffairs.org/20050301facomment84201/david-h-levey-stuart-s-brown/the-overstretch-myth.html).*

Another way to look at the current account deficit is that it reflects the excess of imports over exports. The question is: Why is there a current account deficit in the United States, and why do nations such as China have a current account surplus? The answer is that the fundamental personality of the U.S. economy is that it is the world's greatest consumer economy. The issue that is relevant for the forex trader is not the fact that there is a current account deficit; it's the fact that it results in the U.S. Federal Reserve's issuing notes to finance this deficit, and foreign ownership of these securities generates fear in the market. The fear is that if foreign investors of U.S. Treasury notes suddenly became unwilling to buy these notes, the U.S. economy would suffer. Here is what happened in 1997:

> *Foreign ownership of U.S. Treasury securities has often been the subject of considerable public debate. Discussion of this issue arises particularly at times of uncertainty about either the outlook for the exchange value of the dollar or the need for cash in countries holding large stocks of Treasury assets. In June of 1997, for example, there was a flurry of activity in the U.S. financial markets when the Prime Minister of Japan, Ryutaro Hashimoto, suggested that Japan might find it necessary to sell some of its large Treasury holdings.*
>
> *On the day following Mr. Hashimoto's remarks, the Dow Jones industrial average fell by 192 points, its largest decline in a single day since the 508-point*

falloff on October 19, 1987. While the Prime Minster's clarification of his remarks subsequently calmed the markets, it did nothing to alter the potential vulnerability of the U.S. financial markets to sudden decisions by foreign holders of U.S. debt to undertake large-scale sales of their dollar assets. (Laurence H. Summers, "The U.S. Current Account Deficit and the Global Economy," October 4, 2005, The Per Jacobsson Foundation,www.perjacobsson.org/2004/100304.pdf)

The U.S. Treasury issues a report called "Major Foreign Holders of U.S. Treasury Securities (www.treas.gov/tic/mfh.txt). The fear that someday foreign ownership of U.S. Treasury securities will stop and cause interest rates to increase and destabilize the U.S. economy. The trader will find that this fear continues to resurface in newspaper headlines and will likely become part of the U.S. national political dialogue.

When the U.S. Treasury report comes out, it can move the forex market. We can see from the latest reports that the United States has over $2 trillion of foreign holders of U.S. securities (see Table 8.2). From a fundamental view, this is supportive of the dollar. We can see that the Organization of Petroleum Exporting Countries (OPEC) accumulates dollar surpluses from its petrodollars. It also purchased more U.S. treasuries. Monitoring the levels of foreign owners of U.S. securities is an important part of sensing the true dollar sentiment in the world. Forex dollar bulls can point to the fact that essentially a consistent stream of buyers of U.S. treasuries has provided a floor against a steep and quick fall of the U.S. dollar.

TABLE 8.2 Major Foreign Holders of Treasury Securities (Billions of Dollars)

Country	As of Jan-07
Japan	648.8
China	353.6
United Kingdom	249.3
Oil exporters	102.4
Korea	65.6
Taiwan	63.1
Caribbean banking centers	62.9
Germany	56.4
Hong Kong	54.7
Brazil	53.7
Top 10 Total	1710.5
	76% OF TOTAL
Total	2239.7
T bills	181.4
T bonds and notes	1135.4

Source: www.treas.gov/tic/mfh.txt.

Economists are in agreement that the effect of foreign purchasers of U.S. Treasury securities is to lower interest rates. Without such purchases, U.S. rates might be nearly 1 percent more. Here is how analysts at the U.S. Treasury Department portrayed risks to the United States related to foreign ownership of U.S. Treasury securities:

- Treasury ownership by itself does not present a risk, but the "special" role of the dollar in private and official dealings has meant that:
  - The dollar has been stronger.
  - The trade balance has been weaker.
  - Econometric evidence suggests that recent heavy central bank buying has helped keep interest rates low.
- If the dollar's role were to fade, interest rates would be pushed up and the dollar down:
  - Central banks would diversify reserve currencies away from dollars.
  - U.S. investors would increase exposure to foreign securities.
- A decline in the role of the dollar, were it to occur, would likely be gradual . . .
  - Central banks are very conservative by nature.
  - The institutional structure of global trade payment system would change gradually.
- . . . and thus does not present a risk of a sharp or destabilizing financial market event (www.treas.gov/offices/domestic-finance/debt-management/adv-com/minutes/mm-2005-q1.pdf).

In the long run, evidence exists that there is a trend toward diversification of foreign holders away from dollar assets. As other economies grow, the incentives to reallocate reserves away from U.S. dollar assets to more local assets will rise. Even rumors of such diversification lead to selling U.S. dollars in the market by traders who do not want to risk holding dollars. This has an effect of weakening support for the dollar.

Find the Top 10 Holders of U.S. Treasury Securities

Go towww.treas.gov/tic/mfh.txt and answer these questions:

- Has there been a change in the trend of foreign holders of U.S. Treasury securities?
- When is the next Treasury International Capital System report coming out?

CHAPTER 9

Conducting Your Own Fundamental Analysis

The forex trader today is very lucky. The Internet provides unprecedented access to information and data—perhaps too much information. A good technique to use that provides an efficient way to pull information out of the World Wide Web is to use the search engines and input the right terms. For example, as the trader prepares to evaluate a currency to trade, he or she should also scan the latest news. Here is how to do it:

1. Go to Google, click on the ***News*** link and then click on ***Sort by Date***.
2. Input search terms (U.S. dollar, Australian economy, etc.).

For example, if you input the term *Australian interest rates*, the results will quickly point to the latest article on it.

Using Google or any other search engine effectively will depend on which terms are entered. The trader should enter a variety of terms to maximize the items retrieved. Here are some useful terms to start with:

U.S. dollar

U.S. economy

U.S. interest rates

Bloomberg on U.S. Dollar

European economy

European interest rates

German economy

German interest rates

Bernanke

Trichet

Zhou Xiaochuan

Bank of China

Fukui

Australian interest rates

Australian economy

Canadian economy

Canadian interest rates

Governor Dodge

Bank of Japan

The idea is to search for the latest analysis while you are scanning the charts, which will help you gain an understanding of what forces are moving the charts while you trading.

DEVELOPING A FUNDAMENTAL OUTLOOK

Developing a fundamental outlook is part of the evolution of a forex trader. When you first begin trading, the focus tends to be on technique and tactics because learning how to put on the trades and how to read the charts is the most important task at hand. But as a forex trader develops an understanding of the fundamentals, he or she will eventually ask the following two questions:

1. What currency pairs should I be trading?
2. What direction is my next trade?

It is helpful to be able to group currencies by their fundamental personalities. We can see that some currencies are stronger than others and that some currencies are fundamentally at extremes; those groups become more interesting to trade. A fundamental view leads to the understanding that the major causes of change in the relative value of currencies are real or perceived changes in interest rates, inflation, or economic growth between their economies.

The relationship between fundamentals and forex prices is not a direct relationship; rather, it is more akin to fuzzy logic or a chemistry of forex. Fundamentals remain in the background and provide important conditions conducive to a currency's strengthening or weakening. By forming a fundamental view of currencies, the trader is able to get in line with the powerful economic forces that currencies ultimately reflect.

To guide traders in conducting their own fundamental analysis, they need to have their own fundamental forex checklist and action plan. The purpose of the fundamental forex checklist is to make sure you have the information to make some trade strategy decisions.

Fundamental Forex Checklist and Action Plan

1. Scan and list current global data on gross domestic product (GDP), interest rates, and inflation levels.
2. Scan price patterns in commodities such as oil, gold, copper.
3. Review the Trade-Weighted Index (TWI) of each currency to determine if any are probing key support or resistance.
4. Check the U.S. Dollar Index (USDX) at www.ino.com and compare it to the TWI of the U.S. dollar.
5. Scan global interest rates and try to group currencies by:
   a. Countries expected to raise rates
   b. Countries expected to keep rates the same
   c. Countries expected to lower rates
6. Choose which currency pairs to trade.
7. Choose the preferred direction of your next trade. If you do not have a preferred direction, that means you are choosing to trade in either direction.
8. Watch the calendar for economic releases.

Prepare your own Fundamental Outlook Report

Try to write a paragraph describing in your own words the fundamental outlook for a currency. Send it to learn4x@earthlink.net will be reviewed, and you will receive advice on how to improve it. Here is a sample:

Fundamental Outlook Report on the Currency Pair (_______)

The CURRENCY PAIR is in a strong position fundamentally because its economy is experiencing growth at a GDP rate of (_______) per year. Its inflation rate is now at (_______). The central bank has indicated (1) a bias toward increasing interest rates; (2) a neutral stance on interest rates; (3) concern on slowdown of the economy. The Trade-Weighted Index has shown a trend (up) or (down).

The biggest risk factor for this currency pair is:

1. Unexpected rise in inflation
2. Further slowdown in housing
3. Direction of oil prices, etc.

In other words, put in your own words a summary of what's going on with the fundamentals affecting the currency that you are looking to trade.

PART II

Timing the Trade with Technical Analysis

The question in every trader's mind is: Just when and where should I pull the trigger? Technical analysis supplies the tools for answering that question, but there is no single answer. There is no single technical indicator that can be exclusively relied on to produce winning outcomes, because the markets are too complex. No one, to date, has produced a consistently reliable technical trading system for any market, let alone forex. This is because technical indicators can never capture all of the variables that influence price movements. Financial mathematicians, known as "quants," try to come up with algorithms (equations) that improve predictive ability, and they get millions of dollars to try. They've tried every conceivable methodology, such as Fourier analysis, wavelets, and neural networks, to try to gain even the smallest increment of predictive value. Yet none can replace the seasoned experienced trader. The reason should be obvious—technical analysis provides a snapshot of market moves that have already occurred. The resulting snapshot is a picture that is always lagging and limited in resolution. In contrast, the smart trader has evolved a successful mixture of analytical tools that sense repeatable patterns in the market.

Yet technical analysis is not without its value. Technical analysis of chart movements, when used correctly, can improve trading, not by predicting but by providing a "map" revealing important aspects of what the price has been doing and how it got there. Technical analysis can help sort out the "noise" of price movements and reveal patterns that can be traded with a high probability of success. The forex trader's main challenge is to use technical analysis of charts to achieve actionable "knowledge" of market conditions.

Whatever analysis techniques are used, the single most important question that the forex trader has to ask and answer is: Where is my next trade? By asking this question, the trader prioritizes information and analysis and separates what is useful from what is not. For example, the forex industry is filled with a great deal of information flow. We might even call it information overload. Traders have numerous chat rooms to visit; there are a number of news feeds pushing the latest headlines to the trader. Blogs have added to the noise as well. Every forex firm seeks to gain a competitive edge by providing the latest "analysis" of market conditions. *The challenge is to pull the information that helps shape your next trade.* How to shape your next trade is the goal of Part II of this book.

Becoming a forex trader is not an instant process—it's an evolution. Beginners to forex do not even know what they need to know. Trades are put on without a plan, and beginning trades are really trial-and-error experiments. Winning trades occur but don't seem repeatable. The beginning forex trader experiences the market but doesn't leverage his knowledge. At this early stage, the exposure to quick and large losses usually wipes out the trader within the first month of trading.

The second stage of the evolution of a forex trader is the discovery of indicators and technical analysis. At this stage, the trader tends to use too many indicators. The trading results are not much better, but this stage is characterized by hunting trades. The trader overtrades due to a desire to put on trades as often as possible.

The final stage in the evolution of a forex trader occurs when the trader has sharpened his tools and has acquired an ability to let the market come to him. This is achieved when knowledge and experience combine. While the biblical adage that there is no wisdom without pain still rings true, much of the pain that new traders experience in unnecessary losses can be avoided. The best traders in the world lose perhaps 40 percent of the time but are still able to become profitable.

How does one evolve to his or her level of maximum forex competence? While everyone cannot become a master trader, everyone has the capability of raising their level of competence. *Competence* is the ability to apply forex knowledge with consistently profitable results. Therefore, the purpose of technical analysis is to help the trader shape a trade that offers a high probable profit within acceptable levels of risk. The process of becoming competent in forex trading started with understanding what forces move forex prices. It continues with understanding how to map the market. Let's start.

CHAPTER 10

Mapping Price Action

Finding the Geometry of the Market

The purpose of this chatper is to explain the first steps in conducting technical analysis of forex prices. These steps involve finding support and resistance, trend lines, and assessing where the price is in relationship to these geometric points.

PROJECTING HORIZONTAL SUPPORT AND RESISTANCE POINTS

Where is the currency pair price and what is it doing? This question is quite basic but it involves many levels of analysis. Understanding the location of the currency pair is a foundational beginning of technical analysis and will reveal a great deal of information that a trader can use in formulating trading strategy.

But how do we know where to look? The basic technical measurement of horizontal support and resistance provides the ground floor of technical analysis. Whenever you look at a currency pair, you have to ask where support is and where resistance is. The answers provide the first mapping of the market.

Support is where the price stops falling, and *resistance* is where it stops rising. The process for locating support and resistance is fairly straightforward. Figure 10.1 includes several support and resistance lines. Those lines that form floors and ceilings are outer support and resistance containing the price action within a range. Those lines that are inside these larger lines are inner support and resistance.

What is most significant about horizontal support and resistance lines is that they are not lagging. In contrast to indicators, they are projections and form psychological hurdle

FIGURE 10.1 Horizontal Support and Resistance Lines for Monthly EURUSD.
Source: www.tradesignal.com.

zones. When price establishes support or resistance, the market recognizes that location as a zone or hurdle that has to be overcome. The immediate future price movements need to probe and penetrate a support or resistance line. *One of the first principles of trading forex is to locate a trade near support or resistance.*

Once we know where horizontal support and resistance are, we need to also determine the strength of that support and resistance. There are different ways of forming an opinion about the level of strength in the S/R lines. In Figure 10.1, we can see that the 1.2500 level offers strong support because over six months that price point was unable to be broken down and the euro–U.S. dollar (EURUSD) held above it. In contrast, the resistance levels show only one test of the previous high. The trader can conclude that there is greater strength on the support side at 1.25. If the price moved toward the previous high (1.3367 on December 31) and failed to go through it, confidence that resistance was stronger at that level would increase. The time interval on a chart also can be used to weight one's confidence about how strong the S/R levels are. The longer time frames

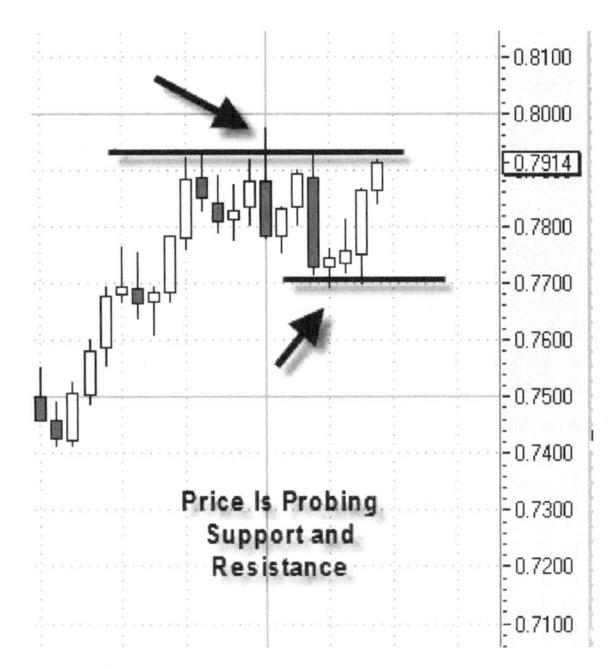

FIGURE 10.2 Price Is Probing Support and Resistance.
Source: www.tradesignal.com.

such as monthly and weekly resistance and support are more robust. After all, a great deal of money has had the chance to go through those levels but did not.

In constructing support and resistance lines, the trader needs to realize that there is a degree of judgment. In Figure 10.2, the support and resistance lines are drawn where there appears to be a set of highs and lows. Some of the candlewicks are penetrating the lines. Those penetrations would be viewed as creating temporary levels of new support and resistance, with the stronger levels being those connecting more points. Drawing support and resistance lines need to be done with the perspective that these are zones and not exact lines.

TREND LINES

The trend is your friend—until it is at an end.

After finding the geometry of support and resistance, we come to the most classical tool used by chartists—trend lines. Trend lines provide a projection of support and resistance that links past behavior into the future. A trend line is used to map whether there is ɩency in highs and lows. While simple in its construction, knowing the trend is a .c foundation for trading forex. Once a trend is identified, detecting a potential change . . the trend becomes a focus for the trader because trading at the break of a trend or the failure to break a trend line is a high probable point of success. Figure 10.3 shows a downtrend in place and the price twice coming to the trend line, and then failing to stay above. Although the price actually created a high above it (where the arrow points), it failed to follow with another candle at that high point. Thereafter, the return of the price under the trend line and the resumption of the downtrend would be recognized by an experienced trader as a sell condition.

The main benefit of trading with a trend is one of probabilities. An upward trend presents a greater number of buying opportunities to the trader. It doesn't mean there are no good selling or contratrend opportunities. We can see in the charts that there were countertrend moves, but much fewer than trend-aligned moves. A prudent trader will seek opportunities that provide a higher probability of success. Trading with a trend

FIGURE 10.3 Price Tests Trends and Fails.
Source: www.tradesignal.com.

meets this condition. The question arises: Which trend should the trader align himself with—the week trend, day trend, 4-hour trend, and so on?

Each choice has advantages and disadvantages. The basic trade-off is the increase in price volatility and range when a larger trend time frame is selected. Trading in the direction of the weekly trend means that a trader will see periods of time and maybe days when the price is moving the other way, threatening losses. But in this case, if the day trends are also moving in the same direction as the weekly trends, it represents more confidence that the trend is stable. For intraday traders trading off a 15-minute chart, when the 15-minute trend direction is aligned with the 4-hour trend direction and also confirmed by the 5-minute trend direction, there is a high level of robustness to the trend. The concept of three time zones confirming trading decisions will apply in many areas.

CONFIRMING AND DETECTING TREND CHANGES: THREE-LINE BREAK CHARTS

Three-line break charts are useful for detecting and confirming trend changes. Three-line break charts are increasingly available to retail traders through their forex firms and through charting companies. They are worth using because there is little ambiguity whether a trend is in place and also at what point it would be considered reversed. Therefore, three-line break charts provide the ability to confirm trend direction in any time interval and project where the trend would be considered reversed! Three-line break charts are excellent charting tools to help answer the question: In which direction should a trade be taken, and where should I enter the trade?

Let's explore this chart tool and how it shows trend strength, trend stability, and trend direction. The chart looks like a candlestick chart, but it is not. Each block represents the completion of a new high or new low. The chart therefore shows only consecutive highs or consecutive lows. This provides a snapshot of the sentiment. What the trader is looking for is the predominant direction of the sentiment, whether the sentiment is weakening, and (most importantly) whether it has reversed.

In the example in Figure 10.4, there are 10 blocks (or lines) down and then a reversal. At the point where the reversal block went past the previous three down blocks, we get a reversal signal. The trader can look to buy at that point since the market showed the ability to reverse the sentiment. This is why it is called three-line reversal. Similarly, move to the right of the chart and we can see that after 17 consecutive new highs, there was a reversal down. If the trader is looking to confirm a decision to buy or sell, then the three-line break pattern is used to support that decision. If there is an intention to buy, then the three-line break blocks should, at a minimum, show that the market is in a buy

FIGURE 10.4 Three-Line Break Reversal Points.
Source: www.tradesignal.com.

trend by showing that it is producing consecutive closes of newer highs. The timing of the entry may be based on other setups, but it is even better if the entry to buy occurred on the three-line break reversal from a previous series of down sequences. The decision to sell a currency pair would be confirmed by having the three-line blocks showing a down sequence, and preferably the entry would occur upon the reversal. The trader has the challenge to select the right time frame for the three-line break charts. Using a day chart converted to three-line break chart will show consecutive day closes of highs or lows. This does not mean that there will not be intraday reversals of important magnitude. It won't show up. As the trader selects shorter time frames, such as the 4-hour, 30-minute, and 5-minute three-line break charts, the trader will recognize the strength of the trend sentiment from a multiple time perspective.

The first important use of three-line break charts is to decide to trade with the three-line break direction. But it can be with the day, 4-hour, 30-minute, or 5-minute directions. If they are all aligned, it is the best of all worlds. Using the 5-minute three-line break charts provides a short time frame but still enables the trader to detect trend direction and reversals that lead to magnitudes of 20 and more pip moves that can be captured.

Take a look at the U.S. dollar–Japanese yen (USDJPY) 30-minute three-line break chart right before and after the February 27 sell-off that affected the world's equity and currency markets. We can see that by using three-line break charts, the trader would have had a first reversal at 121.4 for a sell signal. Then the pair proceeded to close 16 new 30-minute lows consecutively before it reversed up briefly; a new reversal at 120.4 occurred, followed by 18 new lows; and then it reversed back to 118.2. The dramatic fall of the USDJPY is seen by the three-line charts as very strong, with long sequences of selling creating new lows consistently (Figure 10.5). There were very few buying opportunities. An alert trader would be to use the three-line chart to join the sentiment ride down, but would know when to get out (when it reversed up) and when to get in again (when it

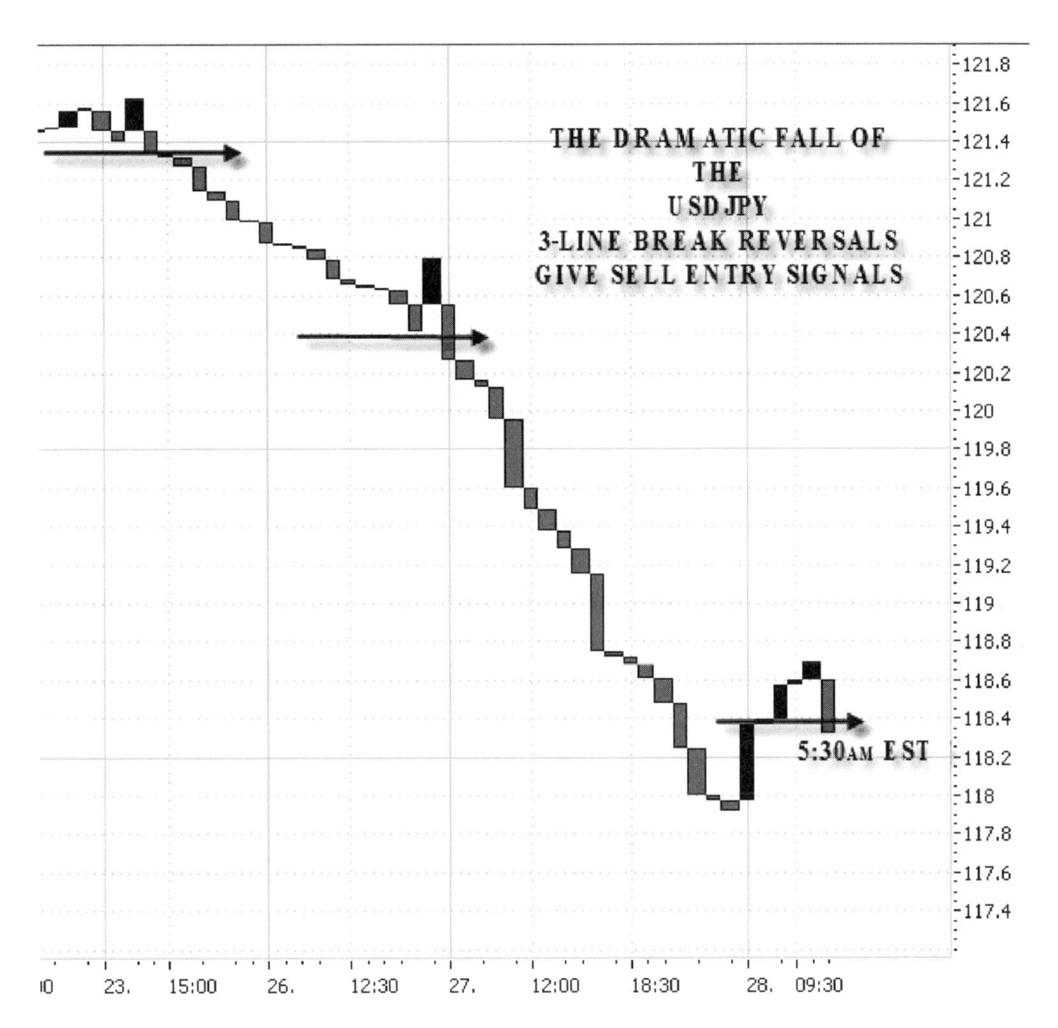

FIGURE 10.5 USDJPY Three-Line Break Reversals on February 27.
Source: www.tradesignal.com.

reversed back down). One of the biggest mistakes traders make is to be caught on the wrong side of the market. Three-line break charts reduce this kind of error by defining the trend in an unambiguous way. Trading with the trend can be rephrased as trading with the three-line break trend.

Using what you have just learned, take a look at a chart of the New Zealand dollar-U.S. dollar (NZDUSD) (Figure 10.6). It is a day chart with a three-line break in it. We can see this pair had very nice alternative sequences of up and down trends. The trader who

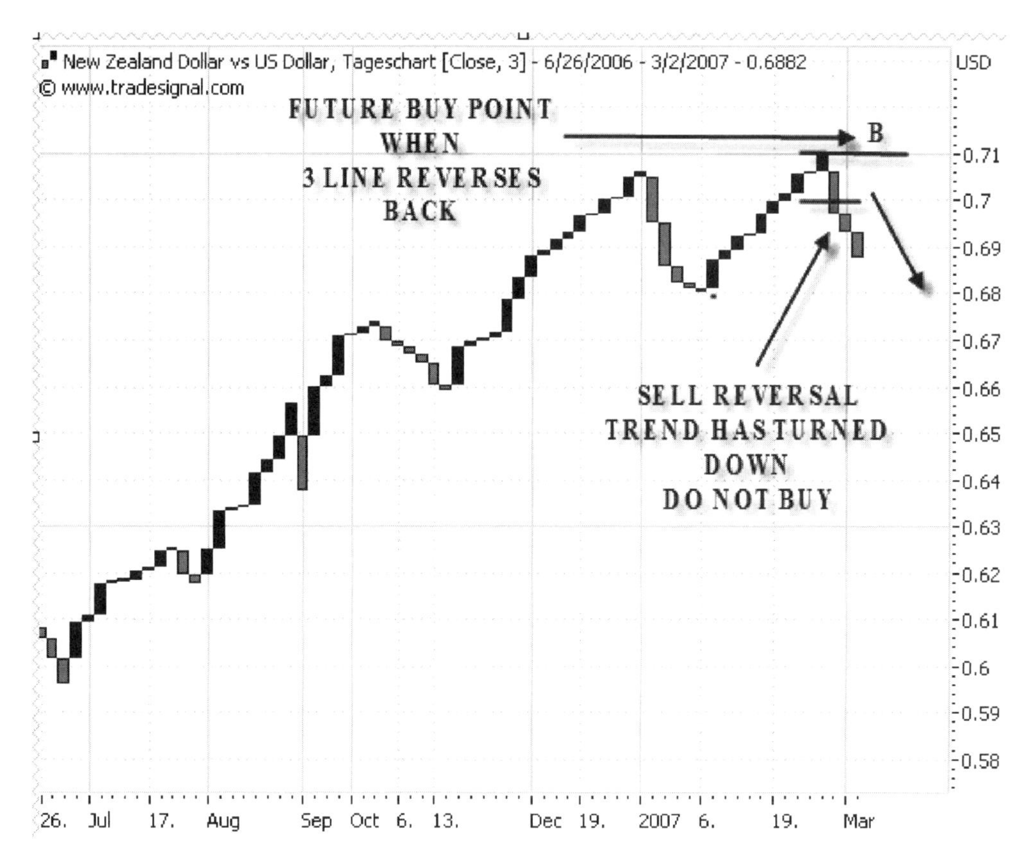

FIGURE 10.6 NZDUSD Day Chart with Three-Line Break.
Source: www.tradesignal.com.

wants to buy would see that the pair is in a downtrend and that the NZDUSD has just reversed an uptrend. The trader would want to wait for a reversal again at point B.

SPOTTING MICRO CHANGES IN TREND SENTIMENT: RENKO CHARTS

Finding the trend direction and points where the trend would be considered being reversed is valuable for entering trades, but one of the largest challenges facing the forex trader is to know when sentiment has changed and turned against the trader and then get out of the way. When it comes to detecting the earliest form of change in trend direction, the trader should consider renko charts. *Renko* means brick in Japanese and provides a way of smoothing out the noise of the market. A renko chart provides an ability to represent a predefined move in the price. While each candlestick or bar provides the low, high, open, and close of a sample period, renko charts provide an additional renko block only if the price has moved and closed at the predetermined setting. In other words, if the trader wants to know only if there is persistence in the sentiment, seeing consecutive renko blocks would confirm that the market is showing the ability to push further brick by brick. This is very useful, and we will show you how to use renko blocks in combination with other indicators to enable precision exiting.

Figure 10.7 compares renko visualization of price action and with the standard candlestick variation. Each renko block is set here at one pip move. This means that if the price closes one pip higher or lower, a new block is added. The time interval is one minute. The trader can choose any time frame and setting appropriate to his or her goals. However, the value of renko blocks is mostly at the smallest setting generating information to the trader about the patterns in the sentiment that are difficult to detect with other charts.

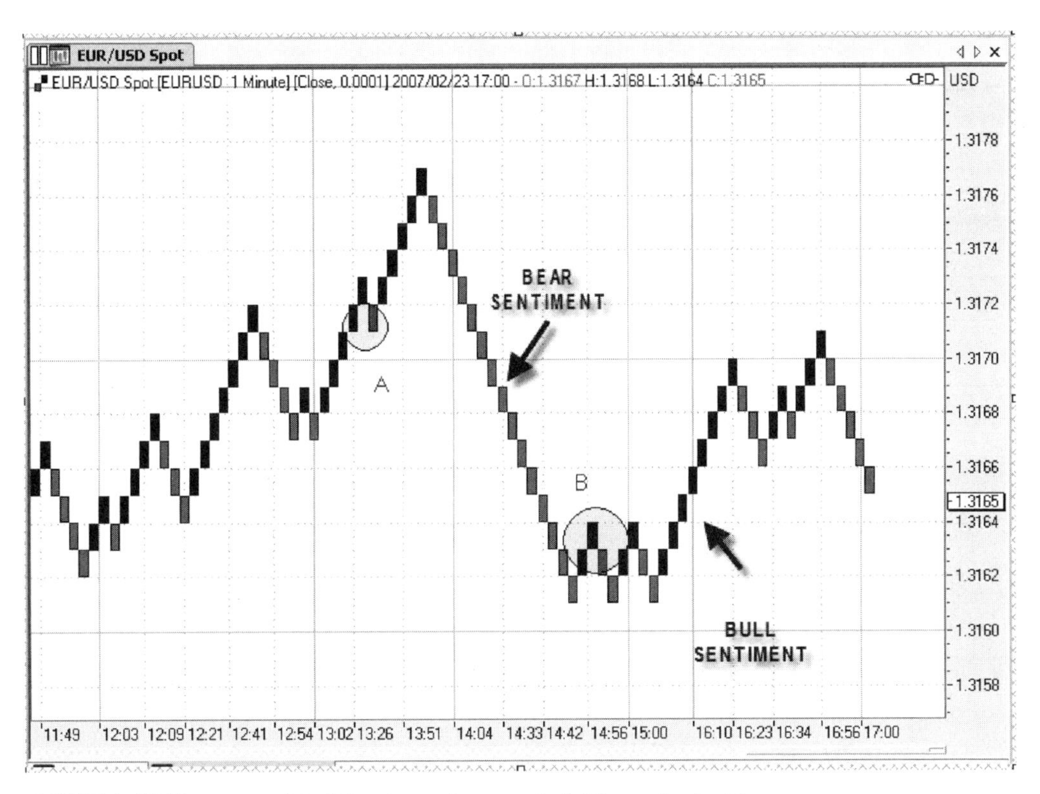

FIGURE 10.7 Bear and Bull Sentiment Patterns In 1-Minute Renko Charts.
Source: www.tradesignal.com.

In effect, we can see that the currency pair exhibits varying degrees of patterns of sentiment. The ability to generate a consecutive series of new up blocks or new down blocks reveals clearly whether a strong micro trend is in place. At points A and B, we see a reversal of the pattern. There will always be some reversals. In this case, one or two renko blocks should not be perceived as the end of the previous pattern. In most recent series of blocks, at the right end we see a downtrend. The trader seeing this chart who was already in a sell position would interpret this last formation as permission to continue to stay in that position. We will demonstrate how to use renko in combination with several setups and strategies later on.

By mapping the price action along key support and resistance lines and finding trend lines, the trader creates a foundation for shaping the trade. We can see that one can go even further by examining intraday, intrahour, and even micro-trend directions using three-line break and renko charts to show patterns of bull or bear bias. The key advantage of using three-line break or renko charts is to reveal whether the sentiment of the market has changed either at the large time frames or the smallest time frames. It is a tool worth exploring.

CHAPTER 11

Finding Significant Support and Resistance

This chapter provides a guide to detecting when support and resistance levels are exhibiting Fibonacci characteristics and their importance. Resistance and support at pivot points are also explored.

FIBONACCI LEVELS OF SUPPORT AND RESISTANCE

Beyond basic geometric measures of support and resistance, there are hidden factors involving psychological forces and patterns in the market that enable the trader to project future levels of support and resistance. Most famous among these forces are Fibonacci levels.

Fibonacci ratios are mathematical patterns of sequences that are expressed in many ways. There are innumerable references to the universality of Fibonacci numbers—a quick Google search reveals over 1,230,000 citations. The Fibonacci sequence describes key ratios from growth in plants, human anatomy, and so on. The forex application is to price movements, which appears to realize Fibonacci ratios. This is particularly obvious on larger time frames such as weekly, daily, and 4-hour time charts. A large move from a low to a high is often followed by an attempt of the price to move back or "retrace" the original move. The profit taking will cause the price to give back a proportion of the move and then rest at support or resistance. These areas of rest are Fibonacci points. For example, let's look at a chart showing a price move on the euro–U.S. dollar (EURUSD) weekly chart (see Figure 11.1).

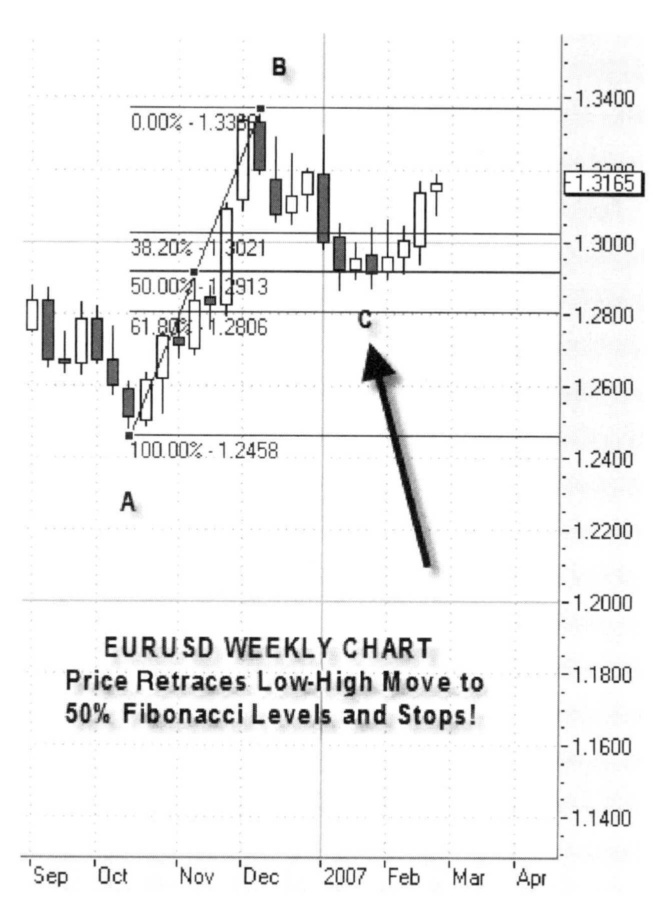

FIGURE 11.1 EURUSD Weekly Chart with Fibonacci Patterns.
Source: www.tradesignal.com.

We can see that the EURUSD made a low at 1.2478 and then proceeded to form a high at 1.3374. Once this move was completed, the trader can use a Fibonacci (Fib) graphic tool, which is available on all platforms to draw a Fib line. Since the price started from the low, the Fib tool assigns the 100 percent level to this origin point. The best way to interpret this is to think of the price going all the way back home to where it started. It would achieve a 100 percent retracement. Once the low and the high are connected, the Fib graphic tool draws the lines and projects it out. Notice that these Fib lines are extended into the future. The trader doesn't know if the price will get there! The trader makes the assumption that if the price is able to get to a Fib level, it will experience strong support or resistance. Also, if the price is able to probe a future Fib level but fails to go through it, the trader can make a reliable assumption that there is key support at that level.

Let's get back to the chart. The price moved from the low of point A to the high of point B and then proceeded to retrace or fall back. What did it do? It probed the 50 percent line but failed to close below it. It was as if it were performing a Fibonacci dance scripted in advance. But a chart using a 15-minute U.S. dollar–Swiss franc (USD-CHF) chart follows a Fibonacci pattern, and we see the price falling and trying to retrace but failing at the key 38.2 percent fib line (see Figure 11.2). Experienced traders would be ready to sell this pair upon these failures.

Figure 11.3 shows a day chart of the EURUSD and another use of Fib lines. The EURUSD completed a move from a high at 1.3293 to a low at 1.2854. Remember, only after it completed the move would a trader be able to put on the Fib levels. The Fib levels then projected out the key Fib lines, which are the projected areas where retracement might occur. We can see that the price moved during a two-day period to point A (the 38.2 percent level) and then failed to close above it. The EURUSD proceeded to move into a three-day trend down nearly 150 pips. It then moved back up and actually went near the 50 percent Fib level but returned below it and proceeded to fall over 100 pips.

FIGURE 11.2 USDCHF 15-Minute Chart Showing Price Failure at Fib Points.
Source: www.tradesignal.com.

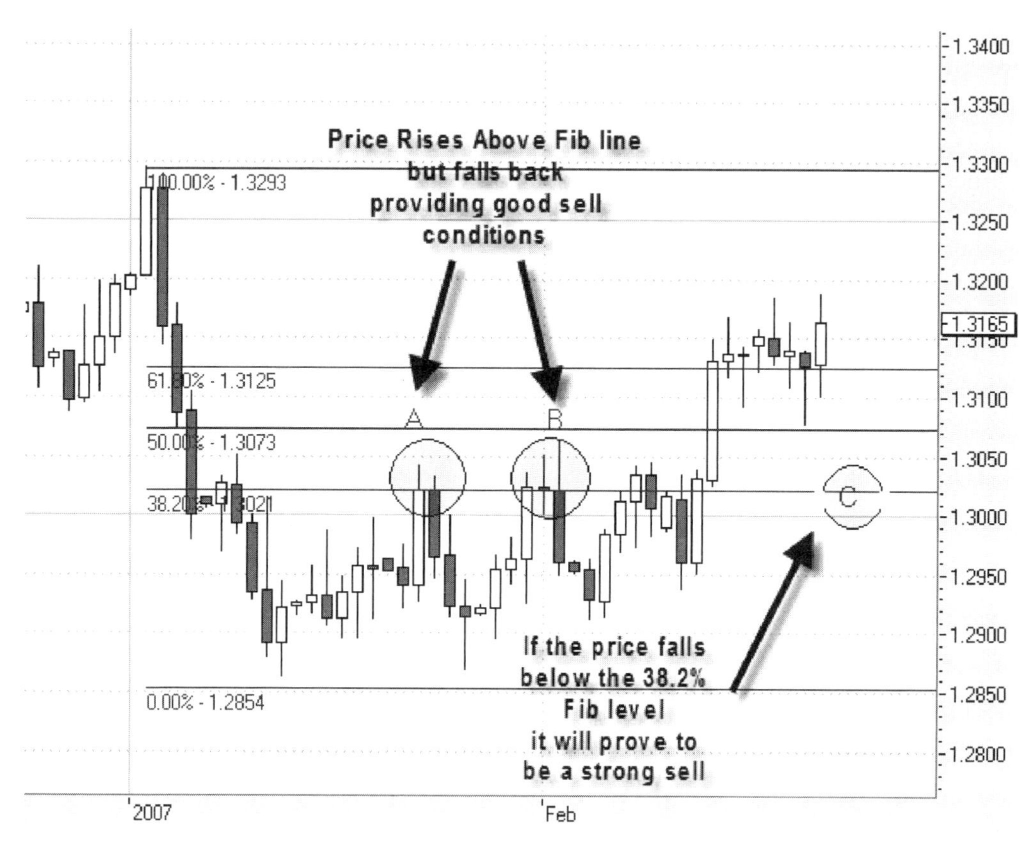

FIGURE 11.3 Sell Conditions Using Fib Points.
Source: www.tradesignal.com.

What is instructive here for the trade is that if the trader were looking to sell, knowing in advance where the Fib levels were meant, while the price was going above point A or B the trader would look to put on a sell trade when the price fell below the Fib lines (of course, confirmed, as we shall see with other indicators). Point C is interesting. If the price falls to point C and stops, the trader with a buying strategy would focus on the price action at this point because stopping at a key Fib line means that support is strong. In contrast, if the trader were looking to sell, the price would have to go below the Fib level at point C to prove it had the energy to keep going.

Let's look some more. In the USDJPY 4-hour chart (Figure 11.4), we see the yen strengthening and probing a key Fib line. Traders looking to sell would be watching this chart. The 4-hour period is particularly important because a 4-hour trend direction represents a great deal of money flowing. Consider the fact that over $2 trillion per day is transacted in forex.

FIGURE 11.4 4-Hour USDJPY Candles Probe Fib Points.
Source: www.tradesignal.com.

Fib lines should not be treated as predictions of what the price will do. They are maps of potential support or resistance. They are areas where great care should be taken by the trader. Rest assured that any professional trader knows where the key Fib levels are. Perhaps because these levels are projected and therefore known in advance, they generate a self-fulfilling process and increase in importance. But the phenomenon of Fib behavior is real and should never be ignored. Take a look at the Fib behavior of the EURUSD in response to the September 11, 2001, terrorist attacks and in response to the July 5, 2006, London train bombings.

WHICH TIME INTERVALS SHOULD WE CHOOSE?

In using Fib lines, the question often asked is: Which lines and which points should be chosen? In answering this question, it's important to be practical. There are many Fib lines in any of the chart time frames used. Even though trades may be taken off an intraday interval, with the 15- and 5-minute time intervals being common, it is still important to use the big Fib levels that are generated off the weekly, daily, or 4-hour charts. The way the Fib lines can be correctly chosen is to start where the price is at the hard right edge. Figure 11.5 shows the steps in drawing a Fib line.

The key is to first ask yourself: Where is the price, and where is it coming from? The trader wants to find the preceding significant low or high and its preceding low or high. Doing so will locate the most recent completed movement. In Figure 11.5, the price was coming from a preceding high, which came from a preceding low connecting point 2 to point 3. Select point 3 as the starting point of the Fib tool, and the Fib lines will be generated. Notice that the 100 percent level is at the low, meaning that if the price falls back to that level it will have given back 100 percent of the move.

Even if the point of start was switched to either point 2 or point 3, what would not change would be the middle three Fib lines. Some firms do not show any Fib levels and simply show the lines.

Knowing basic Fib retracement levels will provide the new forex trader a tool that can be used to help improve an understanding of when to put on the trade. There are many variations of Fib levels. Fib extension levels take the retracement ratios beyond 100. There are graphic tools such as Fib fans and Fib circles. There are even Fib time zones. Whatever tool you choose, the core concept that price behavior often moves in Fib ratios is a major principle of trading forex, and, in fact, Fib patterns are commonplace in many other fields.

THE MUSIC OF FOREX

In *The Psychology of the Foreign Exchange Market* (John Wiley & Sons, 2004), Thomas Oberlechner provides the results of research on how professional traders view the markets. In Chapter 7, Professor Oberlechner demonstrates that traders actually think about forex markets metaphorically. He shows that metaphors are an important way traders organize information, as well as form their own expectations of the market. Professor Oberlechner cites the main metaphors used by forex traders: a bazaar, a machine, a living beast, gambling, sports, war, and the ocean.

Many of us have probably used one or more of these concepts to characterize the forex market. The point of this research is to better understand how one proceeds to trade. The person who views the forex market as sports will look to winning trades as the main focus, but may become emotionally damaged when confronted with a losing trade. In contrast, the person who views forex as an ocean may tend to adopt longer-term views of market moves. Many view the forex market as a war, and as a result may formulate trading strategies that capture pips as if they were the enemy. Even if you do

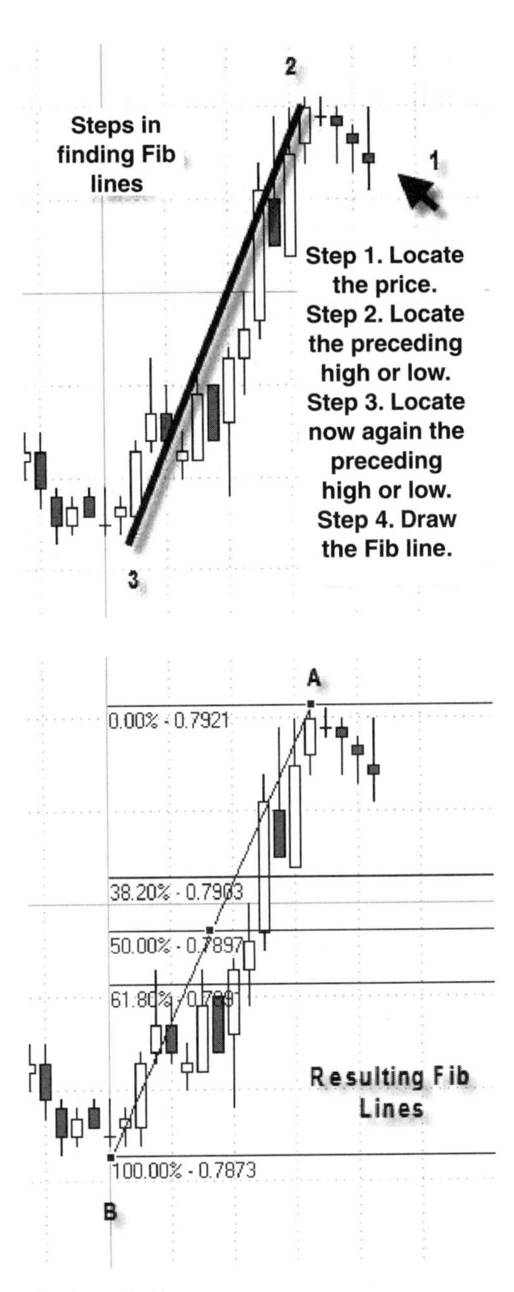

FIGURE 11.5 Steps in Finding Fib Lines.
Source: www.tradesignal.com.

not read the book, it will be useful to ask yourself which metaphor applies to your own views of the forex market and why.

Forex traders also bring to their trading different perspectives based on their job and life experiences. Each perspective provides different strengths as well as weaknesses. Engineers who seek to learn forex often have a tendency to try to model the market and project direction based on equations. In contrast, doctors approach forex trading with the medical mind-set of diagnosing the price action. While the medical workplace provides an environment where patients convey a great deal of respect to their doctors, the forex market provides no such ego gratification. The market is not a patient that returns respect. Those traders who come from a sports background, such as the martial arts, bring a disciplined mind-set and ability to control emotions. Emotions can provide valuable insight into managing a trade, so too much control of emotions may be counterproductive. It turns out that forex trading is a great equalizer among all professions, leaving most people challenged, as never before, in mastering profitable trading.

One profession that appears to provide important insight for forex trading is music, because there is harmony in forex price movements and rhythm in the market. The *Webster Unabridged Dictionary of the English Language* defines harmony as "a consistent, orderly or pleasing arrangement of parts; congruity." What is most interesting is that one doesn't need an in-depth knowledge of music to recognize when one is hearing a harmonic set of sounds or an opposite cacophony of noise. More experienced forex traders focus less on applying more indicators as they become familiar with the inherent rhythm of the market. Yet, those new to forex trading face the huge challenge of trying to separate the noise in price movements and find an inner pattern or harmony.

The entire body of technical analysis has been evolving to provide tools that enable pattern analysis and the ability to smooth out the data. The person new to forex trading seeks to master technical analysis and is challenged by the overwhelming number of indicators and information streaming all day. What is important, and what is permissible to ignore? How does the forex trader know what to pay attention to? Part of the answer derives from looking at forex price movements as a form of harmony. Let's explore this further.

In searching for trades, many traders have a favorite time interval. They could have a day chart or a 1-hour chart and then they apply a variety of analytical techniques and shape a trade. While this may be a rational set of procedures to evaluate the market, an effective technique to consider is to *let the time interval choose you!* To clarify what we mean, consider the everyday experience of driving your car and trying to find a radio station that you would like to listen to. Selecting the scan button allows you to listen for a few moments to each station until the right tune comes along. The driver did not need to know in advance all of the songs being played at every station. All that was necessary was to hear the song that is appealing. Similarly, the forex market is constantly streaming a

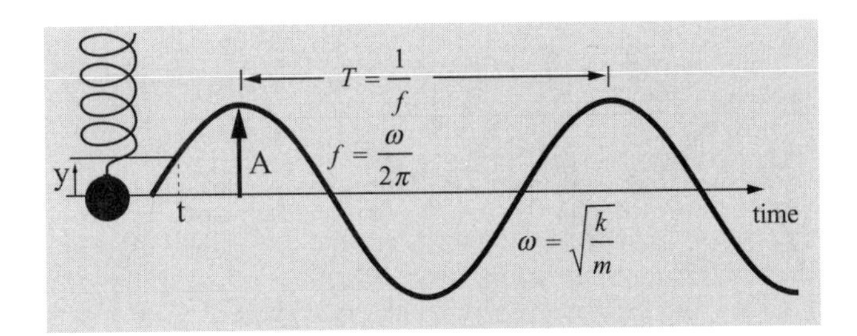

FIGURE 11.6 Forex Prices Often Look Like Sinusoidal Waves.

variety of patterns. There are many potential trades. By scanning through the price action that is playing, a tradable pattern will be perceived.

For example, you might see a sideways pattern (as shown in Figure 11.6) in almost any time interval. If you notice that the pattern has a repetition of the movement up and down the price scale, such patterns reveal an inner harmony. The engineer would recognize this pattern as a simple harmonic motion that is sinusoidal in time with a single resonant frequency. He might even be tempted to formulate an equation to project its path.

A person versed in music would not need equations to sense the pattern as being clearly melodic with a repetition of the tones. Whether the source was the vibration of a string on a violin, or a result of the energy released by the clash of buyers or sellers trading a currency pair, it is an unmistakable nonrandom cycle of self-similarity. Traders with different backgrounds may all come ultimately to the same conclusion about the price action and its structure of movement.

FIBONACCI TONES

In further understanding forex prices and how they move, we cannot ignore the pervasive presence of Fibonacci ratios. It is certainly the case that professional traders know and use Fibonacci ratios to map market patterns. One of the milestones in becoming a savvier forex trader is developing your own understanding of how to recognize and use Fibonacci ratios to shape the trade. Fibonacci is important because currency pairs often move between support and resistance in tune to Fibonacci syncopation. After some base of experience, looking at almost any chart, one can see retracement patterns often along Fibonacci lines. Figure 11.7 shows such a sequence of upward and downward moves followed by retracement stopping at Fibonacci ratios. We can observe that first the pair made a move from a low to a high and then retraced back to 38.2 percent of the way down (point 1) and starting moving back up. It in fact, created a new high and

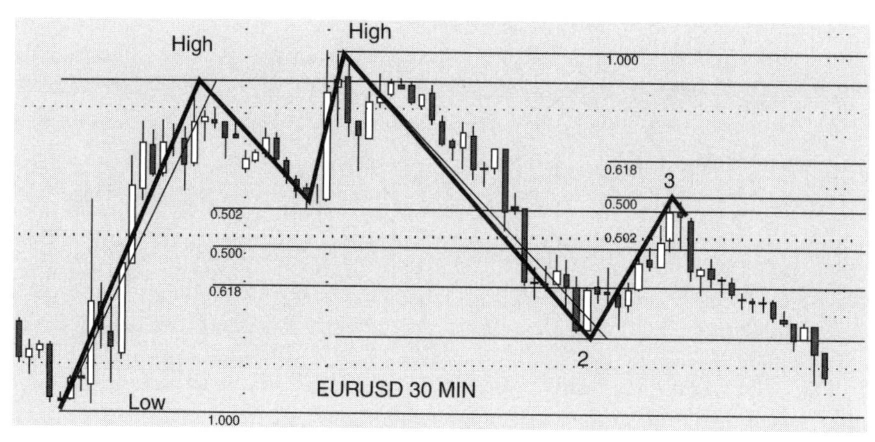

FIGURE 11.7 EURUSD 30-Minute Candles Participate in Fibonacci Rhythms.
Source: www.tradesignal.com.

then moved down to a low (point 2). Having completed that low, it proceeded to move back up again, but stopped at 50 percent of the way up (point 3). This is a sequence that, like music, provides an underlying theme to market moves.

The application of Fibonacci patterns as a universal phenomenon is further underscored, as musicologists have discovered them in the works of many composers including Debussy, Bartok, and the like. The next time you listen to the second half of Scott Joplin's "Maple Leaf Rag," notice the pattern of 13 stressed and 8 unstressed notes. In fact, one can find Fibonacci patterns in the basic structure of instruments themselves. The piano, for example, has 13 notes that separate each octave, which has 8 white keys and 5 black keys. Forex traders will recognize the ratio of 13/8 as a Fibonacci ratio. When using moving average crossovers, try the 13 and 8 time intervals on the charts.

What does this mean to the forex trader? By understanding that currency prices are not linear movements, but expressions of emotions and human behavior, the forex trader begins to move beyond a linear approach to trading. By expanding one's perspective on the underlying tones of the market, he or she will likely see nested patterns that are recursive and, as a result, new trading opportunities. As one trader notes, "Everyone's got the same information at the same time; therefore, you need to find a different way of finding an edge over your competitor" (*The Psychology of the Foreign Exchange Market*, p. 203). The ability to obtain the sought-after trading edge may very well depend on how one looks for it. It would be wise to look for patterns and "listen to the market." It may be playing a Fibonacci melody or, for a brief moment, another profitable tune.

PIVOT POINT SUPPORT AND RESISTANCE

The idea that price patterns follow a retracement ratio is also expressed in the technical concept of pivot points. Pivot points are used by many traders and were developed by floor traders at the exchanges. John L. Person's book, *Forex Conquered* (John Wiley & Sons, 2007), presents a very specific variation on the use of pivot points. We want to introduce the concept here.

The advantage of pivot points is that they are essentially objective in nature. Other forms of resistance projections such as Fibonacci levels, Elliot wave, and so on, have an element of subjectivity, and as a result people may draw those lines differently.

Pivot points focus on the immediate trading session behavior and ranges. They provide a good sense of the psychology of the session. The pivot point equation generates a number that combines the high, low, and close and divides it by three, generating the pivot point number. The basic idea is for traders to assess what happens when the price probes that number. The pivot point number is, in the words of John Person, "the focal point." What is particularly interesting is the pivot point's overlapping or converging with a Fib line or with another important indicator. Figure 11.8 shows an EURUSD hour candle chart where the pivot point converges with a hesitation candle known as the "Doji."

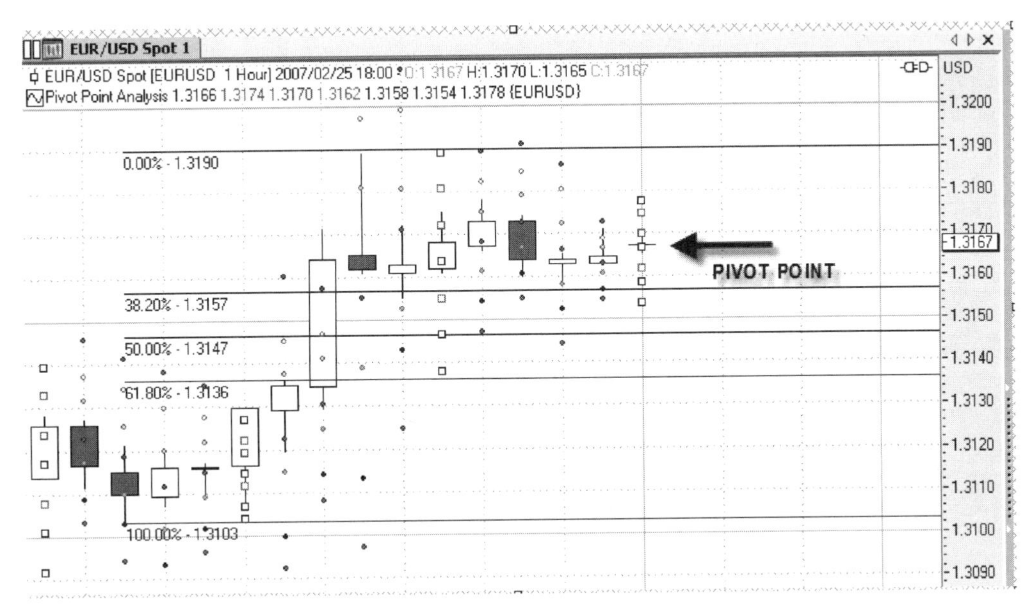

FIGURE 11.8 EURUSD 15-Minute Chart Showing Pivot Points and Fib Lines.
Source: www.tradesignal.com.

In this particular case, it is near a Fib line. Remember that the lower the time interval used, the less stable or reliable are the pivot points.

This is a handy tool, and one you can access at www.learn4x.com/calculator.

PSYCHOLOGICAL SUPPORT AND RESISTANCE

Understanding whether there is psychological support and resistance should not be ignored because hedge funds and institutional investing creates recognizable patterns. Ignoring psychological expressions in the markets increases the risks that the trades will be going against the "smart" money. Psychological support reveals itself in several ways and in many ways is a self-reinforcing process. For example, since traders assign importance to key Fibonacci levels, this results in aggregating more significance to those levels. A greater number of parked orders such as stops and limits become located in Fibonacci zones. Option orders at key strike prices play a key role that the average trader in spot has little accessible knowledge of. Additionally, prices at round numbers such as 1.2500 receive more attention from traders. Finally, psychological support emerges when a key support or resistance level, such as a daily, weekly, or monthly high or low, is being probed by the currency pair.

Up to this point, we have looked at price in relationship to support and resistance lines and pivot points, but mapping price movement is not yet complete. The trader needs to consider the dimension of *time*.

PRICE AND TIME IN FOREX

The language of technical analysis really starts with the description of price in relationship to time. Much of the architecture of technical analysis explores this

A	B	C	D	E	F
Enter -->	High	1180.00	610.00	1520.00	10500.00
Enter -->	Low	1160.00	590.00	1500.00	10400.00
Enter -->	Close	1170.00	600.00	1480.00	10300.00
	SR Value	ES	ER	NQ	YM
	R2	1190.00	620.00	1520.00	10500
	R1	1180.00	610.00	1500.00	10400
	Pivot	1170.00	600.00	1500.00	10400
	S1	1160.00	590.00	1480.00	10300
	S2	1150.00	580.00	1480.00	10300

FIGURE 11.9 Pivot Point Calculator.

multidimensional relationship. Let's start with the fact that the charts themselves are snapshots of what has occurred in a selected time interval. Whether one uses bar charts or candlestick charts, the vocabulary of technical analysis has only four basic words. These words are the *opening*, the *close*, and the *high* and the *low* of the price (see Figure 11.10).

With only these four units of knowledge, the trader can start to talk the language of technical analysis. We can build an entire architecture of trading strategy. We can build trend lines that connect consecutive highs and lows. We can deduce sentiment. For example, when the price closes above the opening, we have a bullish sentiment. When the price closes below the opening, we have a bearish sentiment. Another key relationship that is revealed by looking at the price bars or candles is the *range*, which is defined as the difference between the low and the high action.

The range of a currency pair reflects deeper psychological characteristics of the price action that can't be ignored. As the distance between a low and a high increases, the total energy of buyers versus sellers has increased. Accompanying this increase in range is also the anxiety of the trader. A widening range is a signal of increasing volatility. A narrowing range denotes the ebbing of interest and consolidation as the market needs new energy. Depending on the shape of the range, the trader can employ different strategies. In a sideways range pattern known as a "channel," trading off each side represents a common strategy. But the width of the range should be 40 pips or more to achieve a reasonable chance of capturing 10 to 15 pip moves. If the range is compressing in the shape of a triangle, the trade should be ready for a breakout. There is no guarantee as to which side the price will break out of. More often than not, a breakout in the direction of

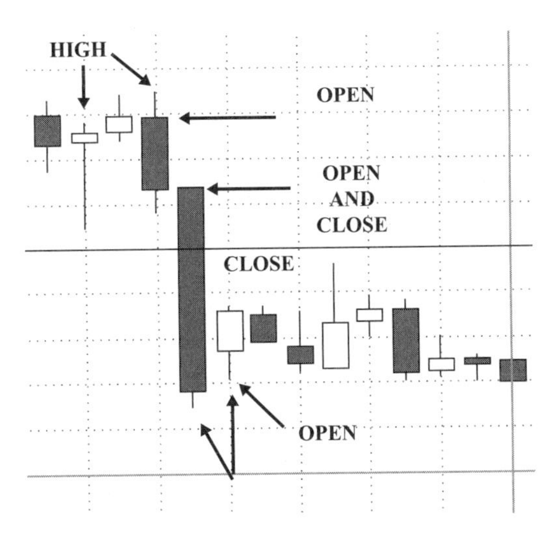

FIGURE 11.10 All Candles Show the Low, High, Opening, and Close.
Source: www.tradesignal.com.

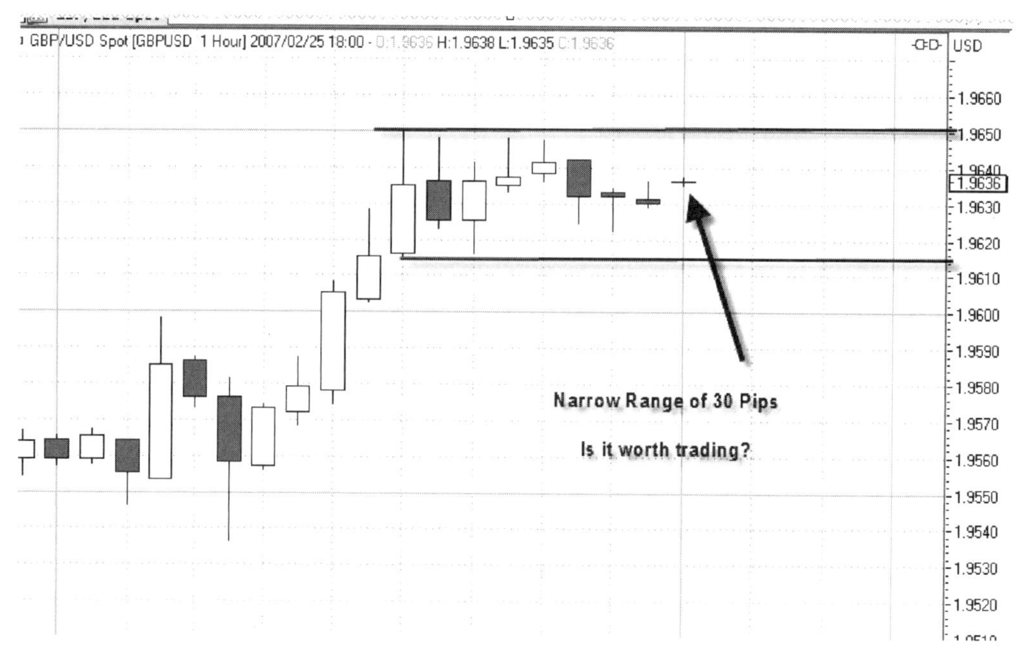

FIGURE 11.11 Narrow Range of 30 Pips in GBPUSD-Is It Worth Trading?
Source: www.tradesignal.com.

the trend is a good bet. If the range is very narrow (less than 20 pips), no trade is preferable because the market is really in a period of noise. Figure 11.11 shows a chart with a range of 30 pips, but notice that the price is near the middle of the range. It would take very good timing to trade this pair from where the price is. Whatever the range is trading near, support or resistance is preferable.

CHAPTER 12

Volatility in Forex and Its Dimensions

This chapter reviews how volatility should be used in helping the forex trader evaluate market conditions. Volatility conditions, when added to classical support and resistance, and trend analysis identify high-probability trading opportunities and patterns.

By identifying currency pair volatility and associated exhaustion conditions, the trader gains knowledge of what the currency pair is doing. What the trader is most interested in is the behavior at prices at the extreme. A currency pair can reach a new daily or weekly high, but it doesn't mean that the price is likely to return to its average or mean price. When a currency is at a high, it is there for a reason. Perhaps new economic information pushed it to that new level. However, it is when a currency is at volatility high that the trader can deduce a potential for a reversal. This is because volatility cannot be infinite, then return to an average level. Understanding the behavior of the price in terms of volatility is a building block of forex technical knowledge.

It's helpful in understanding volatility of currency pair prices to recall our everyday experience with volatility. A strong snow- or rainstorm has periods of varying intensity. But when the storm reaches its most intense period, one knows that it will soon be over. All of us have heard the phrase "the calm before the storm." When the price is quiet, with small ranges and little change over time, it is recognized as a prelude to a breakout—exactly mirroring the phenomenon of the calm before the storm. Trading strategies emerge from applying volatility knowledge. A peak in volatility suggests to the trader that a reversal trade may be shaping up and to be ready for that. A decline in volatility may suggest near-term lack of any significant move, suggesting waiting for conditions to change.

A technical quantitative measure of volatility is the standard deviation of the price range over time. Zero volatility doesn't mean that the price has stayed the same. It means that there hasn't been a change in the price range. The key notion to understand is for the forex trader to observe market ranges and notice whether they are stable or varying.

Once a currency pair starts changing frequently the shape of its range, we have volatility increasing. A surge in volatility may be a prelude to continued movement in the direction of the surge. New energy coming from increased sentiment has to go somewhere. It's important to note when a surge occurs, if it occurs at a key resistance, it may be a reversal indicator as well. Trading volatile markets that have expanding and contracting ranges requires special attention to risk controls because the trader has an expectation that the price can fluctuate more rapidly and more widely.

In Figure 12.1, we see a recent visualization of the volatility increasing. The currency pair British pound-Japanese yen (GBPJPY) experienced a significant increase in volatility right before and after the February 2007 Bank of Japan's decision to increase interest rates. Notice how the volatility ebbed into a very quiet and narrow range afterward. A good clue to volatility is when it takes only one or two candles to pass through the range.

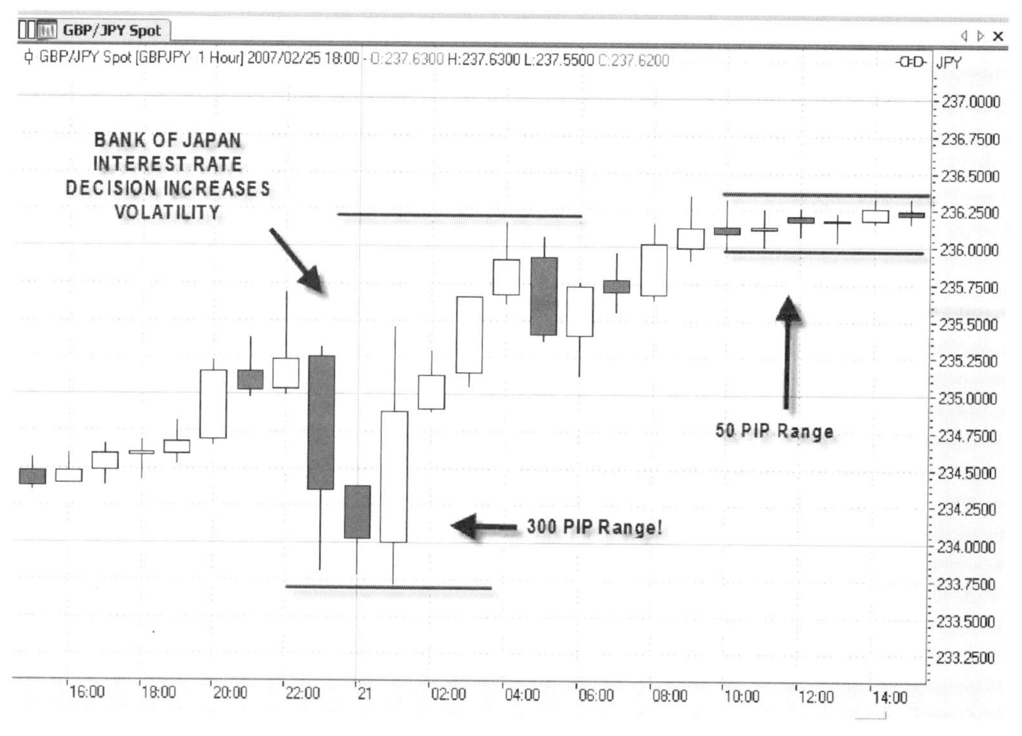

FIGURE 12.1 Volatility Increases for GBPJPY 1-Hour Chart.
Source: www.tradesignal.com.

Visualizing volatility is helped by the use of several technical indicators, which we will discuss in the next section.

14 KEY TECHNICAL INDICATORS

Because we have reviewed the basic geometry of prices and know how to create a forex map of price action, a next step in shaping a trade is to diagnose what the prices are exhibiting in terms of strength and weakness. There are dozens of indicators that accompany many of the forex platforms. This multitude of indicators can lead to confusion for the new trader. Many of these indicators are not all useful for forex trading. Many of the indicators offered by forex platforms reproduce indicators that have been a standard part of the trader tool box for generations in other markets. Whichever indicators are used, they should be evaluated as to how well they contribute to identifying market conditions and help determine the best location and time to put on the trade.

A first step in choosing indicators to use in trading is to understand what they do. Technical indicators are algorithms, which are equations that take price data and generate a smoothing out of the data. The value to the trader of any indicator occurs when they help confirm several technical conditions, as shown in the checklist below:

- How strong is the trend?
- How strong is support and resistance?
- Are there signs of weakness in the trend or in support and resistance?
- Are there signs of volatility or momentum peaks or exhaustion?
- Is there a divergence between the indicator and prices?

The overall goal is to find the set of indicators that increase the level of confidence that the opportunity to put on the trade is at hand. It's useful to think of indicators as ingredients in a recipe to create the basis of a trade. However, the trader needs to also recognize that the key disadvantage of indicators relates to their inherent lagging behind the market and their potential instability when applied to very short time frames, such as under five minutes.

VOLUME INDICATORS: A KEY MISSING ELEMENT IN SPOT FOREX

Volume information is one of the most important components of technical analysis of markets. Volume indicates the quantity of money flow into a particular investment instrument. An increase in volume often precedes an increase in price, and a decrease in volume is considered early identification of weakness. The best equity traders could not conceive of trading without volume data. Yet there is no volume data for spot forex prices when trading through spot forex firms.

This lack of volume data makes many indicators offered irrelevant. Because volume and changes in volume are highly related to indicators of sentiment and market psychology, the forex trader needs to rely on technical indicators that act as a substitute for volume data. For example, knowing that a currency pair is probing a daily support level for a few days represents a great deal of volume at that daily support level. The position of the currency pair price in relationship to support and resistance and how close it is to either level becomes a good substitute for volume. Additionally, when economic data releases comes out, the entire market focuses on the report, and the trader knows that maximum volume is at these news events. Therefore, one of the best ways to overcome the lack of volume data is to trade where there is certainty on maximum volume.

However, for those traders who want the best of all worlds, there is a way to obtain volume data for the spot forex trader. Futures on currency trading include volume data in the form of open interest contracts. This means that all of the technical indicators on the futures side that include volume are valid. While trading the euro-U.S. dollar (EURUSD) through the spot market, a serious trader could also observe the volume data of the futures on the EURUSD contract. While this is cumbersome and involves extra cost, those traders who favor using volume data to gain an edge in their trading are able to overcome this gap. The limiting factor is that the maximum benefit of such volume data occurs during U.S. trading hours only.

An additional volume-related data involves the Commitment of Traders (CoT) Report. This is a weekly report from the Commodity Futures Trading Commission (CFTC; available at www.cftc.gov/cftc/cftccotreports.htm) providing a breakdown of each Tuesday's open interest for markets in which 20 or more traders hold positions equal to or above the reporting levels established by the CFTC. Open interest is broken down by aggregate commercial, noncommercial, and nonreportable holdings. While the data provided by the CoT Report is lagging (the Friday report reflects the previous Tuesday's data), when extremes are reached in positions by the noncommercials, it is a situation that is especially noteworthy for the forex spot trader. The trader can gain greater confidence in aligning his or her next trade in the direction of the noncommercials, which are representative of the sentiment of the "smart money."

Until Forex firms provide the CoT data more conveniently, spot traders need to access this information on their own. It is available at many web sites, as well as from third-party software providers. One such provider, Track 'n Trade, generates CoT charts with effective visualizations of the data. Lan Turner, the developer of Track 'n Trade software, observed the following (see Figure 12.2):

Following the Commitment of Traders, as it relates to the March U.S. dollar contract traded on the New York Board of Trade, you can see how the large speculators, depicted in the indicator windows below our chart [Figure 12.2], has been following the ebb and flow of the market as the value of the dollar increases and decreases. The large speculators, as represented by the histogram, consist of large banks and hedge funds, organizations who manage large amounts of money for speculative investment. It's often asked: Is this a case of the dog wagging the tail, or the tail wagging the dog? Because these organizations manage and control such large amounts of cash, do they react to the market, or does the market react to them?

What we're seeing represented in this graph is the percentage of large speculators who are long versus short the market. For example, looking at the above chart, you notice that the large speculators represented by the high point during mid-October is over 85 percent, which means that over 85 percent of reported large speculators were trading long or had long positions during that time frame. Also notice that as the market begins to drop, how quickly the large speculators reverse their positions, where we then see a pictation where the majority of large speculators are now short the U.S. dollar during the month of December. Also take a close look at the open interest line as it increases in volume; this is an indication of an increased number of short positions being added to the market. It is very common to see the open interest line increase in relationship to the market trend during a strong downtrend, and decrease during a strong uptrend.

An emerging source of volume data is exchange-traded funds (ETFs) on currencies. One of the leading traders in the country, John Person, effectively uses these volume data sources. ETFs on currencies are fairly new opportunities for forex and equity traders.

TREND-RELATED INDICATORS

While trend lines remain the most effective ways of determining whether a trend is in place, many indicators have arisen that go further in detecting changes in the trend. Moving averages and their variations are often used by traders. Let's consider some of them and how to apply them to help understand the trend.

The basic technical indicator used to help interpret the trend line is the moving average. It has many variations. The most popular is the simple and exponential moving average. Other variations, such as the weighted and adaptive, have been developed to provide traders different views on filtering the price information. What is important is to realize what the moving average does and what it cannot do. Moving averages are inherently late to the party. They lag behind the information and therefore have limitations on their use as triggers to put on a trade. But they are valuable in mapping the contours of changes in the trend.

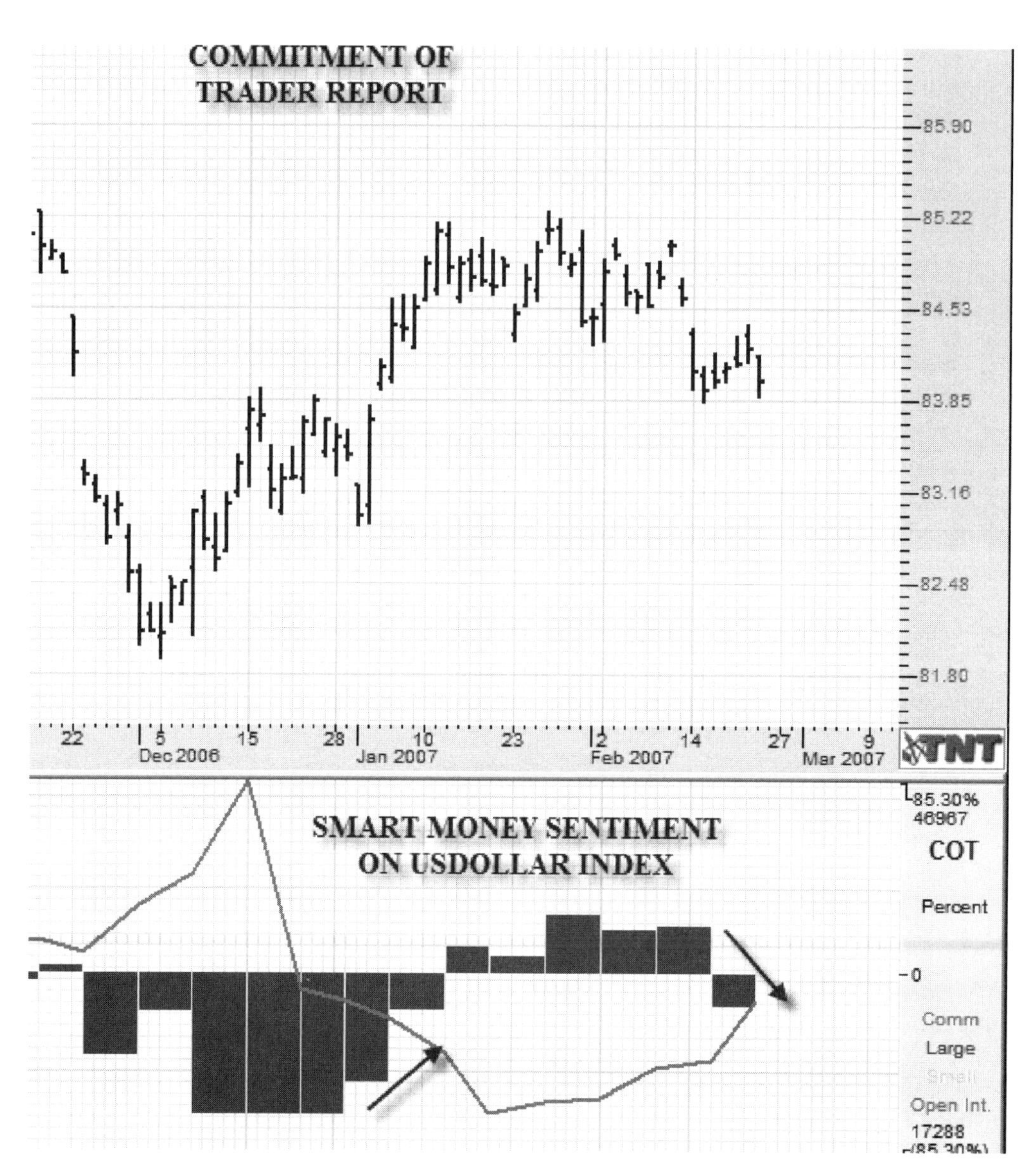

FIGURE 12.2 Commitment of Traders Chart. Chart courtesy of Track 'n Trade Pro. Copyright © 2007 Gecko Software, Inc.

The simple moving average acts as an easy way to smooth out the price data. It's a basic algebraic average that adds a new period and drops the first as time moves on. In the simple moving average, each period gets the same level of importance. This has disturbed some traders because earlier periods are overvalued. The exponential moving average provides greater weight to the most recent periods being considered, and this reduces the lag of the resulting curve. There are many variations emerging on how to minimize the inherent lag of moving averages, such as adaptive moving average, fractal adaptive moving average, median adaptive moving average, and triangular moving average. The triangular moving average weights middle periods more than the earlier and later periods. Traders are always coming up with new moving average versions to test out.

Which moving average is better? That depends, of course, on how the use of the moving average contributes to trading success. In Figure 12.3, compare the simple moving average to the exponential moving average and the triangular moving average. It's hard to answer that question. They are very close. For the trader, consistency in use is more important.

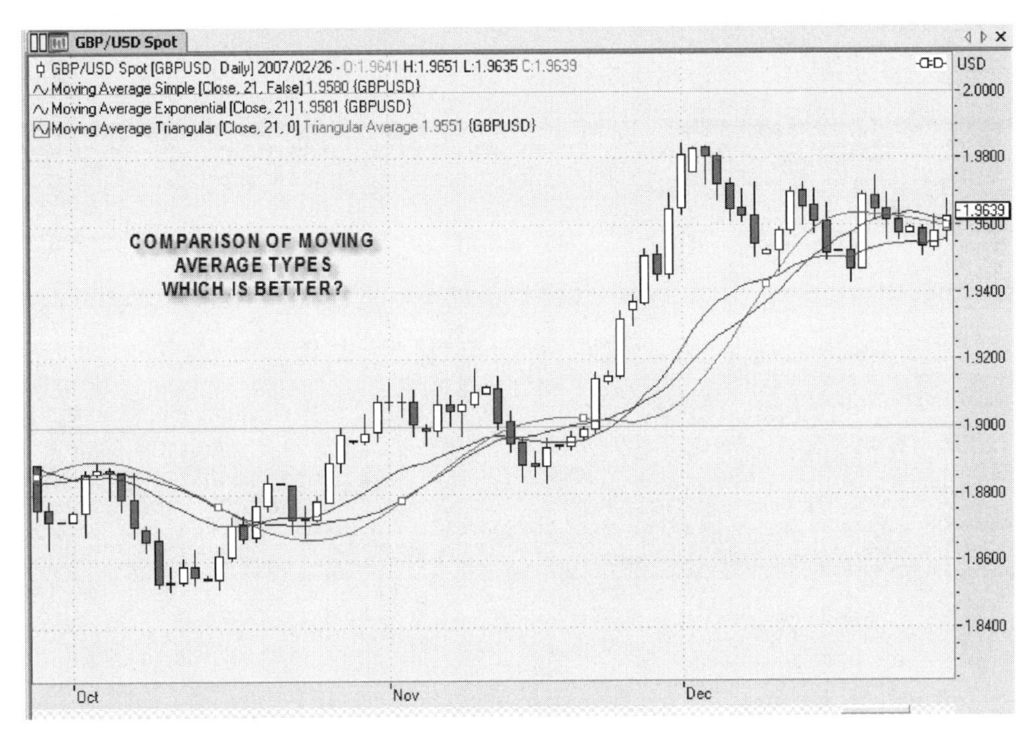

FIGURE 12.3 Comparison of Moving Average Types.

A consideration for the trader is to choose which time period to use for the moving average. The 50-period is considered an important hurdle, and when it is probed or penetrated, the trader needs to pay closer attention because it is considered important.

Combining two moving averages where one period is longer than the other creates the moving average crossover. The idea behind it is to overcome the lag of one moving average. There are many variations of periods to use in a crossover. The 55-period versus the 5 and the 13 versus the 5 offer examples of how to use them. When a crossover occurs, traders will look to enter a position or exit one that assumed the previous direction, providing further confirmation is achieved.

MOVING AVERAGE CROSSOVERS

Crossovers provide several uses in interpreting price action. We can see in the chart for the GBPUSD 30 minutes (Figure 12.4) that the crossovers were of limited value in sideways patterns, but did provide buy zones when the crossover turned up. Also note

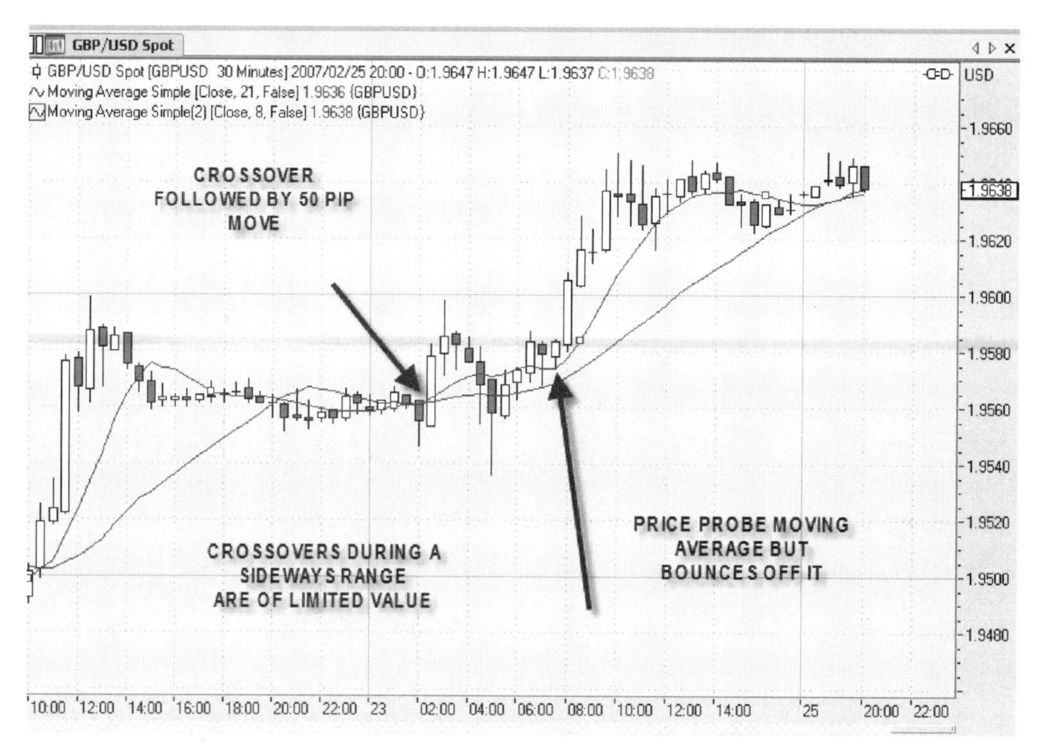

FIGURE 12.4 Moving Average Crossover Followed by 50 Pip Move.
Source: www.tradesignal.com.

that the moving average acted as a firm support later on. Notice that the moving averages look ready to cross over again, pointing down. If the candle probes below these moving averages, traders looking to sell will have strong confirmation.

Which crossover periods should be used? In the previous example, the 21 versus 8 simple moving averages was used. But the selection of the moving averages is quite arbitrary unless they are back-tested. The experience of the trader is the most important variable to use.

MOVING AVERAGE RAINBOWS—MULTIPLE MOVING AVERAGES

A very effective utilization of moving averages occurs when several are plotted at the same time. The effect is to reveal areas of major convergence and also display visualization of changes in momentum. We can see in Figure 12.5 how a cluster of moving averages provided important clues to a shift in trend direction and momentum.

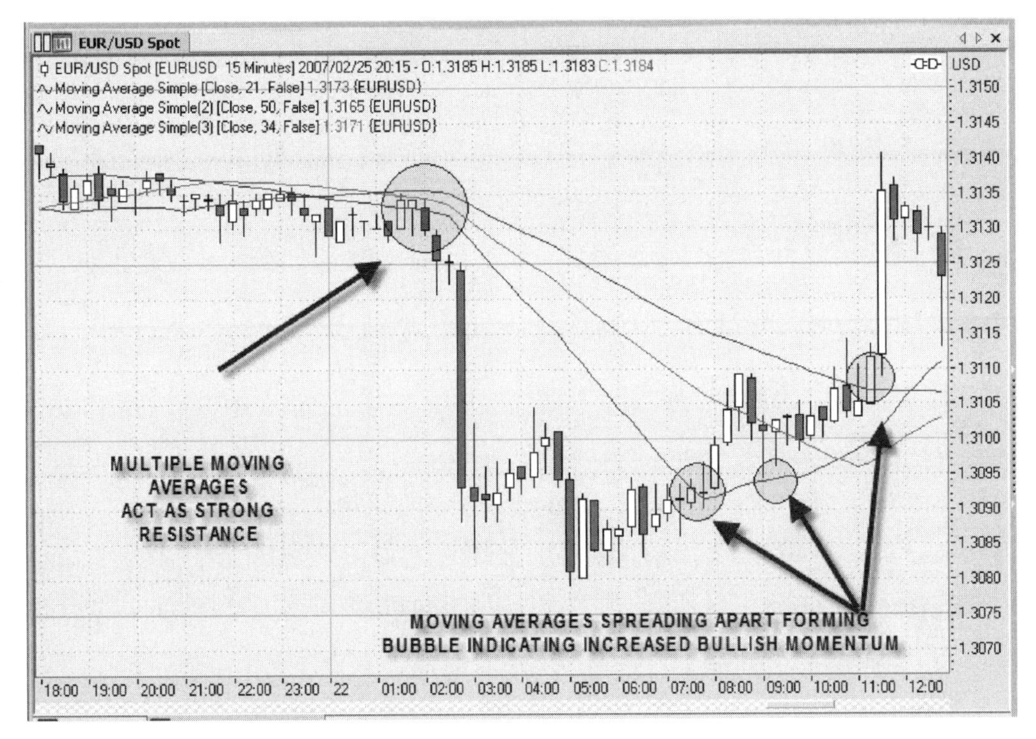

FIGURE 12.5 Multiple Moving Averages Converge.
Source: www.tradesignal.com.

MOMENTUM INDICATORS AND OSCILLATORS

Another group of technical indicators available for forex trading are those that measure changes in momentum by comparing extremes in value. These are also called oscillators. The goal of using indicators from this group is to identify whether a currency pair is approaching extremes of being overbought or oversold.

Moving average convergence divergence (MACD) is a popular indicator that gives the trader a sense of a change in momentum by comparing two exponential moving averages (see Figure 12.6). The settings used are the 24-period exponential moving averages and the 12-period exponential moving averages. So what we have is a moving average crossover. MACD goes further and adds a 9-period exponential moving average of the difference between these two. The result is a visual clue when there is a turn in the sentiment from being bullish to bearish, and vice versa. When used with other confirming indicators, MACD increases the confidence of a new trader for high-probability trades. The MACD tool is a standard part of the set of indicators, but

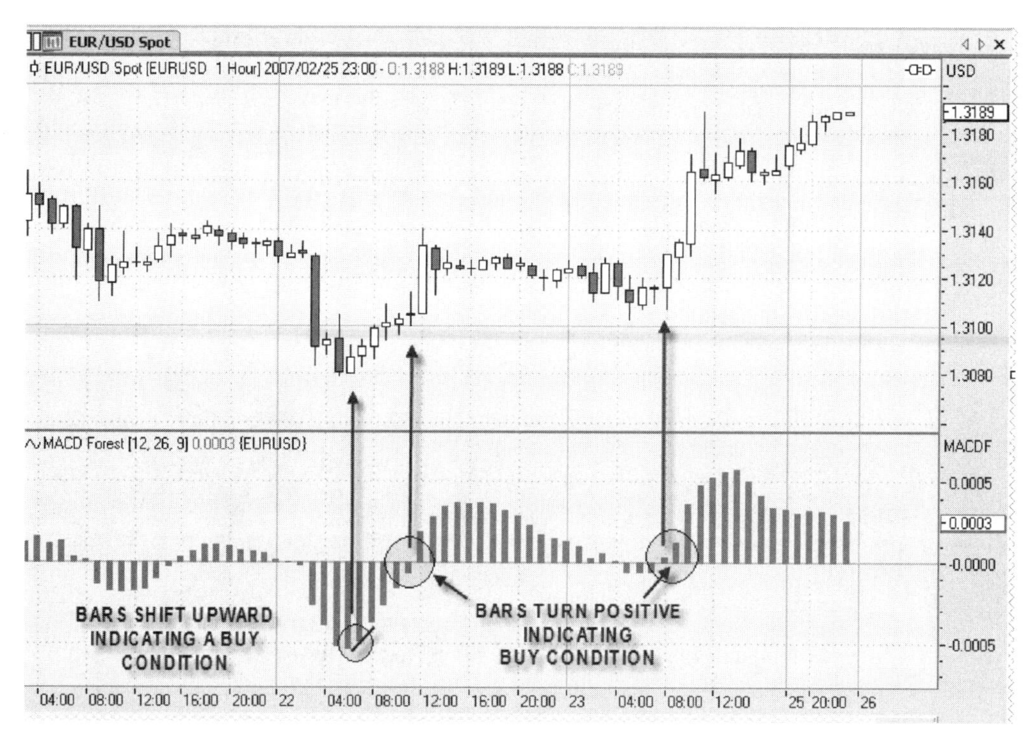

FIGURE 12.6 Example of MACD Histogram or Forest Chart.
Source: www.tradesignal.com.

there are variations in how it is presented. The difference between the two exponential moving averages can be displaced alone. Also, the MACD indicator can be presented with bars (histogram) showing more clearly whether the momentum is changing. This later version of MACD is also known as MACD Forest and is very agreeable and easy to use.

Note that Figure 12.6 is an hour chart, and as a result the trader has to wait longer to detect a shift in the MACD condition. However, we will see that by shifting to a shorter time frame, this waiting period can be reduced. Figure 12.7 shows a 15-minute chart, where the MACD histograms provide, in effect, permission to enter a trade on the buy side.

An important observation for the trader is to spot whether there is a divergence between the MACD indicator direction and the price. When this occurs, the trader needs to be careful in assuming that the price will continue in its direction. Figure 12.8 shows the price's being essentially flat while MACD is shifted down. Traders who are already in a buying position would be looking to get out and sellers would be looking to get in.

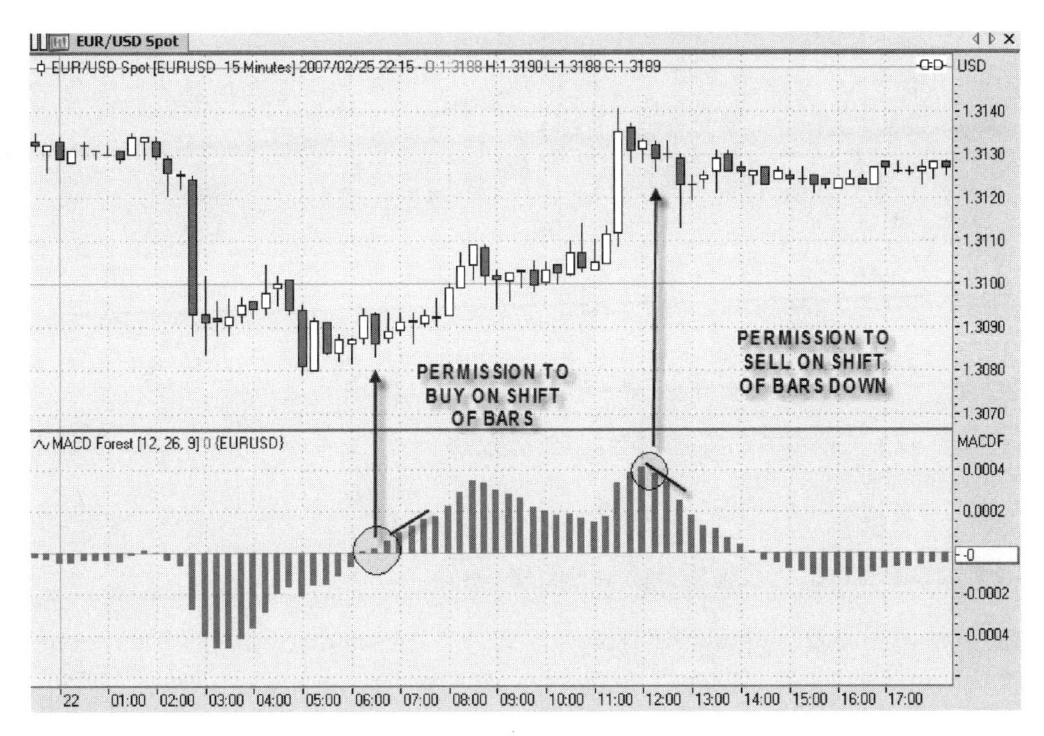

FIGURE 12.7 Buy and Sell Signals Using MACD Forest.

FIGURE 12.8 Divergence between Price and MACD.
Source: www.tradesignal.com.

RELATIVE STRENGTH INDICATOR (RSI)

The relative strength indicator (RSI) provides clues to whether the currency pair is overbought or oversold. It compares averages of period closes that are up against period closes that are down. It is an oscillator that has a range of 0 to 100. Traders using RSI should note that when RSI reaches below 20 or above 80, it is considered to be peaking in its strength. But these levels do not mean they are automatic buy or sell signals. Applying

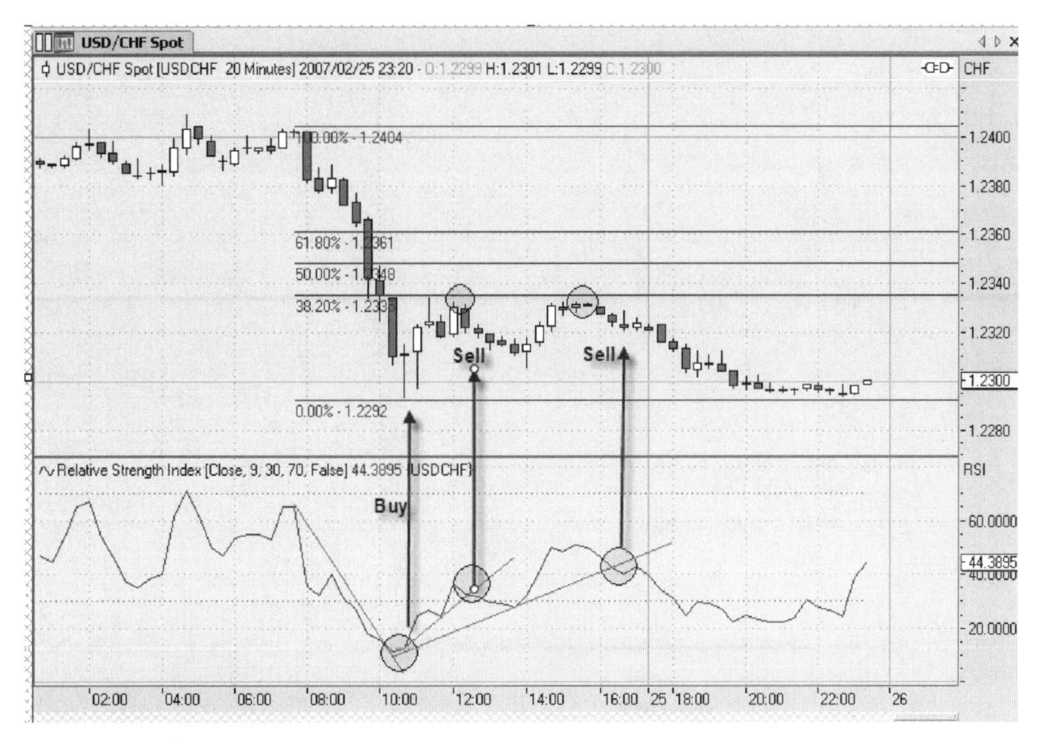

FIGURE 12.9 Trade Signals with RSI.
Source: www.tradesignal.com.

trend lines to the RSI indicator is a more precise approach to when and where one can put on a buy or sell trade. In Figure 12.9, the trend-line break in the RSI coincided with the failure of the price to retrace above the Fib line. This provides added confirmation of a weakening condition, and it is appropriate to apply trend lines on indicators that are oscillators, such as RSI. We see a similar RSI trend break failure in Figure 12.10.

RSI has default settings at 14 periods, but traders can reduce this period to 9 to eliminate some of the lag and make the indicator a bit more sensitive to the recent actions. Traders should also note that there are variations in the RSI index formula producing different RSIs. But they all are relatively close, and personal preference will decide which one you choose.

THE STOCHASTIC GROUP OF INDICATORS

Stochastic analysis is a general term describing a process of sampling random data to generate information. In evaluating price action and in forex, the stochastic group of indicators has the goal of providing insight into whether the price has lost its ability to

FIGURE 12.10 Break of RSI's Trend Lines.
Source: www.tradesignal.com.

close at the highest or lowest level. In simple terms, when a currency pair is strong, one aspect of this strength is that it achieves closes that are higher. At some point, it loses its strength and creates closes away from the top or bottom. The formula shows that the stochastic compares the most recent closing price with the low of a preset period of periods (14) and compares it against the high of the same period. The result is the equation called %K:

$$\%K = 100[(C - L14)/(H14 - L14)]$$

Then the stochastic indicator creates a moving average of the %K this is called %D. A three-period moving average is usually used. A crossover effect is generated when the %K line crosses the %D line.

Once again, a technical indicator is trying to smooth out the data to show something of value. A high %K, for example, of 81 means that the price closing is percentage-wise 81 percent of the range of the period measured. So the ability of the price to stay that high will be more difficult.

Stochastics, like any indicator, are not predicting anything. They provide a useful measure of the power of the trend. There are several variations of stochastic indicators. Most common are slow stochastics and fast stochastics. The difference is that slow stochastics are less sensitive to price movements and therefore provide less risk of too many crosses. The settings for the stochastic indicator are usually defaulted at 14 periods, and 3 for the moving averages. Adjusting the settings to a smaller period of time, such as 8 or even 5 periods, can provide more sensitivity to changes.

The use of the stochastics as supporting a trading decision can be seen in Figure 12.11. If a trader were looking for a buy or sell entry and saw that the stochastic indicator crossed (in the direction of the trade), it would be a green light to buy. If it did not cross, then further confirmation would be necessary. The stochastic indicator

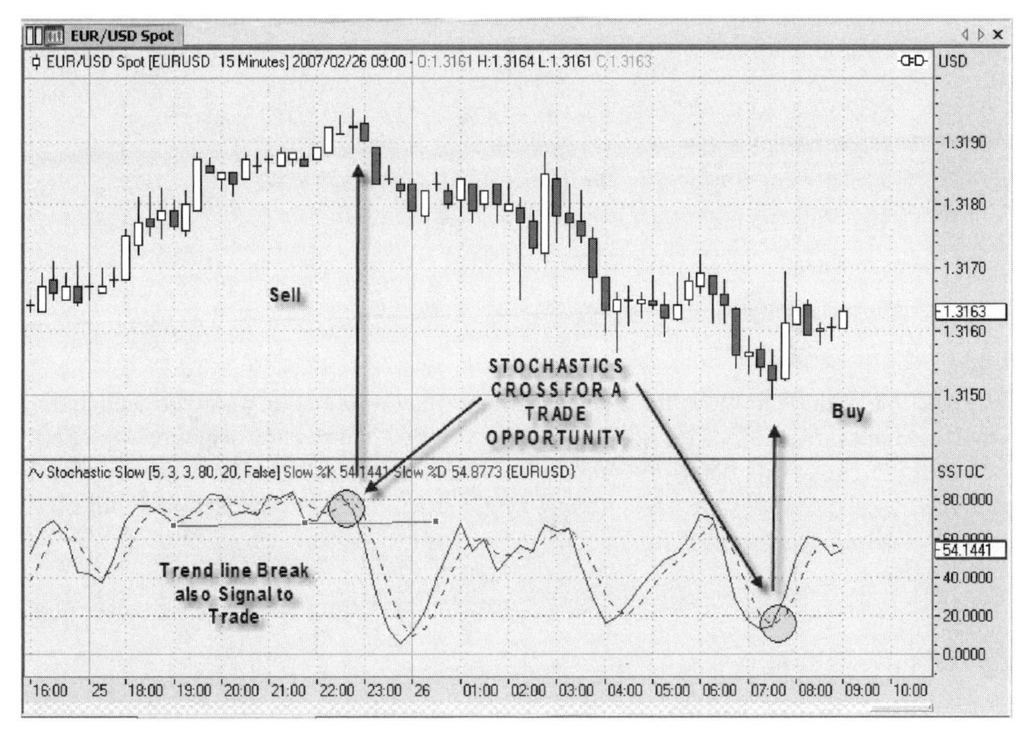

FIGURE 12.11 Stochastic Crossover.
Source: www.tradesignal.com.

acts like a traffic signal. It's always necessary to watch all the traffic, but if the indicator has crossed, then the trader could be focused on pulling the trigger.

The following section explains how the stochastic formula was calculated in more detail (adapted from http://help.geckosoftware.com/40manual/new/use_indicators/fsto/faststo.htm).

Calculation

Parameters:

- Overall Period (3)—the number of periods used to determine the highest high and lowest low.
- %D MA Period (14)—the number of periods used to determine the moving average for the %D value.

Formula:
The first step in computing the stochastic indicator is to determine the n period high and low. For example, suppose you specified 20 periods for the stochastic. Determine the highest high and lowest low during the last 20 trading intervals. It determines the trading range for that time period. The trading range changes on a continuous basis.

The calculations for the %K are as follows:

$$\%Kt = ((Close_t - Low_n)/(High_n - Low_n)) * 100$$

%Kt: The value for the first %K for the current time period.

$Close_t$: The closing price for the current period.

Low_n: The lowest low during the n periods.

$High_n$: The highest high during the n time periods.

n: The value you specify.

Once you obtain the %K value, you start computing the %D value which is an accumulative moving average. Since the %D is a moving average of a moving average, it requires several trading intervals before the values are calculated properly. For example, if you specify a 20-period stochastic, the software system requires 26 trading intervals before it can calculate valid %K and %D values. The formula for the %D is:

$$\%DT = ((\%DT - 1 * 2) + \%K_t)/3$$

%DT: The value for %D in the current period.

%DT – 1: The value for %D in the previous period.

%Kt: The value for %K in the current period.

VOLATILITY/RESISTANCE AND SUPPORT INDICATORS

Understanding the volatility conditions of the market will significantly contribute to trading success because when prices are at extreme volatility they cannot sustain themselves. These conditions generate many kinds of trades. Trades can trade a reversal of the move, or anticipate a reversal and wait for the price to retrace and then enter a trade. There are several good technical indicators that provide quick visualizations and measurement of volatility. This set of indicators includes the classic Bollinger bands, volatility envelopes, STARC (Stoller average-range channels), and Linear regression channels.

Bollinger bands provide an easy-to-see map of whether the price is at its upper or lower ranges. Simply stated, Bollinger bands are a statistical envelope around a preset moving average period of 20. The bands represent 2 standard deviations from this moving average. In other words, the price is considered to be 96 percent of the time ranging between the two Bollinger bands. The Bollinger bands are simply a version of the 100-year-old statistical bell curve that shows probability distributions of a sample population. When a price is probing an upper or lower Bollinger band, the trader should consider it an alert that the price may be getting tired and will return.

Note that this is not a prediction that the price will reverse. In fact, the price may continue to hang on at the bands (this is called "hugging the band") and it may also break beyond it. But the trader using the bands can sense the potential. The shape of the bands becomes important. If the bands are sideways, prices can bounce off the top and bottom more easily. If they are tilted, reversals are less likely. We will also see that when used in combination with other indicators, setups for trades start formulating.

Figure 12.12 shows a Bollinger band with the default setting. Now let's consider the same chart with the addition of another band (see Figure 12.13). On the second band, the setting is 13 periods with the standard deviation of 2.618. This is called an extreme Bollinger band. Jea Yu and Russell Lockhart in *Secrets of the Underground Trader* (McGraw-Hill, 2003) use the concept of extreme Bollinger bands with great success. The addition of this extra outside band provides an outer bounder for sensing whether the price has reached unsustainable levels. Remember that at a 2.618 setting, almost 99 percent of the time the price is between the upper and lower Bollinger bands. If the trading platform does not allow for settings at 2.618, one can approximate with a setting of 3. Its use is most effective when the price reaches an extreme Bollinger band and then proceeds to go back under the original Bollinger band. The forces that put the price at an extreme have changed, and the likelihood of its going back to an extreme are much lower. It will require some new energy. In forex, we can invoke a version of Newton's third law: Prices stay in their pattern unless news moves them out of their pattern. The extreme Bollinger band also can act as an area for stops, which we will explore later on.

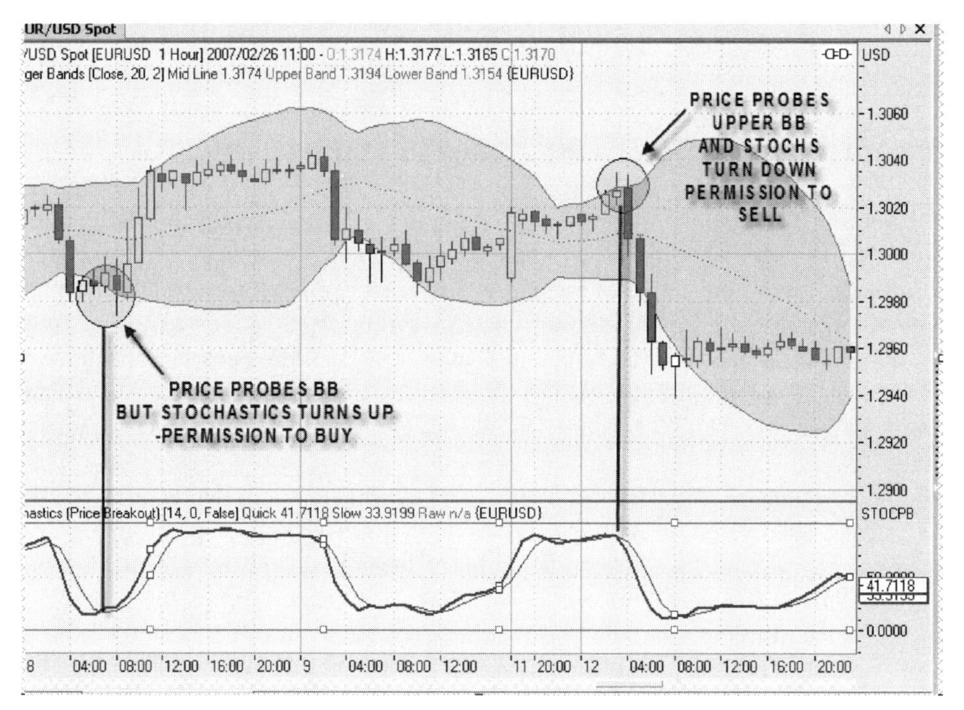

FIGURE 12.12 Standard Bollinger Bands and Stochastics Crossover.
Source: www.tradesignal.com.

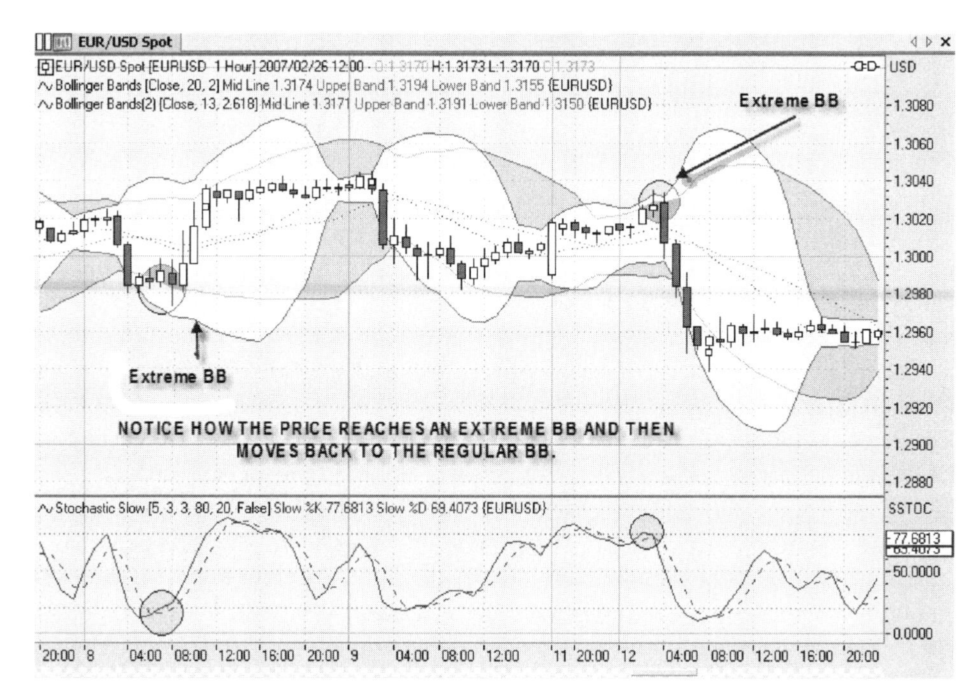

FIGURE 12.13 Extreme Bollinger Bands.
Source: www.tradesignal.com.

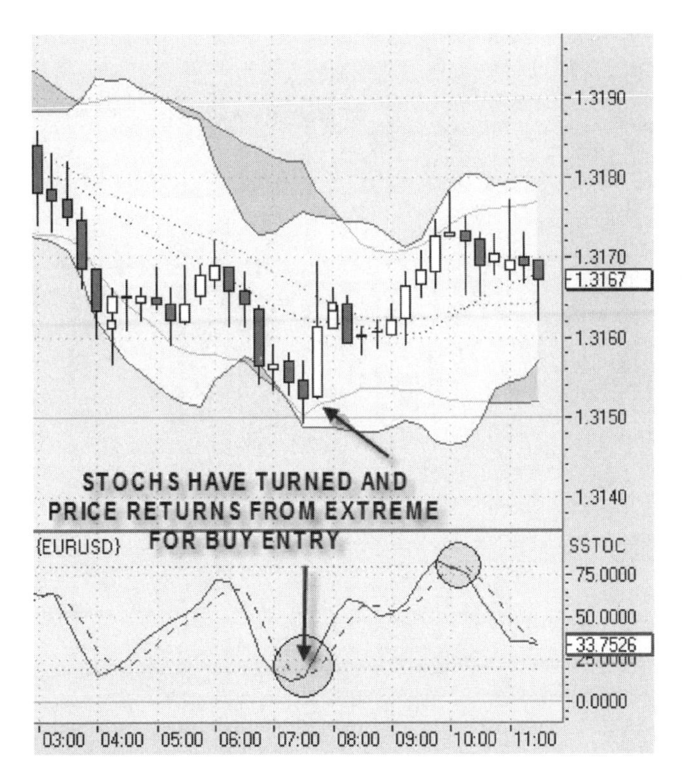

FIGURE 12.14 Extreme Bollinger Bands and Stochastic Crossover.
Source: www.tradesignal.com.

We can see that the addition of the extreme Bollinger band adds a depth of understanding to the forex trader. It provides an entry condition as well. If the price moves to an extreme Bollinger band and then moves back below the standard Bollinger band (as shown in Figure 12.13), then the trader can look to enter a trade. In Figure 12.14 we can see an example of the price reaching the lower extreme Bollinger band and coming back toward the regular Bollinger band, but we see the stochastic also turned, giving extra confidence that the price is ready to reverse (with extra confidence when the stochastic has turned as well!).

There are other volatility indicators that use envelopes similar to Bollinger bands. The STARC band provides another boundary where the price has a tendency to stay between the bands. For example, the same EURUSD chart shown with the extreme Bollinger bands can be illustrated with STARC bands (see Figure 12.15). Notice how the STARC bands form a channel and appear to provide support and resistance.

The linear regression channel is a popular graphic tool that provides another envelope around the prices. If available on your platform, it can be used to project a potential support or resistance area. The channel should be drawn so it extends into the future so

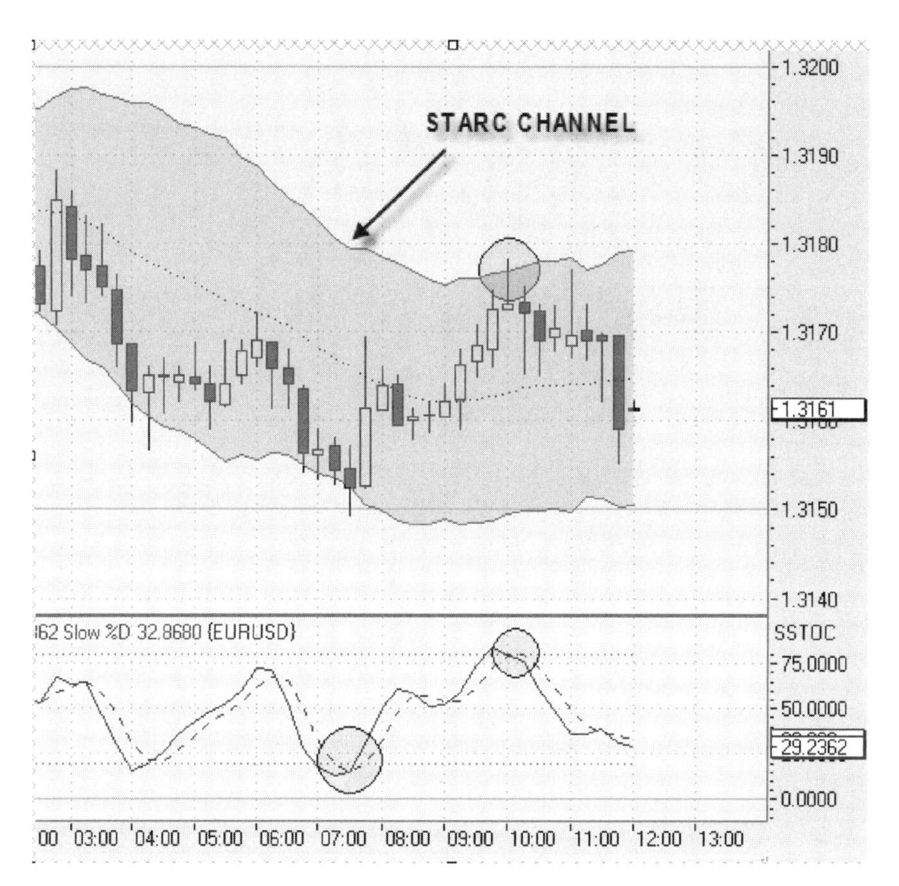

FIGURE 12.15 STARC Channels Act Like Bollinger Bands.
Source: www.tradesignal.com.

the trader can view the upper and lower resistance areas. In Figure 12.15, we see that the price has probed the lower support channel, and watching carefully what it will do can pay off for the trader looking to buy on a bounce off this pattern or looking to enter a sell on the failure of the price to come back. Figures 12.16 and 12.17 are snapshots of how this linear regression channel pattern worked recently on the EURUSD 15-minute chart. In Figure 12.16, we have drawn the linear regression channel from point A to point B. Point C is the future, and the price has not reached there yet. As stated earlier, the linear regression channel points to a zone of support around 1.3153.

The trader does nothing but wait. Using the linear regression channel adds another layer of confirmation. If the price is probing a linear channel, it is also very likely to be probing support or resistance. The idea for the trader is to get as much confirmation as possible.

FIGURE 12.16 Linear Channel Pattern Probed by Price.
Source: www.tradesignal.com.

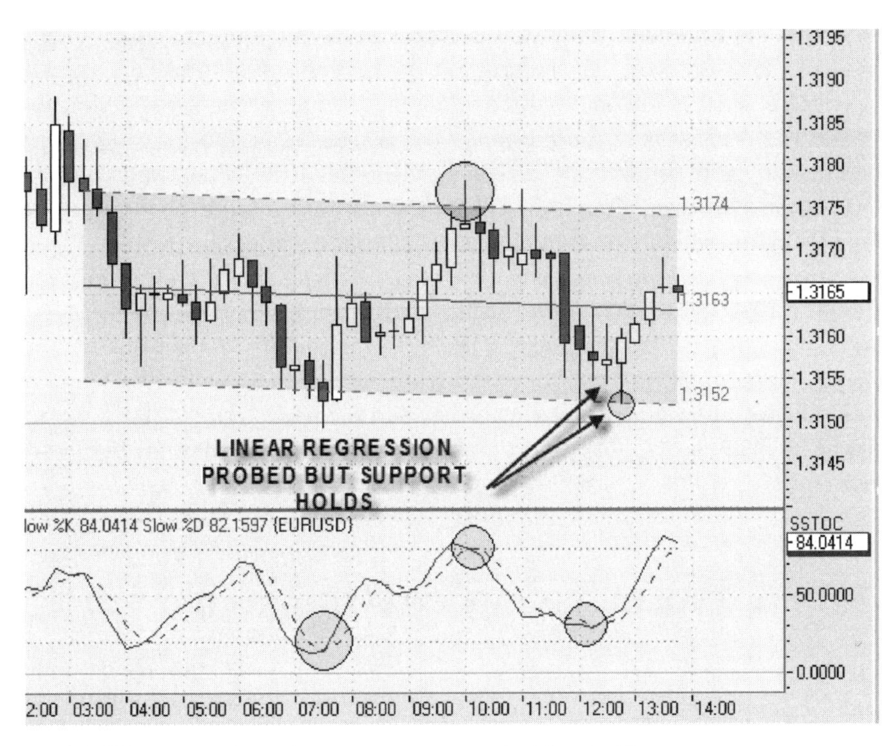

FIGURE 12.17 Linear Channel Pattern Support Probed but Holds.
Source: www.tradesignal.com.

The use of any envelope type of indicator serves to provide an ability to increase confidence that a trade is worthwhile. No single one is itself sufficient.

OPTIMIZING YOUR USE OF INDICATORS

The developers of indicators offer default settings that are intended to be general in their use. However, the settings can be altered. Many traders try to alter the settings without a real understanding of the basis of the alteration. Simple changes, such as increasing or reducing the periods used, aren't particularly controversial. Generally, traders use the default settings on the indicators. These defaults are there because a shorter period makes the indicators more sensitive to price changes, while a longer period smooths out the indicator and increases its robustness. But the question arises as to what is the optimum setting. For example, is 5, 3, 3 on the slow stochastic a better fit to the data than the default 14, 3, 3? It is possible to answer that question if an optimization program or back-testing program was available.

Many platforms and charting services provide an ability to optimize the settings. The first step in optimizing an indictor setting is to identify the time frame for the optimization. A period of price action too far back runs the risk of the trader's optimizing against conditions that are no longer there. Geopolitical and economic conditions change frequently, particularly in forex. This means that the period of optimization should be perhaps very recent, such as the one to three months. Also important is a selection of which candle chart to optimize. Will it be trading off day candles or shorter ones such as the 15-minute candle? Additional challenges face traders using optimizing approaches. A key factor is the stop loss. Even after settings are optimized for gaining the most profits from a trading period, the use of stops and limits will ultimately affect the results.

Once you have developed a trading idea, back-testing is the next step before turning your idea into real, live trades. While paper trading with a demo or game account is highly recommended for getting used to the real-time nature of markets, back-testing can save you an incredible amount of time. By definition, back-testing is a simulation of what would happen if you had traded your ideas in the past. You can test a day's worth of trades up to many years, going back as far as there was a market for the instrument you are trading.

TURNING A TRADING IDEA INTO A TRADING SYSTEM

Before back-testing may begin, your trading idea has to be turned into trading rules that are objective, reproducible, and able to be optimized. One common mistake is to try to back-test a trading strategy or idea that is based on subjectivity. Many popular methods leave out important parameters that you have to guess at. For example, methods under the umbrella of "Elliott wave counting" are notorious for being difficult to back test, because *where* the wave is measured from profoundly affects the back-test outcome far more so than the technique itself.

As you develop trading rules, you will be amazed how many trading slogans such as "The trend is your friend" become meaningless, since they can be objectified into hard, cold trading rules.

Finding the Fittest System

Once an initial set of trading rules is established, you can begin simulating what would happen if they were strictly followed over a period of time. The *time series* is the collection of dates and times when you will be testing the trading system. The *fitness function* is a function or measure that you use to compare systems and the basis on which you optimize a system's parameters. For example, a fitness function could be net profit or loss.

More sophisticated measures, such as the Sharpe ratio, Sortino ratio, and risk-adjusted return, compare different systems as to their performance measured by volatility, loss volatility, and portfolio risk, respectively.

Quick Back-Testing with Excel

Initial back-tests can be easily done in Excel. Simply paste your historical time series into Excel, enter your formula, and apply it to all cells in the time series. The easiest way to express this is by assigning each type of market position by a –1 (sell), 0 (out of market), or a 1 (buy). Then calculate profit or loss, subtracting out a spread and/or transaction cost.

I recommend mastering Excel thoroughly before buying an expensive back-testing tool. This ensures that you know how back-testing works from the ground up.

Typical articles on back-testing typically suggest two contradictory rules for the size of your historical data set. On the one hand, they suggest you use as large a data set as possible, in order to "prove" that your trading system can work under any circumstances. Additionally, it is often said that you should only test your trading system under conditions similar to the current market. Subtly enough, these suggestions again introduce subjectivity. Instead of the trading rules' being subjective to the trading system owner, now market conditions become entirely subjective. For example, you read typically on a web site about a trading system that has an annual return of 22 percent. It has had a consistent winning record over the last 12 months, and you're ready to purchase the system (probably for far too much!) After you buy the system, you trade the system rules exactly. When you fail to realize a 22 percent return and perhaps even a negative return, you are told that the market conditions have changed! So the trading system rules cannot predict market conditions any more than they can predict future prices based on the past!

This phenomenon reveals another common mistake made when back-testing. *Curve fitting* is a term taken from statistics, usually used to refer to nonlinear regression. I will explain with an example. You are back-testing a simple trading idea that takes two parameters. The first time you run the back-test, you get a negative return. However, as you continue to change the parameters, you notice that certain values produce higher, positive returns. If you choose the two parameters that, together, produce the highest returns, you are essentially *predicting* that the time series of market data will look exactly like your historical test in the future. So, counterintuitively, the harder you work at back-testing, the worse your results in live markets. How do you mitigate this inherent problem?

There are several techniques for reducing curve fitting in a back-test. The first technique is to keep your trading idea intact. If you are unable to express your trading idea not only in market actions, but also market action sizes, you need to go back to the drawing board and continue work on your trading idea. Additionally, you can back-test on multiple markets and move the window of the back-test forward and backward to seek out market conditions, setups, or patterns that are ideal for your system. For example, you may want to back-test only on days where a certain economic indicator is released. Back-testing on the most recent data can capitalize on recent market "shocks."

Advanced mathematics provides many back-testing methodologies that are producing results pointing to the fact that volatility and volume exhibit short-term memory. This is because markets are made up of all the information held by the people with positions in the market that intuitively remember the short-term past. This is why long-term back-testing, while at first intuitive, can result in overoptimization and curve fitting.

Market Inefficiencies

It should be obvious that finding trading rules that are able to be profitable is always an ongoing commitment. Remember, you are competing against traders who most likely have far more experience, capital, and research to back up their trades. Finding those market inefficiencies and capitalizing on them with trading rules can be challenging, but there is certainly plenty of market inefficiency to drive huge proprietary trading teams at investment banks, thousands of hedge funds, and many individual traders like you to post double-digit returns year in and year out.

Back-Testing for Risk Management

Banks, hedge funds, and savvy traders also use back-testing for risk management. Managing risk is accomplished by measuring and planning for loss. Even if your trading ideas are sound, not having enough capital for the long-term execution of that trading idea will keep you from realizing maximum success. Standard risk measures include drawdown, value-at-risk (VaR), leverage, and historical volatility. Maximum drawdown tells you the maximum amount, in currency, of your biggest losing streak. This is calculated based on when your trading system or idea would have had a position in the market. VaR is quite different in that it measures, statistically, the 95 percent or 99 percent maximum volatility (movement) in an instrument over a given period of time. This is a far more sophisticated measure of risk because you can compare across portfolios and asset classes (types of instruments). Also, you have a single number that you can apply to many different trading systems for a given market. Back-testing for risk management is probably the most overlooked important piece in a trader's tool kit.

CONCLUSION

At this point we have reviewed the major components of technical analysis, which include support and resistance, trend lines, and volatility. The dimensions of analysis provide a map of what the price is doing. Any technical indicator that is used falls into these categories. But technical analysis is not complete without looking at the patterns that the prices produce. We explore these in the next section.

CHAPTER 13

Chart Formations and Price Patterns You Should Know

The price itself is perhaps the most powerful indicator of all, because when price patterns form the experienced trader gains a strong alert to prepare to trade. Patterns form, appear, and reappear because the forex market in particular is not random in nature. When prices congeal into a pattern, it reflects market sentiment.

Recognizing patterns in fact is the basis of how learning occurs in all fields. A child learns to talk after listening to adults speaking for about nine months to one year because the human brain has the capacity to differentiate patterns in spoken language and that capability makes speech possible. Similarly, when a child tries to walk but falls first, the brain learns which pattern of steps results in successful walking. Every kind of skill can be learned by identifying the patterns that are associated with the successful application of that skill. Ultimately, what intelligent trading is all about is pattern recognition.

The challenge to the new trader in forex is to build a database of experiences in trading patterns. The beginning trader lacks a history of trading. The trader with years of trades accumulated is able to match the pattern he sees with his successful experience with that pattern in the past. The question often arises: How long will it take to become a successful trader? The answer is not one of time duration but one of trades. After accumulating an experience base of 10 trades, there is almost no basis for generalizing about future success. After accumulating an experience base of 100 trades, traders will be able to detect patterns not only in the market but in their own trading. **The critical path to success in forex trading is a constant application of pattern-based trading and knowledge.**

EMOTIONAL CONTAGION AND PATTERNS FOR TRADING FOREX

The first step in learning how to recognize patterns is to understand that the prices reflect market psychology. The trades are signatures of human decisions that move prices in response to market conditions. Trades, however, do not occur in isolation. Traders, whether they are alone at their desktop or in a trading room, are really part of a virtual neighborhood and as a result are influenced directly and indirectly. The result is the presence of market psychology and the phenomenon of market memory.

Patterns in the past influence patterns in the future, because they are behavioral in nature. Observing past patterns actually helps form the next pattern. Therefore, market psychology is about group behavior and the dynamics of how trades reflect group psychology. Market moves are often described as herding behavior because they are similar to how herds of animals, swarms of insects, flocks of birds, and schools of fishes respond to environmental stimuli. In all of these cases there is no real central intelligence leading the group. Instead, patterns of behavior emerge from uncoordinated decisions of numerous single agents. Descriptions such as emotional contagion, crowd-mind, and cellular automaton behavior (www.automatatrading.com) are indicative forms of multiagent behavior. The field of behavioral finance has recently emerged to study these forms of conduct (see Table 13.1).

It is conventional wisdom that the market reflects an interaction between fear and greed. This is simplistic because emotional responses include a much deeper gradient of emotions. For example, there are different forms of fear. There is fear of increased losses and fear of losing profits gained; there is fear of being left out of moves leading to greater gains. There may be fear of spousal disapproval of trading!

TABLE 13.1 Patterns that Reflect Emotions

Emotion	Pattern	Trader Response
Hesitation	Doji	If the doji is at a support/resistance point, look for reversal
Greed or mania	Parabolic path	Wait for price angle to reach 90 degrees
Surprise	Spike and gaps	Stay away; let market recover
Consensus	Channel pattern	Trade signals off channel
	Three-line trends	Trade in direction trend
Boredom	Narrow range	Breakout coming
Anxiety/Uncertainty	Wide range	Range trading scalping
Determination/Enthusiasm/ Despair	Hugging/Sliding on the extreme Bollinger bands	Enter into trend

Now let's look at greed. Greed emerges in several forms when there is a significant increase in buyers. This generates a sharp move up. Uncertainty and anxiety result in a reluctance to trade, and therefore generate narrowing of ranges. Market enthusiasm takes a path of trend continuation. When there is sentiment of consensus about a currency pair, one result is a channel pattern where we see the emergence of equilibrium between buyers and sellers. These are only some of the corresponding patterns that are associated with each of these emotions. Once they are recognized, there are appropriate trading strategies that can be used. Let's explore them.

The doji is perhaps the most famous of the candlestick patterns. It means hesitation. The interpretation of hesitation results from the fact that the opening price is the same as the closing price. This means visually there is no body, and the appearance of a doji candle means that the sentiment battle between the buyers and the sellers resulted during that candle period in no clear winner. When hesitation occurs at a key support or resistance area, it is a sign of weakness. A trader seeing a doji near a lower Bollinger band would be reluctant to enter into a sell order. Stronger sentiment for sellers would put show up as a candle probing the lower Bollinger band with a range around the Bollinger. The opposite is true of doji at resistance. A stronger bull sentiment would not result in hesitation. The market would push the price above the top of the Bollinger band. Several consecutive dojis provide greater confirmation of hesitation. We can see the doji at the bottom of the Bollinger band in Figure 13.1.

When the market is determined to continue a trend direction, a good pattern to trade off is called "hugging the band." We can see this in Figure 13.2. When candles are not reversing after probing a Bollinger band, the trader should not wait for a retracement

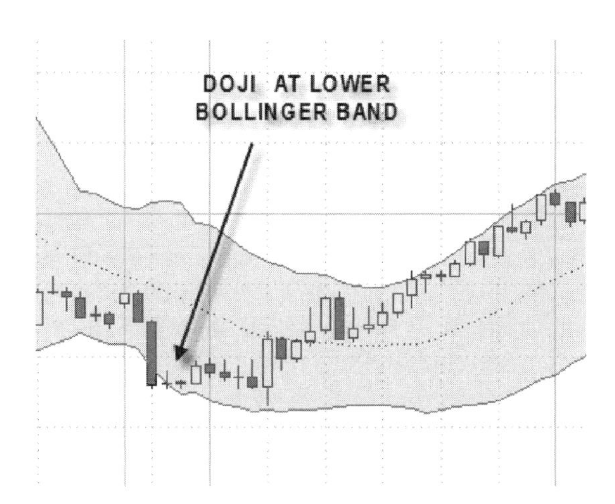

FIGURE 13.1 Doji Touches Lower Bollinger Band before Price Moves Up.
Source: www.tradesignal.com.

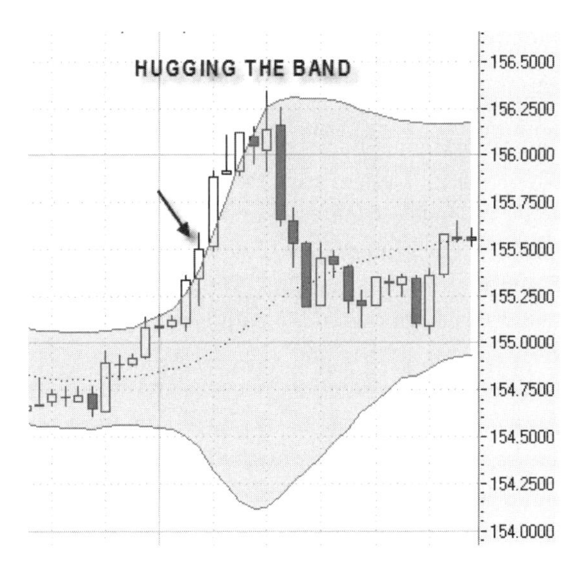

FIGURE 13.2 Hugging the Band.
Source: www.tradesignal.com.

but should consider going along with the pattern by selling (sliding along the path) or by buying (riding the climb up).

SURPRISE, GREED, AND EXHAUSTION

When you see prices follow a parabolic path, trades will follow. The parabolic path is a general phenomenon of energy transfer. Figure 13.3 shows the general equation for what is called a "cubical parabolic hyperbola." This equation closely models the path often taken by forex prices. This should not be a surprise because parabolic patterns are about energy flow and its subsequent loss. When you throw a ball, it follows a parabolic path as it loses energy.

Parabolic paths of forex prices are patterns that show many emotions. First is surprise when the price has a quick and big move. Then there is greed as traders rush in to take a ride on the move and take the path to altitudes approaching 90 degrees. It is unsustainable. At the apex, the trader can anticipate a sell-off. The parabolic is not necessarily a reversal indicator, but it is an indicator of exhaustion. Often, the sell-off works within the Fibonacci levels and the prepared trader can look to trade in the direction of the original move—after the price stops at the Fib level. Look what happened in Figure 13.4 to the euro–U.S. dollar (EURUSD) parabolic and Fib combination.

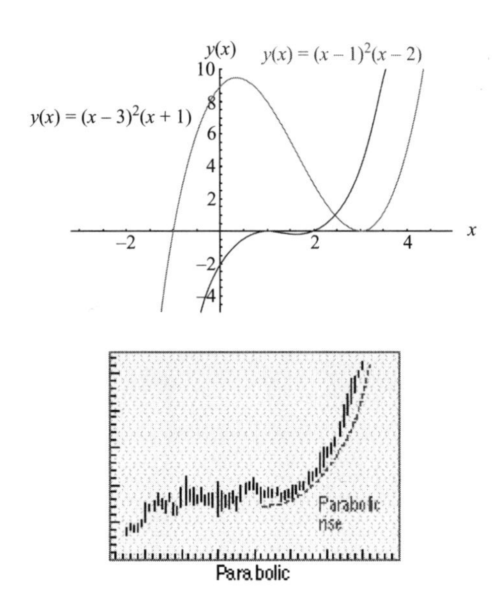

FIGURE 13.3 Parabolic Curves.
Source: Eric W. Weisstein, "Cubical Parabolic Hyperbola." From *MathWorld—A Wolfram Web Resource*, http://mathworld.wolfram.com/CubicalParabolicHyperbola.html.

FIGURE 13.4 Parabolic Showing Sell Off in EURUSD.
Source: www.tradesignal.com.

FIGURE 13.5 Parabolic in USDCAD Followed by Sideways Action.
Source: www.tradesignal.com.

Figure 13.5 shows a U.S. dollar–Canadian dollar (USDCAD) 90-minute chart with a classic parabolic followed by a sideways sell-off and then a downward parabolic.

FRUSTRATION IN THE CHARTS

When sentiment can't find a release, the price compresses and waits for a break. The signature of such compression, frustration, and impending explosion of a breakout are the triangles. Triangles can be equilateral where the angles are all equal or shaped in an ascending or descending pattern. Figure 13.6 shows an ascending pattern because the largest side is trending up. The range is getting narrower, and there is no room for the energy to go. There must be a break. The strength of the break is not known in advance. But the trader seeing a triangle can anticipate that a break will occur.

In the EURCAD cross-pair, an equilateral triangle is spotted, providing an anticipation of a breakout (see Figure 13.7).

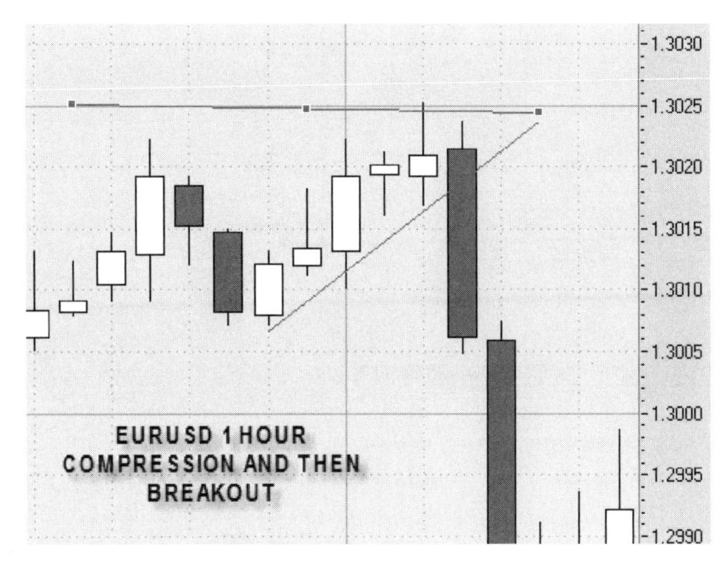

FIGURE 13.6 Compression and Then Breakdown in EURUSD 1-Hour.
Source: www.tradesignal.com.

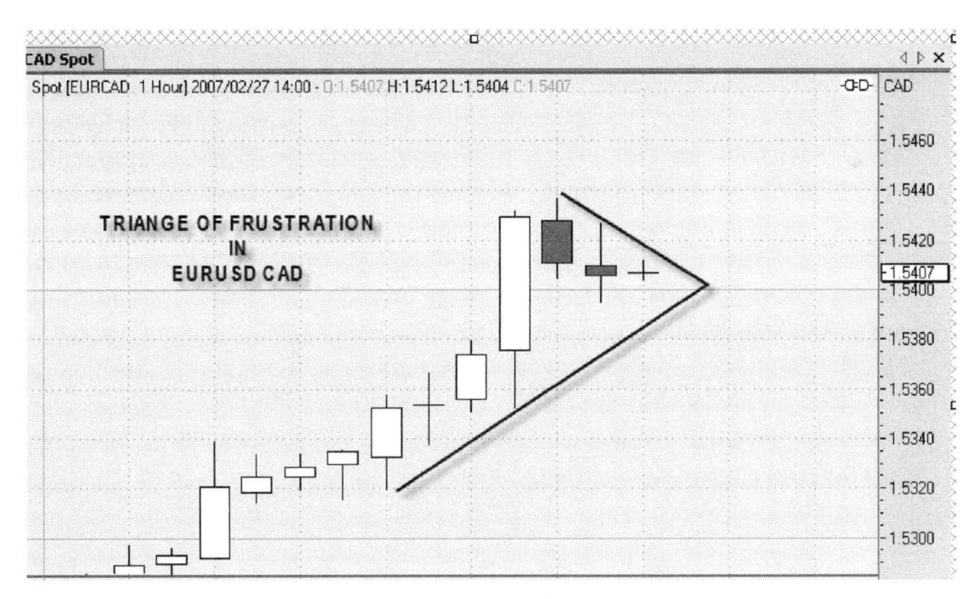

FIGURE 13.7 Classic Triangle.
Source: www.tradesignal.com.

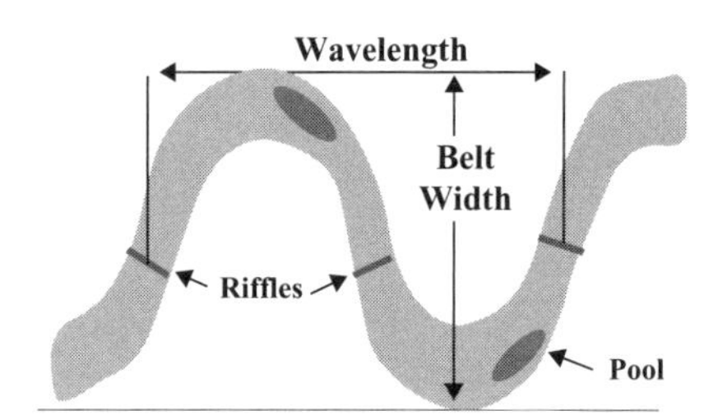

FIGURE 13.8 Wave Equation of Channel Pattern.

STABILITY: THE CHANNEL PATTERN

Patterns that endure over time through 20 or more candles demonstrate sentiment stability. The best visualization of this is the channel pattern. Channels can be sideways or tilted downward or upward. It is called a channel pattern because the patterns are similar to a river channel, and, in fact, the geometry and energy flow of water in a river channel is very similar to the movements prices make when forming a channel pattern. Channel patterns in forex trading are examples of traders using the language of another field of science as a metaphor to describe what they see the price doing (see Figures 13.8 and 13.9). The trader perceiving a channel can decide on several ways of trading it.

The first strategy is to trade in the direction of the channel and, in a downward channel, wait for the price to retest the upper bank. For an upward channel, the best location of the next trade is for the price to sell off and bounce off the lower channel. Channel trading permits countertrend trading because the market is showing persistence in the pattern. The width of the channel should permit trading. This means that the trader needs room for entry off the top or bottom, and assuming that such a cushion requires about 10 pips each, it is reasonable to assume that channels of 30 pips or more are the best size. Four-hour charts provide a very good source of channels.

The channel formation occurs in almost every time interval. Its robustness can express itself even at the most micro levels of price movement. The 1-minute pattern can show a channel and therefore reveal the inherent stability of the sentiment as we see in the 1-minute U.S. dollar–Japanese yen (USDJPY) chart channel in Figure 13.10.

Most recently, as the EURUSD pair reached historic levels, it formed a clearly identifiable channel pattern (see Figure 13.11).

TIME AS A TOOL OF ANALYSIS: MULTIPLE TIME FRAMES

Once you become familiar with trading setups, using time as a variable of analysis is appropriate. In a real sense, the forex trader is a time traveler moving from the

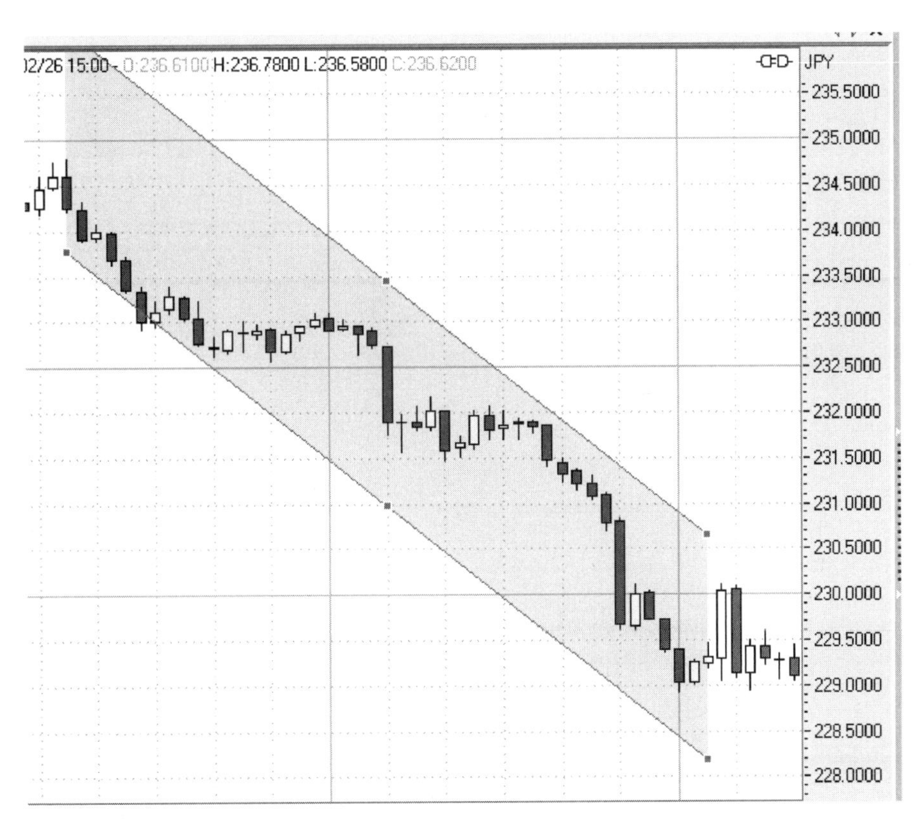

FIGURE 13.9 Mississippi River Channel Pattern.
Source: www.tradesignal.com.

FIGURE 13.10 USDJPY Showing 1-Minute Downward Channel.

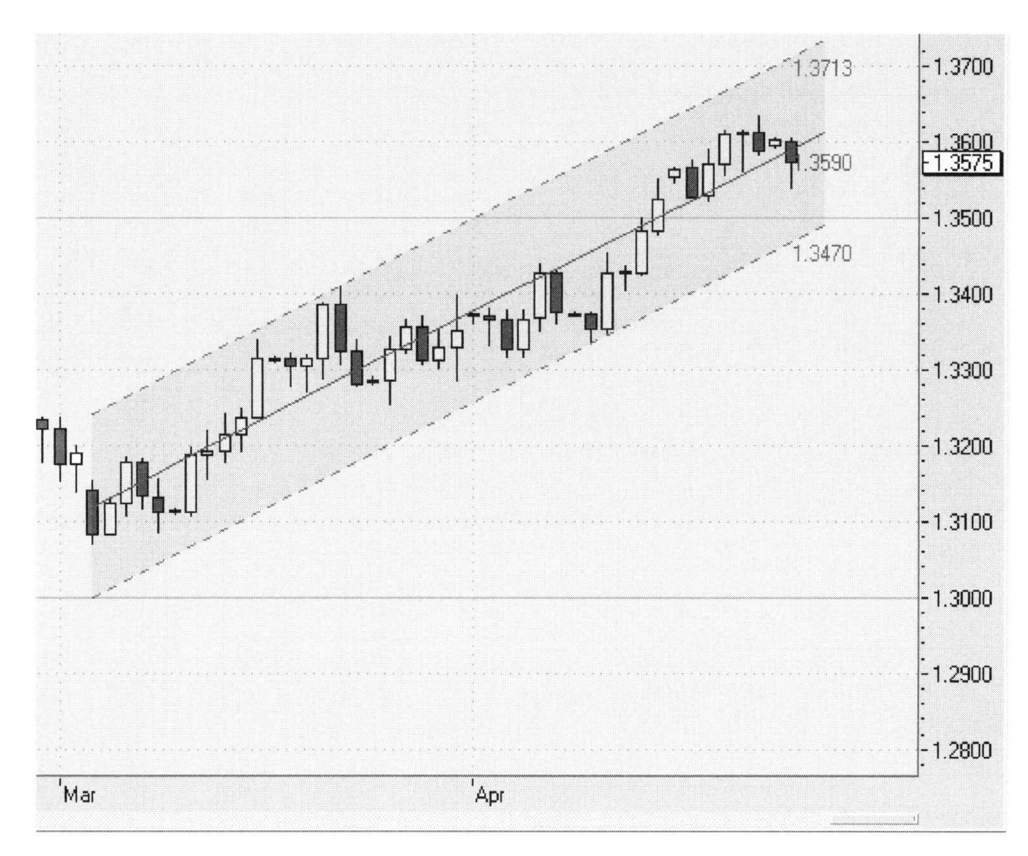

FIGURE 13.11 EURUSD Channel.

intrahour chart worlds to the outer reaches of weekly and monthly charts. The question often arises: Which time interval frame is the best to use to put on the trade?

The answer is that each time interval generates trade-offs that the trader has to consider. A short time interval such as a 5-minute or 15-minute chart provides less risk exposure to wider moves, but also involves the risk that the pattern traded is not reliable and has more noise than information in it. A longer time frame such as a 4-hour or day chart generates a much wider price range and great potential for larger pip profits.

At the same time, it is also associated with risk of larger losses since a wider range increases volatility. The proper way to utilize time is to compare and align different time frames. This allows time itself to be a confirming indicator, increasing confidence in the decision made by the trader to put on the trade.

SUMMARY

Technical analysis, when applied to trading forex, must also include recognition of price patterns. When forex prices form patterns, they represent a variety of emotions. Understanding patterns and whether they are stable is a key milestone in evolving into a knowledgeable and skilled trader.

CHAPTER 14

Trading Styles and Setups

One of the major reasons that forex trading has such a wide appeal is the presence of different trading styles that can be applied. Those traders looking for very quick moves can adapt scalping strategies and tactics. A great portion of forex traders put on trades that have moderate-size intraday durations that allow the currency pair to move through a range. These traders go for 10 to 30 pip moves. Multiple day trades allow for larger profit objectives of 100 pips or more. Forex trading can also include the goal of trading for income. This goal is featured in carry trades and is a dominant strategy of large hedge funds and institutions. But carry trades are also possible for the average retail trader.

The beginning trader should explore many of these styles and strategies by creating trading setups that use a combination of technical indicators, and chart patterns to pinpoint conditions for a trade. Table 14.1 provides a matrix for grouping the strategies and the appropriate technical analysis tools to implement them.

As we can see, there is no single style of trading, nor any one technical indicator or methodology that will be sufficient. Successful trading of forex is a combination of fundamental knowledge, technical tactics, and experience in pattern recognition. While there are many paths to success once you choose a particular style, there are setups that have proven successful for each style as summarized in the matrix above. Let's discuss each one with some illustrations of their application. The order of these styles does not reflect any priority. All the styles are valid for use in forex trading.

TABLE 14.1 Trading Styles and Associated Setups

Style of Trader	Profit Goal	Duration of Trade	Tech Tools And Tactics	Best Pattern
Scalper	5–10 pips	15 minutes or less	5-Minute Trend-Line Charts	Parabolic
			Renko 1-minute charts	
			Three-line break charts	Fib lines
News trader	5–9 pip scalp on news breakout	5 minutes to 2 hours	Pivot points + renko charting	Fib lines
Post news trader	15 pip moves	15 minutes to 2 hours		
Intraday trader	15–30 pips	1–2 hours	Use basic setups:	Sideways channel
			Bollinger bands	
			Fib lines	
			Stochastics	
			Relative strength indicator	
			Moving average convergence divergence	
			Setup enhancements:	
			Linear regression	
Bounce trader	20–40 pips	4 hours	Bollinger bands	30 minutes
			Stochastic turn	4 hours
			Market structures	
Reversal trader	Scalp	15 minutes to 2 hours		Three-line break
			Fib breakdown	
			Stochastic turn	
Trend trader	15–50 Pips	15 minutes to 2 hours	Bollinger band hugging	Trend lines
			STARC channel break	Channel patterns
Set and forget	30–150 pips	2 hours to several days	Variety of setups	Channel patterns
Carry trader	3–5% per month return on equity	Several months	Monthly and weekly trend lines	

BOUNCE TRADER

The bounce trader waits for prices to enter into sideways ranges. The price could be coming from an uptrend or a downtrend, but there are likely to be pauses along the way. The bounce trader will select a direction to trade and then wait for either the failure of the price to penetrate resistance or support. The price could in fact close above resistance or support but then proceed to fall back. Using a setup to confirm the reversal the bounce trader is looking for a 15+ pip move. In the U.S. dollar–Japanese yen (USDJPY) 15-minute chart shown in Figure 14.1, we see a set up with standard Bollinger bands, slow stochastics (5, 3, 3) and moving average convergence divergence (MACD) histogram or Forest version. These indicators are all lined up and provide a high confidence that the setup for the trade is reasonable. The setup aligned itself for several bounces off the top and bottom trades. Important to note in the setup is the convergence of the upper channel line with the upper Bollinger band. The range is about 40 pips. This means the trade has to conserve slippage and trade off the top or bottom.

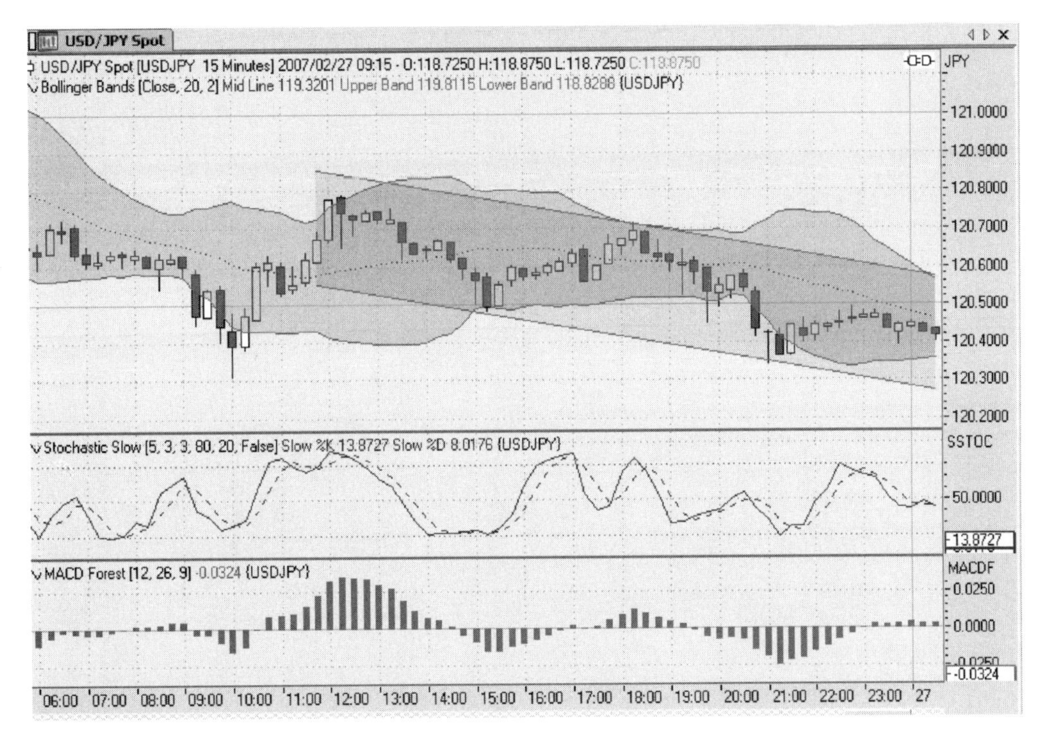

FIGURE 14.1 15-Minute USDJPY Forms Bounce Pattern.
Source: www.tradesignal.com.

INTRADAY TRADER

The intraday trader has more patience and wants to go for a bigger move than the average goal of 15 pips. This requires trading off larger time intervals such as the 30-minute and 4-hour charts. The intraday trader is looking for wider ranges of 60 pips or more to locate a trade preferable near support or resistance. This trade requires a "sniper" mind-set to wait for the right pattern.

TREND TRADER

The trend trader (slide or hug trader) isn't looking for reversals but wants to go along with the crowd. When a pattern confirms trend continuation, this trader enters into the trade. Many times, one hardly needs any indicators at all to recognize that a trend continuation pattern is intact. This occurred in a classic way on February 27, when the USDJPY pair proceeded to enter into a downtrend with increasing momentum (Figure 14.2). The

FIGURE 14.2 30-Minute USDJPY Forms Multiple Trend Lines.
Source: www.tradesignal.com.

chart reveals several shifts in the trend line, creating a fan of outer to inner trend. Trend patterns such as this one are irresistible, and entering into the trend is a high probable trade provided stops are placed above the trend lines.

The pattern shows crowd behavior, as there are very few corrective moves up. This usually occurs when the price is sliding down the Bollinger band or hugging the band on an upward move. The major technical tactic is using the trend line to confirm where the trend reversal would occur. Also, determine if an oscillator is appropriately aligned in the direction of the trend (see Figure 14.3).

Let's look at how the trader would use renko blocks to determine whether to get out after going into a slide trade. We see a very clear hugging-the-band situation in the USDJPY 15-minute chart (Figure 14.4). Assume the trade was put on at 8:00 after seeing the price stick right on the band. The question is: Should the trader get out? By using

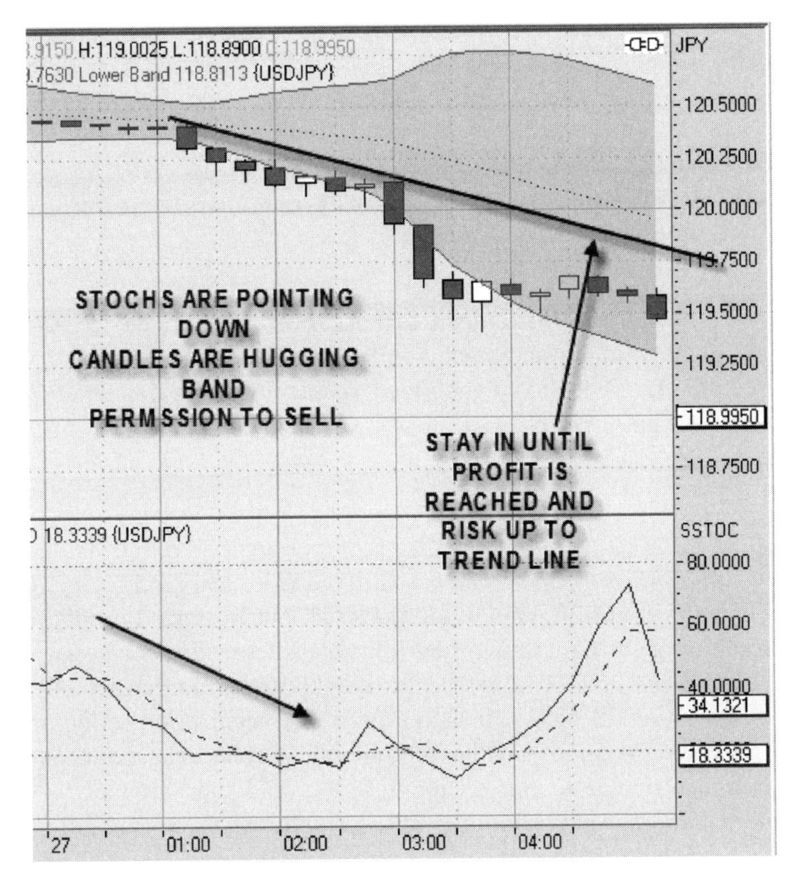

FIGURE 14.3 Trendline Provides Resistence.
Source: www.tradesignal.com.

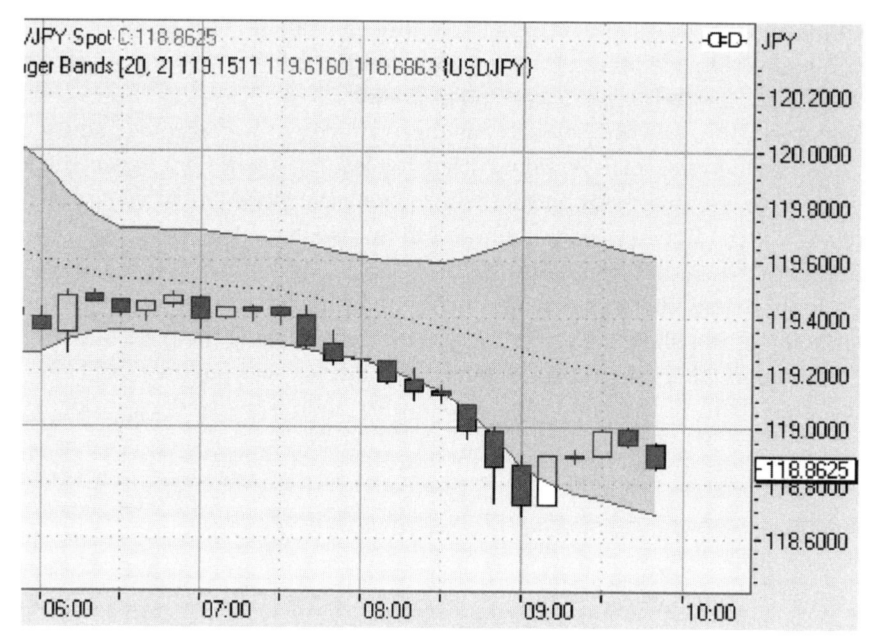

FIGURE 14.4 USDJPY 15-Minute Shows Hugging-the-Band Pattern.
Source: www.tradesignal.com.

trend lines and renko blocks, the trader gets the answer. If the trader sees that the renko blocks are staying in a selling sentiment (red), as we see in Figure 14.5 and also that the price is below the trend line, it is a good idea to stay in for the ride and not get out on small countermoves up.

SCALPER

The scalper has the goal of a quick trade for small but leveraged profits. The scalper prefers to trade frequently for small moves instead of working for larger moves. The scalper focuses on the goal of taking profits quickly from the market and trades in a very limited time frame. Scalpers focus on the most recent price action and on small time intervals, from 10-minute candles to 1-minute candles. The trader seeing a high probable trade can decide to put on multiple lots and then attempt to obtain 5 to 10 pips or more. Parabolic patterns are excellent conditions for a scalp. After a parabolic move up, the probability of a fading of the sentiment is great. The scalper has to minimize the risk of a whipsaw. There is no perfect strategy, but the use of renko blocks

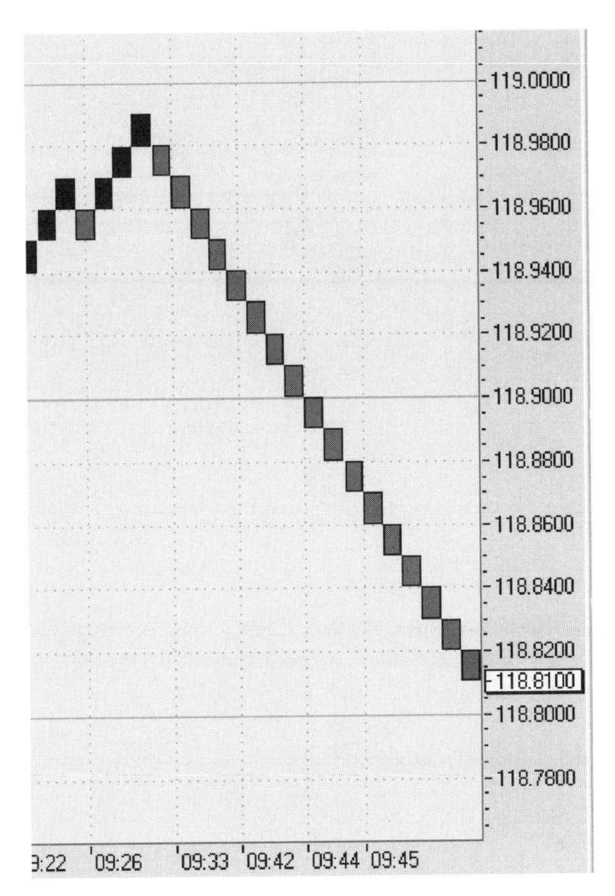

FIGURE 14.5 Renko Blocks Showing Initiation of Bear Sentiment.
Source: www.tradesignal.com.

will clarify more precisely than candlesticks when to get in and out of a scalp. Figure 14.6 shows the situation facing the euro–U.S. dollar (EURUSD). There was a parabolic move up, indicating a potential reversal. The question was when to get in and out for a scalp.

Let's see how a renko scenario would have worked. Mr. Ashkan Balour is a professional forex scalper trader who focuses on capturing moves like a hawk looking for prey. It takes experience in pattern recognition, but Ash is an example that forex trading can become a profitable endeavor. Figure 14.7 is an example of one trade he did; his own description of it follows. Ash is quite a good trader and was able to pick off 15 pips without 1-minute candles. Compare his candlestick view with renko. The newcomer to forex scalping should use renko to help out. (See Figure 14.8.)

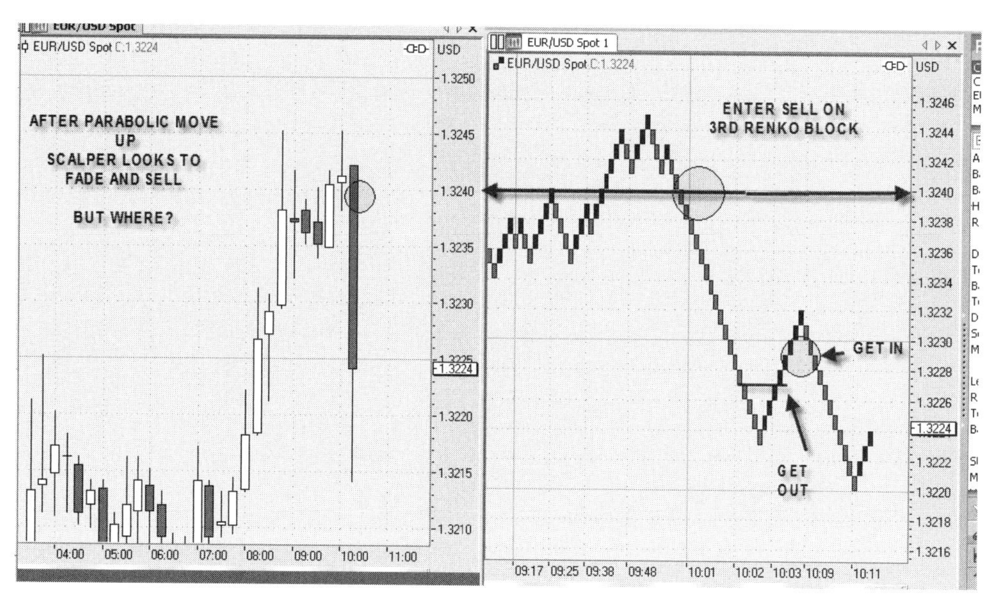

FIGURE 14.6 Parabolic Move Up on EURUSD.
Source: www.tradesignal.com.

FIGURE 14.7 Scalp Setup.
Source: www.tradesignal.com.

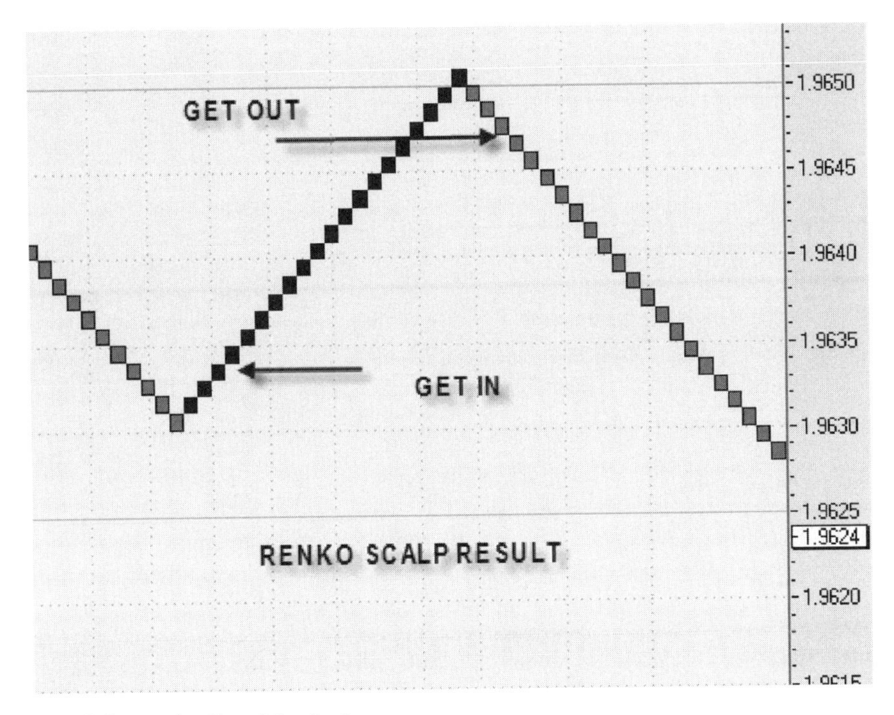

FIGURE 14.8 Renko Signal for Scalp.

I just finished this trade. The dollar has been weak all day. It came down from the top of about 1.9673. It did one wave down to around 1.9645, then started to form a pendant and went lower. I was looking to go long the whole time. I waited till it did a three-wave sequence down under the pendant. On the third wave, it entered an area of support in the 1.9630 area. I read a comment that there were buyers here around 1.9630, which is not my reason to trade this area but gives you some confidence. On the first up candle I was long, 1.9636; I waited until the first red candle and bagged 15 pips easily. Most trades aren't this quick and easy.

SET-AND-FORGET TRADER

The set-and-forget trader is playing fundamental direction and is seeking very large moves of 150 to 300 pips. This trader doesn't want to sit and watch the screen but play the longer moves and forces behind forex. This requires trading off 4-hour, daily, and even weekly charts and setting with risk control to target a 3-to-1 ratio of pip profits over losses. Trading cross-pairs such as the euro–Japanese yen (EURJPY),

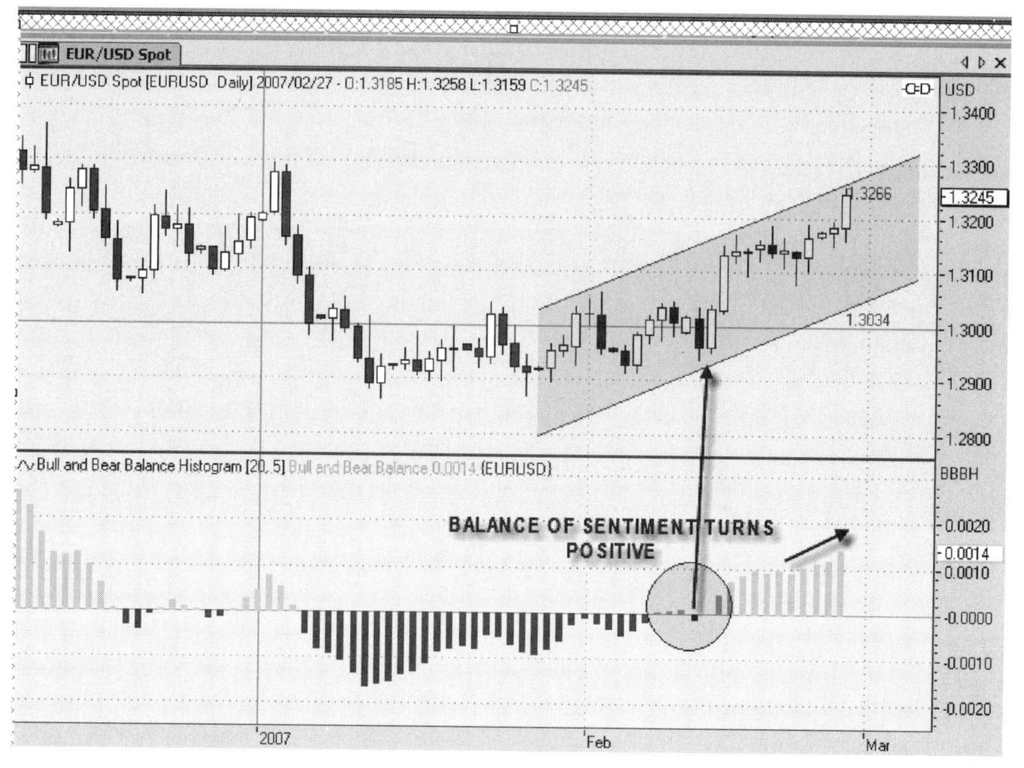

FIGURE 14.9 Bounce Off Channel Line.
Source: www.tradesignal.com.

Australian dollar–Japanese yen (AUDJPY), and euro–Canadian dollar (EURCAD) provide wide ranges. One disadvantage is psychological. Set-and-forget trades are slow and take a long time to complete. In contrast, an advantage is that all it takes is three out of seven wins to be profitable.

The trader wants to enter on the side of the predominant trend, put on the trade with proper limits and targets. Channel patterns fit this style. In Figure 14.9, we can see the EURUSD day chart was in an upward channel, and sentiment for the strengthening EUR is confirmed by the bull sentiment histogram, especially when it turned positive.

CARRY TRADER

The carry trader is interested in playing the interest rate differentials for receiving income by buying the pairs that pay income to the account. The goal of a carry trade account is to get a superior return on the equity through interest. The carry trade will almost always be part of forex as long as interest rates around the world differ. Money tends to flow where it is perceived to get the best return. The most famous of the carry trade pairs is buying the New Zealand dollar–Japanese yen (NZDJPY). The NZD offers 8.0 percent interest, while the JPY offers 0.50 percent. This means that the gap between them is 6.75 percent paid to the trader if done right. Another part of any carry trade portfolio has been the AUDJPY playing off the 6.25 percent interest rates behind the aussie. A third pair common to carry traders has been the British pound–Japanese yen (GBPJPY) using the high rates of the pound at 5.75 percent. Carry trades have been the domain of very large institutional trading, but they are available to new traders.

Carry trading has become extremely popular. A sure sign that the success of that strategy was coming to an end was a taxi driver's asking about carry trades. The risks of carry trades need to be recognized. The risks of large drawdowns while one waits for interest to be paid is substantial. Let's first take a closer look at the mechanics of the carry trade for the retail trader.

The first concept that needs to be learned is how a carry trade account works differently from a regular forex account. The account is the same, but the trader has two important focuses. The first is the balance of the account. As interest payments come in, the balance totals will increase. The second is the equity of the account. This is the liquid value of the account if everything was sold. There will be volatility in the equity because the value of the pair bought will vary. The concept is that even though there is risk of losing equity, ultimately, if you hold on, the interest rate will reimburse the account. This is a tricky trade because there can be substantial volatility in the equity values.

Figure 14.10 shows the weekly NZDJPY and GBPJPY. These are the two major carry trade currency pairs. We can see that for a substantial period of time those buying these pairs and holding them not only got high interest rates but also benefited from the fall of the yen. But as interest rates in Japan increase, the carry trade becomes less attractive and holds greater risk of losses as the yen rises against the other pairs. A carry trade portfolio looks to capture interest rates, but the equity value of the account will be volatile.

A real-world example shows this very well. The trader trading a $30,000 account had on a mix of pairs. Until a major sell-off of the yen on February 27, this account performed approximately 5 percent per month. But it incurred a loss of equity of $6000, or 20 percent, in one day. Those who held on to the carry trade positions the week after February 27 suffered further losses. But the carry trade was not eliminated. The difference in interest rates in the carry trade pairs continued to appeal, and the prices recovered weeks later. It's important to keep leverage low in carry trade accounts to enable sudden large

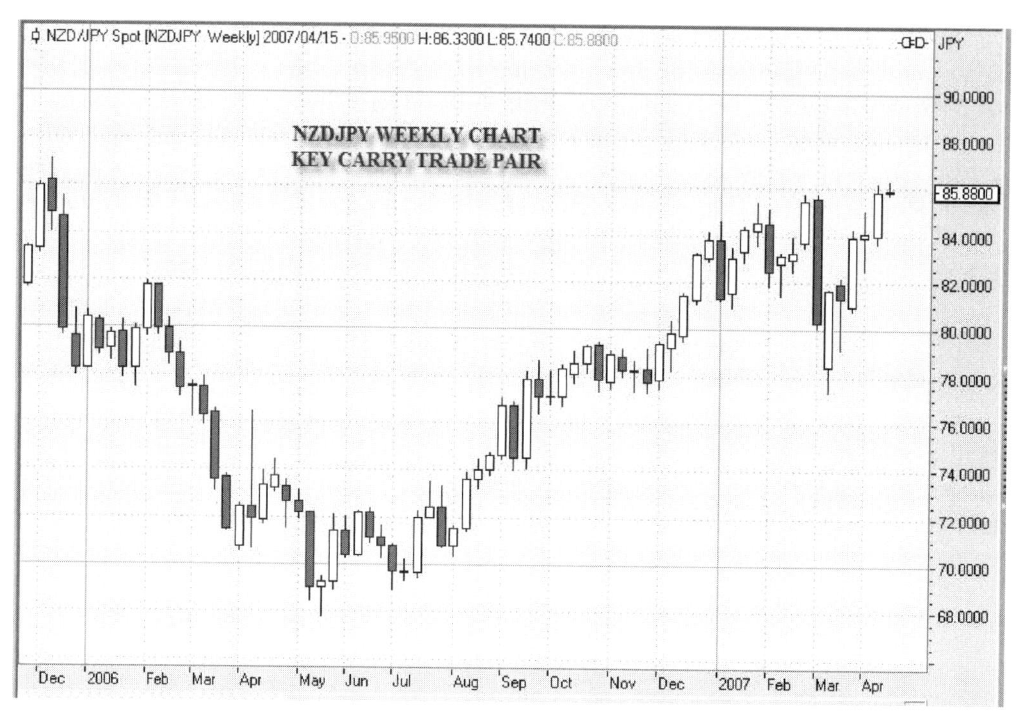

FIGURE 14.10 NZDJPY and GBPJPY Are Popular Carry Trade Instruments.
Source: www.tradesignal.com.

moves to be sustained. Jes Black, a forex trader and money manager at Black Flag Capital, observed that:

> *Typically, the carry trade is leveraged. With a $10,000 account, and trading minis, you should not exceed 10 times leverage. If you have more trading capital, you should look to diversify the various carry trades to reduce your risk. You could also look to do hedging strategies whereby you equalize your U.S. dollar exposure to net zero. Example: long USDCHF and short USDMEX. Both collect a carry, and you have effectively brought your dollar exposure to zero, much like a long/short equity manager attempts to do.*

NEWS TRADER

The news trader focuses on trading economic news releases. A great advantage is that the strategy offers effective trading in a short period of time. News trades should be considered seriously by those who cannot do forex trading on a full-time basis.

The market patterns relating to the news trade display three distance phases (Figure 14.11). First, the price patterns go into a sideways pattern. This is because there is hesitation about the outcome. Then the news release occurs. A surprise result causes a sharp move in one direction or the other through the formed support or resistance levels. After the initial impulse, the market will sell off and try to retrace. It may succeed in returning to the original sideways range, or simply go to a point of retracement and then pause and resume the move in the direction of the break. These phases are part of every economic news release responses by the market.

Tactics for News Trading

There are three essential tactics traders can use:

1. *The Hedger*. Put on a hedge trade by buying and selling the currency pair at the same time right before the news. When the news is released, the trader gets out of the losing position and stays with the winner.

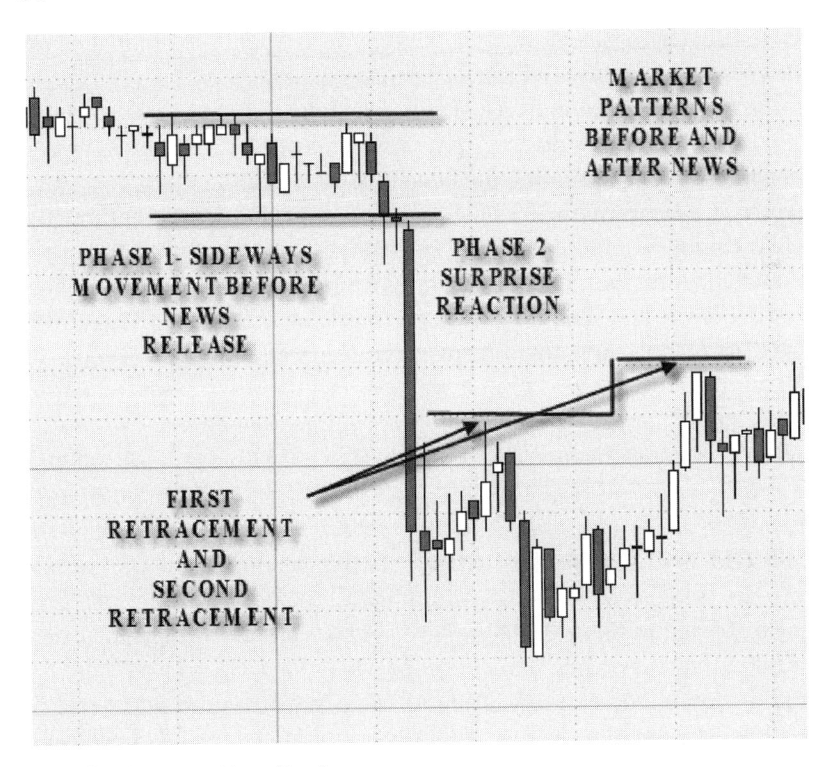

FIGURE 14.11 Phases in News Trades.
Source: www.tradesignal.com.

2. *The Bull Ride.* Trade on the break of the news by entering the market in the direction of the break and trying to ride out the move.
3. *Post-News Retracement.* Wait for the economic data to be released and allow the market to move and complete its first wave. Once the move is over, the trader will wait for a post-news Fibonacci retracement and enter the trade after this retracement.

Each tactic has its advantages and disadvantages. Trading the news is a very efficient way to trade forex because the trader knows in advance that the market will move. Let's look at the strategies in greater detail.

Riding the Bull or Bear—Anticipating Results (Most Aggressive Strategy) The trader has an intuitive feeling (a hunch) for the outcome of the economic data. It is not a wise strategy to put on a trade before an economic news announcement. But if the trader has an informed point of view, putting on the trade before the news announcement is an aggressive play that can be very profitable if correct. The key risk of being wrong and having the price move against you is important to minimize.

Tactics for the aggressive strategy are as follows: About 15 minutes before the economic data release, locate the 5-minute or 15-minute chart. Locate support and resistance levels. Use the average true range (ATR) at the default setting of 14 periods. Place a market order in the direction you desire. Place a stop loss order at 2 times the ATR. Should you put on a limit order? In trading the news, the idea is to be ready for a big move But we don't know if a big move will come. So a small limit order targeting 10 to 15 pips would be like eating cake with artificial sweeteners. If you're going to trade the news, focus on controlling the risk. The idea is to take a ride on the bull or bear, get on before the break of the news, and then try to stay on to get the most out of the move. So I don't recommend a small limit. You might want to put on a larger limit of 75 pips.

Getting off the trade in a news event requires a high level of skills in identifying shifts in sentiment. Renko charts are a powerful tool for this. Remember, riding a bull or bear represents high risk. But if you want to try it out, do it with small lots on and test your skills.

Trading on the Break (the Bull Ride) In this version of the news trade, the idea is to get into the trade as soon as the data release breaks. The trader needs to have the ticket ready to go and jump in. The risk here is of a whipsaw, where the price reverses. This risk is not as high as people think because when the news breaks, there is maximum energy and the market will respond. The risk of no surprise does occur and that results in a small move, causing the risk of smaller losses than a whipsaw because essentially the price doesn't move beyond a previous range and there is little room for profits. But if you're on the bull or bear trade and it is a big move, you have the same challenge of when to get out. The advantage is that you are not immediately wrong.

Playing Both Sides at the Same Time (the Hedger) In this strategy, the trader wants to participate in the news breakout but doesn't want the risk of prediction and the costs of waiting to decide direction. This strategy means you are buying and selling the currency pair at the same time. As soon as the news breaks out, a decision has to be made as to which side to get out of. Should it be the winning or the losing side?

The first tactic is to get immediately out of the losing side. This may cost you 20 pips or more on a strong move, but it also means you're in on the winning side. So the price for the ride depends on how quickly you can get out. Getting out of the loser first follows the logic that at the break of the trade there is maximum momentum, and being in at this point is, in fact, the best time to be in. This strategy works well when there is a big move. Figure 14.12 shows a classic breakout in response to positive dollar nonfarm payroll news release. The hedge strategy would have worked out, with the loss of about 20 pips on buying the EURUSD, offset by a gain of up to 60 pips with buying the USDCHF. Few traders could get the maximum gain out of this kind of move and would more probably achieve a 15- to 25-pip move in about a 15-minute period.

Getting out of the winner first is a variation of this strategy. In other words, keep the loser and get out of the winner because the first minute is when there is maximum energy. Then manage the losing side. The idea is to wait for a retracement on the loser. This strategy can backfire; if there is a small move on the news, both sides can lose.

News trades can occur on any currency pair because all countries have key economic data releases. There are many hedge combinations for trading news that affect currency pairs. The same principle of going long and short at the same time applies (see Table 14.2). Some forex firms now allow hedging in the same account. Other firms allow the creation of a subaccount. For example, one can buy EURUSD in one account and sell the EURUSD in the other account. But when this is not permitted, there are other ways to employ a hedge strategy. If one is doing the EURUSD news and buying also the USDCHF, there is a pip differential. The EURUSD moves $10 per pip (per $100,000), and the USDCHF will vary. To obtain an actual hedge, one needs to rebalance the trade. For example, if a trade were put on when the USDCHF was at 1.22, it would move $8.20 per pip. So a trader doing a hedge would trade 10,000 for the EURUSD and 12,500 for the USDCHF to balance out the move.

The trader will find that the implementation of these news trading strategies may vary, based on the forex firm involved. One should test them out to determine if a great deal of slippage occurs at the firm you are considering.

FIGURE 14.12 Currency Moves in Response to Nonfarm Payroll Report.
Source: www.tradesignal.com.

POST-NEWS RETRACEMENT TRADER

This strategy is by far the most consistently productive and should be part of the initial set of strategies used by beginning traders. The idea is that after the break of the news, there will be retracement—the price will move from a high to a low, or from a low to a high and then retrace. The trader waits for the retracement failure and looks to enter a trade on the direction of the original break. The retracement failure point is most likely

TABLE 14.2 Hedge Combinations for Different News

U.S. news	Buy EURUSD and buy USDCHF
British news	Buy GBPUSD and buy EURGBP
Japanese news	Buy USDJPY and sell GBPJPY

to be a Fibonacci-based pattern. After a news release, there is the initial move, but there can be many retracement attempts and therefore many opportunities to trade.

An aggressive version of this is to wait for the move after the release of the news, and then when it stops and reverses, put on a reversal trade. This strategy of fading the move adds a scalping tactic and provides more opportunity. But the far greater percentage payoff is on trading post-news retracement. If the price does retrace to a Fib point, then the trade can employ the setups that work in other times.

SUMMARY

Which economic data release should you trade? Every currency pair has economic news that affects that pair. It's hard to know in advance which ones will be important. The key factor is whether the market is surprised. Check your economic calendar and highlight key news releases. Focus on those releases that will report on inflation, job growth, and housing data. Initially, be sure to use low leverage or test your skills in simulation.

CHAPTER 15

Alternative Setups and Trading Strategies

This book is designed to provide traders new to forex knowledge that helps shape trades. This knowledge includes fundamentals, charting analysis, technical indicators, and market psychology—to name just a few. The act of trading becomes the application of these areas of knowledge with the forex trading mixing-and-matching techniques and tactics. The setups used will vary along with the trader.

Charting companies such as eSignal, VisualCharts, TradeSignal, and Prorealtime are examples of current excellent forex chart providers. These providers often offer many indicators, including some that may not be relevant to forex trading. For example, indicators that show volume cannot be used for spot forex. Some companies include experimental indicators that are developed by traders but have not been proven. This chapter examines alternative setups and compares them with traditional setups that use more common indicators. Which is better? That will depend on the skills of the trader. Forex trading success is not a process of instant creation but a process of evolution. You should try different setups and determine which mix is best for you.

STRATEGIES FOR STOP LOSSES AND PROFIT LIMITS—ESSENTIAL COMPONENTS OF RISK CONTROL

Even if you mastered all of the elements of fundamental and technical analysis, trading success would still require risk control. The most frequent question asked is: Where should I put my stops? There is no definitive method for stops, but the most important first step is to determine the risk per day that a person wants to tolerate. For example, if you have a $10,000 account, and the risk per day is 2 percent, this means that the trader will tolerate a loss up to a limit of $200.

Any level of risk has the consequence of providing a boundary for the trading. Unless you have an unlimited ATM machine to replenish your account, risk discipline is a critical factor. The consequence of having $200 risk per day is that the trader needs to decide how much risk a particular trade is worth. Is the next trade worth the entire risk of the day? A $200 risk must also be translated into pips. Trading at standard size amounts of $100,000, the value of each pip move is $10. This means that putting on a trade that results in a 20-pip loss would result in using all of the risk for that day. The trader in this situation would be foolish to risk a whole day's trading capital on one trade unless it was a fantastic setup. The trader should make room for several trades by choosing smaller amounts to trade. Mini lots that involve putting on $10,000 would mean that the value of a loss of 20 pips would be only $20. There is room for 10 more losing trades that day!

The concept of a risk per day can be better understood as having two accounts. The first account is your real account with the capital in it. But the second account is the risk capital account. Ask yourself how many pips you are willing to lose per day. By putting on trades of $10,000 on a currency pair, many more trades can be taken. Yes, it does limit the gains, but during the critical formative period where beginning traders are learning trading, staying alive is more important than the magnitude of profits.

After selecting the level of risk per day, locating a stop loss becomes a choice of the geometry of the price action. The first approximation for a stop loss location should be the answer to where you would get out if the market moved against you. In other words, if you were to buy a currency pair, then the stop loss would be where one would sell it—and vice versa. The trader will look to the trend line and support and resistance lines to find the location. But it's not that simple in forex. Remember, there is noise in the forex market. There is no precise location for the price, since it is a bid-ask market. One of the most frequent sources of losses for beginning traders is being stopped out very quickly. They place the stop close to the entry. In forex, the noise may take up three to five pips easily.

The response to this situation is to allow the prices to vibrate through its range. Here is where looking at larger time frames is important. You may trade off a 5-minute chart, but remember the price pattern of the 5 minutes provides a close look. Zoom out to the 15-minute and 30-minute charts to find more secure levels of resistance or support. This translates into putting one's stop loss above or below the 15-minute support or resistance, or above or below the 30-minute support or resistance. If you're trading off a 4-hour chart, then day support or resistance is an appropriate level for locating a stop.

Another method for finding an optimal location for a stop is the level of volatility. Putting a stop above the extreme Bollinger band is one solution because that would recognize that the price would have to go to new extremes to get stopped out.

Another tool for locating the stop is the average true range (ATR) indicator. The ATR provides a measure of the "reaching" ability of the price in terms of its lows and highs. Remember that the range is defined as the difference between support and resistance. The ATR compares the range's behavior to previous closes, highs, and lows. The ATR is the greatest of the following three values:

1. The difference between the current maximum and minimum (high and low)
2. The difference between the previous closing price and the current maximum
3. The difference between the previous closing price and the current minimum

The ATR becomes a smoothing indicator of the true range over the periods selected. How do we apply it to stops?

When the trader chooses to trade off a specific time interval, such as the 5-minute chart, the range of that time interval is expected to be less than the range of the 15-minute chart. Generally, the larger the time frame, the larger the distance between support and resistance. By watching the ATR, the trader can get a sense of whether the candles themselves are increasing in volatility.

Tablc 15.1 gives an example of two currency pairs and their associated ATRs for different time periods. If the ATR with a period 14 indicates a level of 9 pips, let's say on a 15-minute chart, this means that the lows and highs could have been 9 pips higher or lower on the average for the previous 15 candles. A good way to understand this is to visualize any candle to stretch beyond its highs and lows 9 pips either way. So if the trader places the stop near or at the ATR level, it is inviting being stopped out by the natural tendency of the market to swing in the plus or minus 9 pip range around a candle. Here is how to use this: A good rule of thumb is to use two times the ATR for your stop. If one is trading on the 15-minute chart, then two times the ATR of the 15-minute candles provides room to breath.

Alternatively, one can use the 30-minute ATR as the stop distance, even if one is trading off the 5-minute or 15-minute chart. By doing so, the trader is acknowledging the natural vibrations of the price. Try to test this application out by putting on two trades in your simulation account. Place a stop on one of the trades based on your own selection

TABLE 15.1 Comparative ATRs

	Average True Ranges for 14 Periods					
Currency Pair	**5-Minute**	**15-Minute**	**30-Minute**	**4-Hour**	**Day**	**Week**
GBPUSD	3	9	15	36	101	295
EURUSD	5	5	9	28	62	179

criteria, but for the second lot, put the stop on two times the ATR of the 15-minute chart. See how your frequency of being stopped out is reduced. In Table 15.1, we see that the ATR of the British pound–U.S. dollar (GBPUSD) pair was 9 and that the ATR of the euro–U.S. dollar (EURUSD) was 5. Using the rule of two times ATR, traders looking to put on a trade in the GBPUSD would be sure to have a stop above 18 pips. Those looking to trade the EURUSD could place the stop above 10 pips, since the ATR was lower in value.

Very often, the question arises: Should the stop loss be a ratio of the profit? In other words, if the trader were going for a 20-pip move, should the stop be 60 pips? The idea of a positive ratio of reward to risk is at the surface a good one. Having bigger winners than losers is critical to profitability. But having an arbitrary ratio between a profit target and a stop loss is just that—arbitrary. It does not reflect the reality of the dynamics of the price movements and actual conditions facing the trader. It does not take into account whether there have been increases in volatility in the range. Additionally, if a trader is achieving a very good win-loss ratio, then it is possible to be profitable even if there are more losers than winners.

Consider the situation where a trader has a ratio of 60 percent wins. If the trader had a risk of 20 pips per trade and a profit of 20 pips per trade, the result would be (6 wins × 20) – (4 losers × 20), or +40 pips. In contrast, a trader with a ratio of 40 percent wins and an average profit of 40 pips with an average loss of 20 pips would result in a net of (4 wins × 40) – (6 losers × 20), or the same 40 pips. In other words, the reward-to-risk ratio depends on the performance results. A very good trader can, in fact, have a high negative ratio and still be profitable.

TRAILING STOPS

The question of trailing stops is always a topic of controversy. Should one have trailing stops? Where should a trailing stop be placed? There are a variety of approaches that provide different answers. First, the trader is new to trading and has not accumulated many trades, and putting on a trailing stop could be detrimental to improvement in performance. This may not seem obvious. However, a trailing stop is a predetermined pip increment that is distant from the price. If the price moves further by 10 pips, a trailing stop set for a 10-pip trail would adjust further. The problem with this approach is that it is delegating to the market the decision to get out of the position. The trader should be watching the position, and putting on a trailing stop may be an incentive not to watch. Additionally, an arbitrary trailing stop such as 10 pips may be an invitation to being stopped out because the natural noise and vibration of the market could easily exceed that trailing stop (remember the ATR discussion). Finally, when traders are trading for relatively small targets such as 15 to 20 pips, it's important to get good at achieving those targets and not focus on pushing the profits further. Keeping in a position after it reaches one's goals may not be as productive as simply adding another lot to the original position. It is easier to get a 40-pip total profit from two lots than to use a trailing stop to try to get another 40 pips.

Rather than trailing stops, a valid approach is to move a position to break even when possible. If the target has been reached and the trader wants to stay in, moving the stop to a breakeven point results in a free ride on the trade. A good rule of thumb would be if you sold a currency pair, the breakeven stop loss would be 5 pips above your entry. If you bought the currency pair, the position of the breakeven stop loss would be 5 pips below the purchase. In multilot trading, where a trader can capture profits on some of the lots, it makes sense to move the stops down to a breakeven location.

Finally, mental stops are very popular and very dangerous. A mental stop is one that can easily be changed with the onset of an emotional whim. Mental stops violate the cardinal principle that all trades should have three components: the entry order, a stop loss order, and a profit order.

For those traders interested in avoiding stops, using options instead of stops is an area worth pursuing once they have experience in trading.

PROFIT LIMITS

Profit limits are orders that are designed to close a position with a profit. Technically, if the ongoing trade was to buy, for example, the EURUSD at 1.3200, then the profit-limit trade would be a sell limit at 1.3220 if a 20-pip profit was desired. The price would have to go through it to execute the trade. The limit order guarantees that price or better, but not worse. But the price has to go through the position. Many new traders see the price hit the limit and think it should have been executed. The question arises of how to form profit targets. This is the other side of the stop loss issue.

The major difference between being able to formulate a stop loss risk-control strategy and being able to formulate a profit-limit strategy is that one has total control over stop losses. Where to set them is up to the trader. But achieving profit targets is not under the control of the trader. Market conditions vary and setups vary, with the potential for small profits, from 5 pips to bigger moves of 50 pips and more. The best approach is to become proficient in getting small moves. A good medium ground for setting a profit target is 15 pips on the trade. This target falls within the ranges offered by the market under even small time frames. It is achievable, and coming close to it is acceptable. The goal of the trader should be to become competent in achieving an average 15 pips per trade. Once this is achieved, gaining more pips can be accomplished by adding more lots and by becoming skilled in managing the trade. This brings us to the issue of multiple-lot trading.

MULTILOT TRADING

Putting on more than one lot is a milestone in the evolution of the trader. Multiple-lot trading provides enormous efficiency for the same effort. But it comes at a price. The risk of quick and large drawdowns is proportionally greater. Multilot trading becomes a double-edged sword. The new trader needs to learn how and when to put on multiple lots.

The first rule of multiple-lot trading is the rule of three. Each trading decision can be broken down into three components:

1. Financial
2. Technical
3. Psychological

All three converge to trigger a trade. The trader makes a financial decision on how much to risk. At the same time, there is a technical decision on quality of the setup. Finally, there is an unquantifiable factor on whether the trade feels good. It is very difficult to quantify how each component contributes to the final trigger of the trade. Because it is impossible to separate these three factors, the best approach by a trader is to think of three lots as the best way to trade multiple trades. Each lot, in a sense, serves a different master. The first lot calibrates with the financial objective of the trade and would get a limit of the average goal per trade of 15 pips. The second lot would be aligned with the technical aspects of the trade and get a limit that is related to the range. It would be more than the first and would be designed to capture more profits. In other words, if the range is 50 pips, the first lot is always set at 15 pips, and a second lot is set at 40 pips (just short of the other side). The last lot becomes the wild card—it serves the psychological needs of the trader. You can decide to have a very large limit, such as 70 pips or more, or even leave it totally open. The effect of this approach is that when three lots are put on, the trader will be able to manage the trade without overreacting to the market. The fear of missing a big move is eliminated.

The challenge becomes identifying when to put on multiple lots. When do you put on more than one lot. How do you differentiate between conditions that justify two lots from those that justify three lots? The multilot decision should not be an arbitrary one. While there is no rule set in stone on this issue, an effective approach that has worked very well is the *confidence indicator*. The purpose of the confidence indicator is to be able to determine when to put on multiple lots. Each trader should develop his or her own confidence indicator. It is not difficult, but it becomes a powerful way to improve trading.

The process is straightforward. For each trade setup that the trader is using, the trader should assign a number from 1 to 5 (5 being the highest rank). If the trader sees a setup that has many elements of confirmation, then it gets a 5. An example would be a setup that has Fibonacci levels at resistance or support, the price is probing the Bollinger band, there is alignment with the trend, and so on. The 15-minute and 5-minute setups are similar and supportive of the trade. This deserves a 5. If the trade setup generates a feeling of high confidence with good features, but not the best, it gets a 4. A 3-ranked setup is one that the trader has a "hunch" about. Maybe it will work. It may be a guess. A 2 ranking is one where there is divergence and the situation appears to be not tradable. It may be a narrow range, or the price may be in the middle of a range. A 1 is the lowest ranking. A ranking of 1 represents conditions that experience shows are very dubious for a successful trade. A ranking of 1 results when the trade is countertrend and when the indicators are not agreeing with the trade, showing divergence.

The idea is that, over time, by ranking each trade that is about to happen, the trader will be able to have a strong correlation of the confidence index with profitable trades. As traders become more experienced, more of the profitable trades should consist of higher-ranking setups such as a 4 and a 5. In the beginning, during your first 50 trades, many of the trades are hunches. So the distribution of winners should, over time, be with highly ranked trade setups. During the first 50 trades, many losing trades would consist of high-ranking setups, which is an indicator that the trader is misevaluating the trading setups. If a large number of the winning trades are ranked 3 as hunches, consider yourself an intuitive trader and keep doing what you're doing!

Using your own confidence indicator ranking system provides a powerful tool for self-improvement. Traders who experience a series of losses and then go back and review the trades in terms of their rankings will more quickly perceive what the nature of the error was. Having an archive of your trades ranked by confidence levels becomes the equivalent of having a snapshot of your thinking right before a trade. A key tool is to take an image of the chart when you put on the trade and place the ranking on it. Using the "print screen" function achieves this capture. A very good and popular software tool to do this is SnagIt (available at www.techsmith.com). Take a snapshot of your next trade, and rank it right after you put on the trade. Then evaluate your own ranking. Did it deserve the number you gave it? Over time, your ranking criteria will also improve.

Here's an example: Early on the morning of February 28, at the opening of the London session, a high-confidence setup was observed (see Figure 15.1). Evaluate this setup. We see the price probing an upper band. We see the Williams %R indicator pointing down, and we see a reversal in the renko blocks. This was a nice 4 rating (in my mind) and it fit the criteria for a multilot trade worthy of two lots of USDJPY for a Sell@118.57. Placing a stop order for 118. 36 (not quite twice ATR) and one limit of 20 pips for the first lot, the second lot would have a limit of 30 pips. Both objectives were met within a short amount of time.

FIGURE 15.1 High Confidence Setup for a Trade.

SUMMARY

Ultimately, where and when to enter a trade is answered by the trader's observation of whether the conditions providing a high probable winning result are being observed. Aggressive traders would put on a trade more often with less confident setups. More patient traders would wait for a 4- or 5-ranked setup. Traders new to forex need to build within them an archive of winning setup experiences. Remember, before you learn to speak, you listen for about one year. For speaking the language of profitable forex, it's not time that counts, but the number of trades that accumulate an actionable knowledge base.

PART III

Putting It Together

At some point in time, you need to transition from observing the market and acquiring knowledge to applying that knowledge in putting on real trades. Some accelerate the process by quickly opening a forex account and beginning to trade. Many start a demo or virtual account and then proceed to trade. Both approaches are deeply flawed. Immediately starting a real-dollar account provides the realism of facing emotions in real trading, but the result is usually large and quick drawdowns. Those using demo accounts often experience beginner's exuberance by putting on trades with large lots, only to see their real trading totally disconnected from the successes in simulation.

The point is not that it is wrong to go and trade with a real account as soon as possible, nor that it is wrong to simulate trades. The common flaw is that of inadequate preparation. One does not go into war without training, and one should not start trading forex without appropriate training. The shift into live trading should follow several milestones of phases that enable a constant cycle of learning, pattern recognition, and risk management. Even the best traders never stop learning.

How to get ready to trade is the overall theme of this section. There are many ways to start and many ways to start *wrong*. Many traders start with too much money and too much leverage and quickly get caught in major drawdowns.

There is a better way that persons with various degrees of available trading capital can use. This section provides guidance on the essential ways of getting started and achieving adequate preparation.

CHAPTER 16

The Right Way to Use Simulation Accounts

One of the most useful tools to prepare for forex trading is the demo or simulated account. All firms provide these accounts. They enable a person to practice trading without the risk of loss. The trades go through an identical platform that would be used in real trades, but they do not execute. Instead, the profit and loss are hypothetical but tracked in the account history. The demo accounts are viewed and used by the forex firms as marketing tools for converting prospects into customer accounts. They are not designed to train people on trading. The result is that many people have observed the experience in going from simulated accounts, where they were making large profits, to real accounts with sudden and large losses.

Their conclusion has been that simulated accounts are not a valid way to prepare for trading. That is a wrong conclusion. While the real test of one's capability is in trading real dollars, testing one's strategies and tactics through simulation can be very useful if done under a plan of action that follows rules. The idea that one can start trading forex effectively by simply opening an account and beginning to trade invites too many pitfalls. Trading for the sake of trading is learning by trial and error. The risks of major drawdowns are too great. Getting started in forex trading begins before one trades. It begins with building fundamental and technical knowledge, testing skills without risk, and then applying those skills in real accounts with varying amounts of risk and capital.

Let's explore this further.

WHY SIMULATION WORKS

Training and simulation, when applied correctly under a well-planned sequence of instruction, work very well. It is inconceivable for airline pilots to fly jets without extensive simulation. Simulation allows for testing one's strategies and tactics to discover weaknesses and does not have discovering strengths as a priority. War games are designed to discover the strategic vulnerabilities of the battle strategies, not to predict a particular battle. It is essential, in preparing for forex, to correctly use a simulated account to test-drive your skills. The question arises: What is the best way?

We have already provided the hints of an answer. The best way to use a simulated forex trading account is to use it to simulate strategies and tactics that are intended to be used. Trading $100,000 in a simulated account when the real account will be $5,000 is misapplying the concept of simulation. Putting on two lots instead of one to test your skills in multiple-lot trading is an excellent way to use simulation to stretch your boundary of experience. The test-drive of forex skills in a simulated account should be seen as an opportunity to identify what you know and don't know about your own level of competence. Of course, the results are hypothetical, but if trades are put on as realistically as possible, then the results will have preparative value in moving ahead to real trading.

WHEN SIMULATION DOESN'T WORK

The major weakness cited in relationship to simulated accounts is that they cannot reproduce the emotions associated with trading real money. The fear and pain of loss, the anxiety of anticipation, and the joy of winning are not produced by the simulated account. The simulated account may be a clone of real trading, without a soul. Yet, this is a narrow view and, in fact, misunderstands even the drawbacks of simulation. Not being able to reproduce the emotions associated with the trading situation may be simulating the best psychological state of them all—no emotions. Having practiced trades seriously, without the emotional angst of each trade, the trader has in fact reproduced an advanced state of trading.

HOW TO USE A SIMULATED ACCOUNT

Even if the critique of simulated trading is correct, the benefits far outweigh the costs. Let's proceed with how to use the simulated or virtual account.

1. Set the account size to the level anticipated for opening an account.
2. Apply the sequence of trading challenges that are outlined in the previous chapter and test them in the virtual account.
3. Test yourself in the following challenges:
   a. *Sequential wins.* Try to get 9 sequential wins in a row of 10 pips or more.
   b. *Stop loss test.* Place an extra lot on each trade and place a stop loss of 50 pips on the second lot. Compare whether you improve the percentage of being stopped out.
   c. *Profit-limit test.* Place an extra lot on each trade, and place a profit limit on one with your average pip goal, and on the other leave it open.
4. Select a currency pair you have never traded and put on 20 trades on that pair in simulation before you try it in real time.
5. When trading a real account, place the identical trade in a simulated account and vary the stops, limits, or lot sizes to compare performance.

One of the greater challenges that the simulated account offers an opportunity to test is that of discipline. If one can't follow a trading strategy and rules in a simulated account, it may be a prelude to the lack of discipline in a real account.

PREPARING TO TRADE

Preparing to trade is not a linear process; you're *always* preparing to trade. But we are focusing here on key steps to take that promote a winning mind-set. These steps are effective because they are rituals of behavior that reinforce practices:

1. Scan yourself. The most important scan to undertake is a self-scan. When you wake up in the morning or right before you come to the screen after a break, observe your own state of being.
2. Take a walk and clear your thoughts.
3. Read the *Financial Times* while you're having a cup of coffee or your favorite morning beverage.
4. Turn your cell phone off.
5. Scan fundamentals and select the currency-pair's predominant direction of your next trade.
6. Scan monthly, weekly, and daily charts for key areas of support and resistance.
7. Check the trade-weighted index charts for each currency pair (www.iboxx.com).

The result of following these steps is more than formulating an evaluation of market conditions. The process generates greater confidence in taking on the trades that follow and the trader mind-set is ready for the challenges ahead.

Following are 10 key principles to guide the beginning experiences of forex trading:

1. Trading in simulation is effective as a learning tool *only if it is guided by a sound methodology*.
2. Training to trade needs to approximate the actual level of capital intended to trade.
3. The first 50 real trades are all test trades.
4. The first 100 real trades should be at no more than 2-to-1 leverage.
5. Losing trades are as valuable as winning trades: Don't fear losses—learn from them.
6. A trading plan won't work if it's somebody else's.
7. Success in trading is more than just profitability—it is repeatability.
8. There is no best time to trade there are only best patterns to trade.
9. Analyze the market by yourself before you read someone else's analysis.
10. Don't waste time looking for better trading platforms; focus on better trading.

SUMMARY

Ultimately, it is a personal decision when one is ready to test one's skills in real trading. The best approach is to look at simulation as a first step in testing one's real trading—not as the end of training but as an evolutionary step in becoming a forex trader. Therefore, simulation and real trading need to occur in a context of principles that guide the trader. These principles reflect a commitment to achieving excellence in trading.

CHAPTER 17

Strategies and Challenges for Different Account Sizes

The experience of trading can be greatly affected by the size of an account. Traders starting with relatively large amounts of money often have the belief that more money in the account leads great success. Often, the opposite is true. Having a large account before you have acquired proven skills is an invitation to simply losing more money. Yet, size does matter in trading forex because alternative account sizes generate different combinations of strategies and tactics. In a sense, each account size could be seen as presenting different challenges that should be mastered. Let's explore some of them.

LEVEL 1: THE $5000 FIRST-100-TRADE CHALLENGE

In beginning to trade forex, the account size should not be less than $5000. At $5000, one has the ability to put on trades and strategies that can be used in any size account. In a $5000 account, one should put on a standard lot amount ($100,000) only when they recognize a very high probability setup. A 20-pip loss in such a trade would represent a $200 decline, which is a 4 percent decline. In the early stages of trading experience, a sequence of losses with big lots could wipe out the account.

The best approach for a $5000 account size is to trade at $1 per pip and the most $2 per pip. This means placing $10,000 trades and $20,000 trades. The objective at this stage is to achieve a measure of competence, not a measure of profitability.

A $5000 account size should be viewed as a training account to get one into shape for the marathon of forex trading. With that view in mind, there are warm-up exercises and strategies to test out for your first 100 trades. Each strategy should apply to a sequence of 10 trades to allow for a reasonable ability to quantify performance and learn from that analysis. Think of the trading as a series of challenges:

1. Select one currency pair to start your trade.
2. Set a goal to achieve an average pip win of 10 pips for your first 25 trades.
3. For your next series of 25 trades, set an average pip win of 15 pips.
4. For the third and fourth sequence of 25 trades each, select a different currency pair with the same profit targets of 10 pips and then 15 pips.
5. Set a risk per day of 4 percent of equity ($200) to allow for the expectation of being frequently wrong during your first 100 trades.
6. Don't do any trades using less than 5-minute candles.

LEVEL 2: THE $10,000 FIRST-50-TRADE CHALLENGE

Whether one starts with a $10,000 account or grows to that level, one gets the ability to test and train with more strategies than at $5000. The biggest difference is to trade with two currency pairs at a time. The $10,000 account should still trade with mini lot sizes, but we increase the lot level to a maximum of three lots. The strategy for effectively phasing into a $10,000 account requires that you first select the currency pair or pairs you will trade. An important consideration is formulating a pip profit target that you want to achieve each day. Determining your risk tolerance is a critical task. Let's take a step-by-step look:

1. Select two currency pairs to start your trading. One is a currency pair you like as your favorite, and the other is a pair that your scan of the markets suggests is presenting good conditions to trade.
2. Set a goal to achieve an average pip gain of 10 pips for the first 25 trades on one pair and 20 pips on the second pair.
3. The maximum risk per day should drop down to 3 percent risk per day, or $300.
4. When using multiple lots, use an all-in and all-out strategy.

The Trader Log of Ross, A Real Beginner

Following is a real-world example of getting started. Ross, a beginning trader in London, takes a controlled approach. After learning *how* to trade at Learn4x.com, Ross opened a real account with approximately $10,000. A careful examination of his actual trades (Table 17.1) shows a remarkable discipline. The initial trades were put on with small sums to test his skills. Greater amounts per trade were slowly put on.

TABLE 17.1 A Log of the First 50 Trades

Date	Currency	Entry	Stoploss	Exit	Quantity	Total Pip	$ PIP	Result	P/L (£)	Comments
3/5/2007	EUR/USD	1.3130	1.3098	1.3132	13,000	2	$1	Won	5025.21	Exit news release 8.55 am
3/5/2007	GBP/USD	1.9251	1.9213	1.9351	10,000	10	$1	Won	5029.21	USD ISM – bearish
3/5/2007	EUR/USD	1.3106	1.3067	1.3107	13,000	1	$1	Won	5030.73	USD ISM – bearish
3/5/2007	EUR/JPY	152.26	151.93	152.31	13,000	−28	$1	Lost	5016.71	JPY is still overbought**
3/6/2007	EUR/USD	1.3116	1.309	1.3126	13,000	0	$1	B/E	5016.67	Sideways action
3/7/2007	GBP/USD	1.929	1.9254	1.9278	10,000	−12	$1	Lost	5010.33	EUR factory order: should have stayed with position news bearish
3/7/2007	GBP/USD	1.9286	1.9252	1.9294	10,000	9	$1	Won	5013.72	
3/7/2007	GBP/USD	1.9290	1.9320	1.9189	10,000	3	$1	Won	5015.72	Sideways Action – US Oil Inventory Data out 3.30 pm
3/7/2007	GBP/USD	1.9317	1.9285	1.9319	10,000	2	$1	Won	5016.65	Exit – Fed Gov Walsh Speech at 7 pm
3/8/2007	EUR/USD	1.3161	1.3196	1.3151	13,000	10	$1	Won	5023.96	$ rising before expected ECB rate hike (ECB 3.75% expect)
3/8/2007	GBP/USD	1.9341	1.9311	1.9346	10,000	5	$1	Won	5031.34	
3/8/2007	EUR/JPY	153.57	153.22	153.67	13,000	10	$1	Won	5026.33	
3/8/2007	EUR/ USD	1.3155	1.3120	1.3160	15,000	5	$1	Won	5037.78	Exited: ECB rate announcment 12:45 pm
3/8/2007	GBP/ USD	1.9320	1.9286	1.9325	10,000	5	$1	Won	5032.10	BOE as exp. Keeps rate at 5.25% – riding mkt reaction
3/8/2007	GBP/USD	1.9296	1.9261	1.9306	10,000	10	$1	Won	5042.95	Bad Entry – mkt went down before up
3/8/2007	EUR/USD	1.3138	1.3110	1.3139	13,000	1	$1	Won	5043.18	Bad Entry again – let it test resistance retreat then enter
3/9/2007	GBP/USD	1.9299	1.9273	1.9299	10,000	0	$1	B/E	5043.18	Let it bounce retreat then assess bull/ bear strategy
3/9/2007	EUR/USD	1.3148	1.3113	1.3158	13,000	−1	$1	Lost	5042.28	Wait until the downmove exhausts itself
3/9/2007	**GBP/USD**	**1.9315**		**1.9317**	**10,000**	**−2**	**$1**	**Lost**	**5040.37**	**ERROR: Platform put order into mkt/ not my actions*** **
3/9/2007	EUR/USD	1.3152	1.3172	1.3148	13,000	4	$1	Won	5042.59	Stocks say stay in trade longer: keep checking

(continues)

TABLE 17.1 *(Continued)*

Date	Currency	Entry	Stoploss	Exit	Quantity	Total Pip	$ PIP	Result	P/L (£)	Comments
3/9/2007	EUR/JPY	154.39	154.06	154.49	13,000	7	$1	Won	5047.11	US non farm payroll suggest moderate expansion** no explanation
3/9/2007	GBP/USD	1.9298		1.9293	10,000	−29	$1	Lost	5034.30	Stupid Stupid: WAIT FOR THE NOISE TO CALM AFTER A NEWS REPORT
3/12/2007	USD/JPY	118.15	117.85	118.13	20,000	−2	$2	Lost	5040.51	Disaster: Bought at 118.15 collapsed eventually broke 118 level
3/13/2007	AUD/USD	0.7844	0.7879	0.7834	20,000	−76	$2	Lost	4870.08	Stupid: Opened position, spoke to broker forgot to put stop in
3/13/2007	GBP/USD	1.9314	1.9284	1.9320	20,000	6	$2	Won	4892.82	USD Retail Sales more bearish than expected – very imp indicator
2/13/2007	**GBP/USD**	**1.9321**	**1.9283**	**1.9329**	**20,000**	**−10**	**$2**	**Won**	**4895.49**	**MOVED TO SAXO PRO 2 – HAVE TO PAY FEE IF UNDER $50K**
3/15/2007	EUR/USD	1.3210	1.3175	1.3213	20,000	3	$2	Won	4988.86	Seems to be finding resistance despite upbreak – keep checking
3/15/2007	GBP/USD	1.9370	1.9330	1.9375	20,000	5	$2	Won	4943.16	Norwegian raise rates by 0.25% to 4.00% as expected
3/15/2007	GBP/USD	1.9375	1.9380	1.3800	20,000	5	$2	Won	4941.83	
3/16/2007	GBP/USD	1.9473	1.9443	1.9476	20,000	3	$2	Won	4997.08	Worries about US Recession
3/16/2007	EUR/USD	1.3323	1.3293	1.3321	20,000	−4	$2	Lost	4997.08	US Data not as bad as expected: Remember expectations already priced into market
3/19/2007	EUR/USD	1.3297	1.3261	1.3304	20,000	7	$2	Won	4940.44	Below Pivot Support/Resistance Points
3/19/2007	GBP/USD	1.9455	1.9423	1.9457	20,000	2	$2	Won	4979.74	Intra day downtrend in place so exited position

3/19/2007	GBP/USD	1.9434	1.9398	1.9437	20,000	3	$2	Won	4981.46	US Housing Data not a disaster: 36 from 38 last month
3/19/2007	GBP/USD	1.9452	1.9422	1.9457	20,000	5	$2	Won	5014.44	Japanese opening bullish. Aud broke 0.800 resistance other followed
3/20/2007	EUR/USD	1.3288	1.3258	1.3292	20,000	4	$2	Won	5014.44	Bought on pivot point pierce: not sure as has already broken it
3/20/2007	EUR/USD	1.3289	1.3269	1.3290	20,000	1	$2	Won	5014.44	Bought again on break of pivot but daily trend down
3/20/2007	EUR/USD	1.3297	1.3267	1.3298	20,000	1	$2	Won	5014.44	Bought in channel but I think was too high in channel - got out too early
3/20/2007	AUD/USD	0.8025	0.8055	0.8015	20,000	10	$2	Won	5025.91	Mkt at 5 year high - current sideways action - correction?
3/21/2007	USD/CAD	1.1625	1.1605*	1.1630	20,000	10	$2	Won	5059.85	Cad retails sales 12.30pm exp bearish/ plus USD/CAD at extreme low
3/21/2007	EUR/USD	1.3308	1.3278*	1.3313	20,000	10	$2	Won	5059.85	All currencies vs $ rising
3/21/2007	EUR/USD	1.3372	1.3341*	1.3369	20,000	3	$2	Won	5040.51	Channel Play
3/22/2007	GBP/USD	1.9706	1.9744	1.9700	20,000	6	$2	Won	5040.51	Bearish line intra day downtrend
3/22/2007	EUR/USD	1.3355	1.3393	1.3352	20,000	3	$2	Won	5040.51	Channel Play - broke channel bullish but retreated after USD unemployment claims
3/22/2007	GBP/USD	1.9693	1.9657	1.9700	20,000	7	$2	Won	5040.51	USD leading index out at −0.4% vs −0.3% - bearish
3/22/2007	EUR/USD	1.3373	1.3343*	1.3383	20,000	4	$2	Won	5116.57	USD Leading Index - plus broke 1.3366 resistance
3/26/2007	USD/CAD	1.1626	1.1596	1.1630	20,000		$2	Won	5059.85	USD Home Sales out at 2 pm - bullish expectation

(continues)

TABLE 17.1 *(Continued)*

Date	Currency	Entry	Stoploss	Exit	Quantity	Total Pip	$ PIP	Result	P/L (£)	Comments
3/26/2007	GBP/USD	1.9683	1.9718	1.9673	20,000	10	$2	Won	5012.00	
3/26/2007	USD/CAD	1.1610	1.1575	1.1602	20,000	−8	$2	Lost	5012.00	US Jobless Claims bullish - closed without checking properly
3/27/2007	USD.CHF	1.2139	1.2169	1.2135	20,000	4	$2	Won	5068.10	EUR German IFO Business Confidence bullish
3/27/2007	USD/JPY	118.28	117.98	118.35	20,000	7	$2	Won	5068.10	4 hr timeframe suggest buyers in control
3/27/2007	USD/CHF	1.2143	1.2178	1.2140	20,000	3	$2	Won	5068.10	4 hr timeframe suggest sellers in control
3/28/2007	GBP/USD	1.9625	1.9593	1.9270	50,000	2	$5	Won	5089.07	Making a series of higher highs and higher lows
3/28/2007	GBP/USD	1.9653	1.9619	1.9656	50,000	3	$5	Won	5089.07	USD Core Durable Goods bearish
3/29/2007	USD/CHF	1.2153	1.2183	1.2152	50,000	1	$5	Won	5102.00	Hugging Bollinger Bands
3/29/2007	AUD/USD	0.8089	0.8069	0.8087	50,000	2	$5	Won	5102.00	Hugging Bollinger Bands
3/29/2007	USD/CHF	1.2182	1.2152	1.2185	50,000	3	$5	Won	5102.00	US Unemployment Data bullish than exp - should have got in earlier
3/29/2007	GBP/USD	1.9624	1.9654	1.9620	50,000	4	$5	Won	5102.00	Broken support/ bullish US data/only rising above bottom bollinger
3/30/2007	GBP/USD	1.9569	1.9605	1.9567	50,000	2	$5	Won	5116.57	USD Price Index bullish - should have left in longer
3/30/2007	GBP/USD	1.9569	1.9605	1.9564	50,000	5	$5	Won	5116.57	Sold on retracement

3/30/2007	GBP/USD	1.9573	1.9605	1.9571	50,000	2	$5	Won	5116.57	Chicago PMI numbers bearish
3/30/2007	GBP/USD	1.9597	1.9567	1.9599	50,000	2	$5	Won	5116.57	Broke Resistance
3/30/2007	GBP/USD	1.9680	1.971	1.9675	50,000	5	$5	Won	5161.74	Retracement after one masive masive intra day bulltrend
3/30/2007	GBP/USD	1.9686	1.9716	1.9683	50,000	3	$5	Won	5170.61	Retracement after one masive masive intra day bulltrend
3/30/2007	GBP/USD	1.9682	1.9712	1.9680	50,000	2	$5	Won	5175.70	Retracement after one masive masive intra day bulltrend
4/2/2007	EUR/USD	1.3370	News Play	1.3376	50,000	6	$5	Won	5175.41	News Play: USD ISM Manufacturing bearish
4/2/2007	USD/CHF	1.2136	News Play	1.2130	50,000	−4	$5	Lost	5173.91	News Play: USD ISM Manufacturing bearish
4/3/2007	GBP/USD	1.9775	1.9805	1.9765	50,000	10	$5	Won	5201.13	Broke below 200 MA/ Morning reaction
4/3/2007	EUR/USD	1.3353	1.3383	1.3352	50,000	1	$5	Won	5202.91	Triangle developing for an upside breakout
4/3/2007	EUR/USD	1.3368	1.3338	1.3364	50,000	−4	$5	Lost	5193.28	Broke resistance @ 1.3363/ had to go to job interview
4/3/2007	EUR/JPY	158.65	158.95	158.61	50,000	4	$5	Won	5200.34	Hugging Bands sold on retracement/ been very bullish
4/3/2007	EUR/USD	1.3330	1.3300	1.3340	50,000	10	$5	Won	5238.82	Extreme sell off. 4 green bars on renko showing

(continues)

TABLE 17.1 *(Continued)*

Date	Currency	Entry	Stoploss	Exit	Quantity	Total Pip	$ PIP	Result	P/L (£)	Comments
4/4/2007	AUD/USD	0.8075	0.8095	0.8070	50,000	5	$5	Won	5192.00	AUD keep rates at 6.25% mkt priced in a rise bought on retracement
4/4/2007	USD/CHF	1.2189	1.2209	1.2185	50,000	4	$5	Won	5260.93	Hugging 15/30 min bands
4/4/2007	GBP/USD	1.9754	1.9784	1.9747	50,000	7	$5	Won	5216.63	Broke pivot support @ 1.9762
4/4/2007	EUR/USD	1.3372	1.3342*	1.3372	50,000	0	$5	B/E	5281.94	Resistance too strong – may break keep watching
4/4/2007	AUD/USD	0.8128	0.8148	0.8126	50,000	2	$5	Won	5200.11	Hugging 1 min bands/ all currencies vs $ retreating
4/4/2007	GBP/USD	1.9742	1.9722	1.9749	50,000	7	$5	Won	5278.65	USD ISM non manufacturing orders/ factory orders bearish
4/4/2007	USD/CHF	1.2188	1.2158	1.2192	50,000	4	$5	Won	5290.20	Playing retracement after the oversold USD news
4/5/2007	GBP/USD	1.9736	1.9701	1.9740	50,000	4	$5	Won	5301.13	GBP Industrial/Man more bearish: Down move exhausted
4/5/2007	USD/JPY	118.69	118.99*	118.68	50,000	1	$5	Won	5316.46	Bought as broke pivot point but was a false breakout
4/5/2007	GBP/USD	1.9720	News Play	1.9685	**10,000**	−35	$1	Lost	5271.51	GBP Interest Rate Announcement
4/5/2007	EUR/GBP	0.6781	News Play	0.6787	**10,000**	6	$1	Won	5271.51	GBP Interest Rate Announcement
4/5/2007	GBP/USD	1.9699	1.9659	1.9709	50,000	10	$5	Won	5292.35	EUR broke key 1.3389/ GBP followed
4/5/2007	GBP/USD	1.9735	1.9705*	1.9730	50,000	−5		Lost	5323.49	Broke resistance at 1.9727 bought on retracement but gone back through
4/5/2007	EUR/USD	1.3430	1.3470	1.3424	50,000	6	$5	Won	5289.91	Retracement play after big move through res/pivot points
4/5/2007	EUR/USD	1.3422	1.3452	1.3419 (6th)	50,000	3	$5	Won	5330.07	GBP broke through 200 MA/ EUR testing it

4/10/2007	USD/CHF	1.2194	1.2167	1.2185 (11th)	75,000	−9	$7.50	Lost	5326.60	Broke back through 1.2191 5/10 min stocks turning up
4/10/2007	AUD/USD	0.8262	0.8292	0.8256	75,000	6	$7.50	Won	5337.16	15 min/5 min stocks turning/ RSI at 70–80/ all time high
4/10/2007	EUR/USD	1.3430	1.3460	1.3428	75,000	2	$7.50	Won	5341.24	Broken under 1/2 min 200 MA
4/11/2007	EUR/USD	1.3423	1.3453	1.3419	75,000	4	$7.50	Won	5356.83	Broke through 1,2/5 min 200MA / USD/CHF is rising
4/11/2007	GBP/USD	1.9770	1.9800	1.9768	75,000	2	$7.50	Won	5347.91	Broke through 1.9775
4/11/2007	EUR/USD	1.3425	1.3495	1.3426	75,000	1	$7.50	Won	5350.92	Broke through 200 MA 1 min but looked like find res.
4/11/2007	GBP/USD	1.9771	1.9801	1.9769	75,000	2	$7.50	Won	5356.62	FED speech no comments/broke 200 1 min MA/ 1.9775 pivot
4/11/2007	EUR/USD	1.3407	1.3437	1.3397	75,000		$7.50			FOMC meeting int. Rate may prove necessary next month
4/12/2007	GBP/USD	1.9778	1.9808	1.9783	75,000	−5	$7.50	Lost	5356.21	Renko 1 min uptrend formation broken: closed by accident
4/12/2007	AUD/USD	0.8252	0.8222	0.8253	75,000	1	$7.50	Won	5356.21	Broke 0.8250 pivot/ 5–10 min stocks turning up/ renko broken
4/12/2007	GBP/USD	1.9791	1.9823	1.9781	75,000	10	$7.50	Won	5356.21	Mistake: Hugging 10/15 min bands despite what 1 min says
4/12/2007	AUD/USD	0.8280	0.8310	0.8275	75,000	5	$7.50	Won	5356.21	Failed to break 13 yr high res. 0.8284
4/12/2007	USD/CHF	1.2153	1.2123	1.2159	75,000	6	$7.50	Won	5356.21	Retracement play after massive USD collapse
4/12/2007	AUD/USD	0.8289	0.8319	0.8287	75,000	2	$7.50	Won	5356.21	Broke from its uptrend failing/ 15 min stocks turning over
4/13/2007	USD/CHF	1.2144	1.2111	1.2145	75,000	1	$7.50	Won	5424.39	5 min/ 10 min stocks turning over – closed as mkt wknd close at 10pm
4/13/2007										No trading today helping Ispotek with filming

This trader had good initial strengths such as being able to have consecutive wins. A key weakness is not putting on a limit order, and therefore getting out too early. Ross is building key psychological skills in handling more money and facing the pressures that this entails.

LEVEL 3: THE $25,000 FIRST-50-TRADE CHALLENGE

This level of capital presents new opportunities and new challenges. A $25,000 account offers the opportunity to trade a combination of more pairs, larger sizes, and longer durations. More sophisticated strategies can be put to the test. The trader at this level of capital can trade more than one strategy. Therefore, we divide the trade challenge into two phases.

1. **Phase 1: Intraday Trading**
   a. Select two currency pairs to start trading.
   b. Raise your lot size to maximum of five lots. Remember to use five lots only when you have a high confidence level in the setup observed.
   c. Leave your risk per day at 3 percent.
   d. Set the goal to achieve an average pip gain of 10 pips for one pair and 20 pips for the second pair, per trade, for a 25-trade sequence.
   e. When using multiple lots, use an all-in and legging-out strategy.
2. **Phase 2: Multiple-Day Positions**
   a. Take the next 25 trades and focus on opportunities for 50-pip or more gains. This involves using the 4-hour chart to identify large trading ranges.

LEVEL 4: THE $50,000 75-TRADE CHALLENGE

A $50,000 account provides a serious capability to generate results that could provide a path to professional trading. The steps required to meet the challenges of a $50,000 account focus more on being able to handle the psychological pressures that emerge when more money is at stake. Many beginning traders put on too much leverage without first testing their skills in handling the larger risks per trade.

1. Scan all majors and cross-pairs to select to trade.
2. Raise your lot size to maximum of 30 mini lots (two standard-size lots).
3. For the first 25 trades, reduce risk per day to 2 percent.
4. For the first 25 trades, put on multiple lots but leave profit limits open on half of the lots.

LEVEL 5: THE $100,000 TRADING CHALLENGE

There are several challenges here within this level of account size that will enable a trader to prepare for full-time and professional trading. This level should be used if traders have achieved at least a 55-to-45 win-loss ratio. At this level, the trader has evolved to handle the pressures of trades that can result in gains or losses of $1000 per trade. For example, a 50-pip loss on a two-big-lot trade results in a $1000 loss. At a level of $100,000 in the account, such a size loss is 1 percent of the total. If the risk per day is 2 percent, the trader has to be very careful on the trades that follow.

1. Scan all majors and cross-pairs.
2. Use standard lot sizes, with a six-lot maximum.
3. For the first 25-trade sequence, have the goal of trading 7 trades in a row correctly, with a minimum pip gain of 10 pips; if this goal is achieved, repeat the goal of the next 25 trades.
4. For a sequence of 25 trades, put on trades only with the goal of 20 pips per trade.
5. Use a 2 percent risk per day for all trades.
6. Learn to optimize your trading setups by back-testing.

SUMMARY

Some traders will be comfortable with one strategy or focus on one pair. This is totally acceptable. Trading goals and styles should be customized to one's own personality. The purpose of trading more than one strategy is to enable the trader to become flexible and maximize the ability to spot winning trade situations. By scanning the seven majors and several cross-pairs during every day, trading opportunities occur. Market conditions change, and having more than one approach in one's trading tool box will be very useful.

CHAPTER 18

The Path to Success in Forex Trading

Ultimately, the knowledge gained in this book and in training in general needs to be applied to the real world. This involves taking practical steps and choosing a brokerage firm to trade with. Competitive pressures in the industry are narrowing the difference between firms in terms of pip spread, platform, and technology offered the trader. The really important determinants of success will involve how well traders are prepared before they start real trading, and whether the trading itself follows a sound action plan.

FACTORS IN CHOOSING A FIRM

While strategies and tactics are important, ultimately, the trades are placed at a forex firm. The industry is growing rapidly, and forex firms are available throughout the world. Selecting the right broker can make a difference. While there are essential features at most firms, the most important criteria for selection for a trader include the pip spread, dealing desk, customer service, and trading resources.

Pip spreads are rapidly becoming much narrower. Just a few years ago, five-pip spreads were the standard. Today two-pip spreads are available. Remember, if the spread is two pips, then the forex firm is still making money. They are offering you the currency pair with a built-in profit.

The industry is also evolving its dealing desk structure. Firms that have automatic dealing desks are becoming more common, allowing better spreads. But there is no free lunch. Remember, the firms make money on your trades. Customer service is critical. When the net freezes or you have a question about a trade, the ability to call someone on a 24-hour basis is important. Equally important is the ability to communicate. Some firms offer 24-hour service, but the trader connects to a barely competent English speaker. Tech support could be in a third world country. But trading resources is a major tipping point in choosing a firm. Most trading platforms have basic charting. The trader has to go to third-party providers to obtain charts such as three-line break and renko. Firms offering advanced charting packages and discounts on their cost is one criterion for choosing, particularly when accounts are traded with larger capital. Essentially, a good trader can trade profitably at any firm, but an average trader can improve his trading when choosing a better firm in terms of the total services he receives.

The trading environment used by the trader is more important than is usually recognized. Getting started the right way requires having a trading environment that serves the needs of the trade. Having two screens is a minimum suggested configuration. One screen should provide access to charts, and the second screen should enable access to Internet-based information and other activity. Having more than two is not unusual among more serious traders. The forex trader beginning today can use any new computer due to the advances in computer speed and capability. The most important aspect of organizing your own trading room is whether it is dedicated to the trader. The trading room should be isolated from family interference. Trading with kids running around is too distractive. Today's Internet connections provide easy access via high-speed links (DSL, digital cable, etc.). Trading through a dial-up should be avoided, but it can be used as a backup.

GAUGING PERFORMANCE: KNOW THYSELF

Central bank of New Zealand The path to success in forex trading is not measured by profitability alone. Those traders who become profitable have the challenge of consistency. Can they do it over a sustained period of time? The duration of successful trading also requires adaptability. Conditions change in the geopolitical world and its global economic cycles that significantly impact forex. Those who are successful during periods of global growth may not be able to use the same strategies during periods of global stagnation. The key skill of identifying macro conditions comes into play to provide early warnings to reassess trading strategies or choose different currency pairs. If China enters into a slowdown, the forex trader will be very careful about going long on the Australian dollar. If oil is trending up toward the $75+ level, the experienced trader may start including the strategy of going long the Canadian dollar. If the trader observes that Japan's economic performance is showing growth and inflationary tendencies, those favoring carry trades will significantly lighten their leverage or turn to other pairs to avoid equity volatility.

Becoming more successful in forex trading is also about being *efficient.* Two traders may have the same performance record of profitability, but they are not equal in success. The trader who has achieved the pip accumulation with less time is more efficient. Consider two traders who have the same profitability but different win-loss ratios. One trader wins 60 percent of the time, and the other wins 40 percent of the time. Which one is more successful? By measure of profitability, they are equal. But there are huge distinctions in other qualities associated with the trade. The 60/40 trader has a much wider freedom of trading action than the 40/60 trader. The later has to win big and lose small—almost all the time.

One thing that is critical on the path to success in forex trading is what happens after the trade. Being able to evaluate trading performance and apply the new knowledge gained about yourself will be essential to improving. The ability to improve depends on the ability to evaluate.

Performance evaluation needs to avoid being overloaded with information that doesn't lead to improvements. Here are some performance evaluation measures that traders should be able to have regarding their own trading history.

Measuring Performance

To help gauge your performance, the following objective measures should be used:

- Win-loss ratio, standard
- Win-loss ratio, adjusted
- Average win
- Average loss
- Average duration of the winning trade
- Average duration of the losing trade
- Average stop loss distance from entry
- Average profit limit

Measuring Emotional Intelligence

While it is conventional wisdom that emotions are not beneficial to trading, the fact is that they are used by all traders. We are—in the words of Marvin Minsky, one of the founders of the artificial intelligence field—an emotional machine. The profitable trader is using emotions to his advantage. The new trader needs to obtain a high level of confidence about how he or she trades. This is, in fact, a use of emotional intelligence. We reviewed how to rank your trades by confidence level. The goal is to determine what kind of emotional trader you are. Are your winning trades hunch trades, or are they trades that are taken on excellent setup conditions? The effective hunch trader is a very rare species because hunches are hard to replicate. So it becomes important to know the following:

- Distribution of wining trades by level of confidence
- Distribution of losing trades by level of confidence

Compare your first 50 trades against your second 50 trades in terms of how confident you were when you put on the trades. There is a natural shift in percentage of winning trades being highly ranked setups versus hunch trades.

Measuring Performance with the Learn4x Trading Pad

Learn4x has created its own trading pad (Figures 18.1 and 18.2) that provides the ability to have real-time trades in a simulated account. The pad, which can be downloaded at www.learn4x.com/tradingpad, uniquely offers built-in analytics on trader performance, allowing the trader to track the key performance results. The Learn4x trading pad is independent of any Forex brokerage firm and receives the real-time prices from its own feed supplied by Tenfore Systems, a world feed provider.

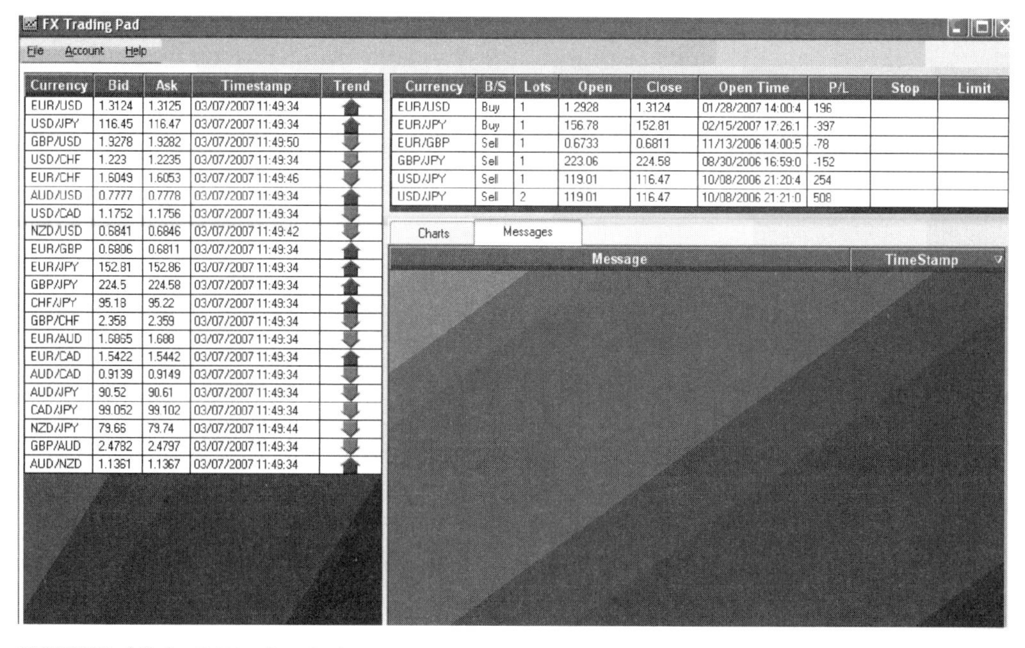

FIGURE 18.1 FX Trading Pad.

Trade Analytics

Total Trades:	56
Winning Trades:	17
Losing Trades:	39
Win/Loss Ratio:	30.4%
Average Profit:	$2,804.66
Average Loss:	($1,328.04)
Average Profit Term:	34,551 minutes
Average Loss Term:	35,018 minutes
Biggest Profit:	$12,077.89
Biggest Loss:	($11,077.98)
Sharpe Ratio:	-4.26
Sortino Ratio:	-4.63

FIGURE 18.2 Performance Analytics.

IN CONCLUSION

Successful Forex trading is not an end; it is an evolving process. It is not easy, but it is achievable.

This book is designed to point the way. Learning to trade forex is very much a self-paced process. There are few shortcuts, but the goal of this book has been to provide guideposts though the fundamental, technical, and psychological pathways that all traders must experience. It is my hope that you have gained an understanding and appreciation of the world of forex and can now use that knowledge to pursue one of the most challenging endeavors available to any individual—forex trading.

CHAPTER 19

Test Your Forex IQ

The following questions test the knowledge you've acquired by reading this book. You are able to take this quiz, place your responses, and find the answers, as well as new questions, at www.learn4x.com/forex IQ. E-mail Abe Cofnas at learn4x@earthlink.net with any questions you may have. Good luck!

1. What is the index that tracks U.S. dollar as an instrument for trading?
2. Which currency pairs are closely related to movements in gold, and which commodities are closely related to movements in the U.S. dollar?
3. Can you name the heads of the world's key central banks?
4. Which time interval is the best for entering a trade?
5. What is the technical basis for locating a stop loss?
6. What are the four strategies for trading a sideways pattern?
7. What information does a candlestick pattern provide that is not in a bar chart?
8. How do you measure sentiment in forex?
9. What is the best time of the day to trade?
10. When is countertrend trading less risky?
11. Which Fibonacci level is the most important?
12. What is the most important report that affects trading the yen, and when does it come out?
13. When the Federal Reserve Open Market Committee meets, what does it decide?
14. What is the name of the Chinese currency?

15. What is the gross national product of the United States versus Europe versus Japan?
16. What is the current interest rate difference between the 10-year U.S. Treasury note and the 3-month Treasury note?
17. Which currency pair allows you to trade the British pound against the euro?
18. When trading forex, what is the cost of the trade when there is no commission?
19. What are the two basic trading strategies for buying or selling that apply to any time frame?
20. If forex prices surge or plunge in response to news, how long should you wait to enter a trade?
21. What's the major problem with using moving averages?
22. What is the average duration of a profitable trade generating 20 pips?
23. When you see a parabolic pattern, what does it predict about the imminent movement of the market?
24. What is the most important fundamental piece of information to track before you decide to trade a currency pair?
25. How do you obtain free and professional advice?
26. How is a cross-pair different than the majors?
27. What pattern always precedes a break of support or resistance?
28. What is the definition of a "false" breakout?
29. What is the best way to spot a trend reversal?
30. If oil prices surge, which currency pair is the most affected?
31. If the Chinese economy slows down or enters a "hard landing," which currency pair is the most affected?
32. Which indicator compares the performance of two different trading systems?
33. Which indicator effectively confirms a reversal?
34. What pattern indicates volatility exhaustion?
35. Which economic calendar release is the most important?
36. How do G7 and G20 meetings affect your forex trading?
37. If gold goes into a downtrend, how do you use gold patterns to determine which currency pair to buy?
38. Which key moving average period should be watched to indicate a trend reversal?
39. When are technical indicators totally useless in determining your next trade?
40. If you are looking at three different time frames, which ones should they be?
41. Which pattern is almost always a reliable predictor of the next move in a currency?

42. Which indicator is the most leading regarding price direction?
43. Which six currencies comprise the U.S. Dollar Index?
44. The index that shows a currency's strength in terms of the country's trading relationship is called ___________.
45. What is the formula for pivot points?
46. Which chart type leaves out time and volume?
47. Which pattern is usually a prelude to a breakout?
48. Name an indicator that shows volatility besides Bollinger bands.
49. The Chinese currency is called the renminbi yuan. What is its value against the U.S. dollar?
50. A trader is losing 70 percent of his trades but claims he is as good as a trader having a win-loss ratio of 60 percent winners. What are their comparable win-loss ratios?
51. If an economic data release is coming out on the British economy and a trader wants to trade it both ways, he will buy the GBPUSD and what other pair?
52. What economic data release report is the most important one issued by the Bank of Japan?
53. What report provides data on foreign owners of U.S. Treasury securities?
54. Who is Japan's biggest trading partner?
55. What is the next number of the following Fibonacci sequence: 0, 1, 2, 3, 5, 8, 13, 21, 34, 55, 89, 144, 233, ___________.
56. What is the ratio between any two Fibonacci numbers?
57. In a recent equity market sell-off, the Dow Jones Index went down, the dollar against the yen fell sharply, and gold fell also. Why?
58. Regarding currencies, what futures industry report provides a clue to where the smart money is?
59. If you wanted to have a 99 percent confidence that the price is between two Bollinger bands, how many standard deviations would it be set at?
60. If the USDX broke support and the trade-weighted USDX did not, which would you use to put on your next trade?
61. What is the difference between a slow stochastic and a fast stochastic?
62. Which is a more aggressive trade: (a) selling before support, anticipating a move down; or (b) selling on the break of support?
63. Which developed country (not third world) has the highest interest rates in the world?

64. If the EURUSD is priced at 1.3150 and a European goes to Disney world in Orlando, how many dollars will he be able to get (assuming no exchange costs)?
65. What does repatriation refer to within the context of the Japanese yen?
66. What technical indicators are leading?
67. If housing starts in the United States showed a surprise increase, what would you expect the EURUSD to do in reaction to this release?
68. If China unexpectedly increased interest rates, which direction would you expect the USDJPY to go?
69. If a trader is using two moving averages, the Simple MA 21 and the simple MA 8, and the SMA 8 rises above the SMA21, is this a signal to go long?
70. If a currency pair closes above the 38.2 percent day fib line, is it more likely to reach the next fib line at 50 percent?
71. If a currency pair reaches the 20-period moving average in the middle of a Bollinger band, and crosses it, is this a signal to sell?
72. If a trader missed a news release and saw the price surge, how many minutes should he wait to enter a trade?
73. If the amount of foreign owners of U.S. Treasury securities significantly declined, what would likely happen to U.S. interest rates?
74. What happens to the value of the average true range when one moves from a 5-minute chart to a 30-minute chart?
75. If the United States increases the rate of exports, what happens to the trade deficit?
76. If a triangle formation forms and it is equilateral, in which direction is the price most likely to break out?
77. If a price is probing a four-hour resistance, does this represent stronger resistance than a price probing a five-minute resistance?
78. If a doji pattern appears at the top of a Bollinger band, is it indicating a reversal?
79. Which has a greater interest rate differential the USCHF pair or the EURCHF pair?
80. If a trader was able to save one pip per trade on the spread and traded five times a day for 100 days, what would the value of the saving be if he were trading the AUDUSD only?
81. Which equity market opens up first, the Tokyo or London?
82. When it is 8:30 A.M. Eastern Standard Time and the nonfarm payroll report is released, what time is it Greenwich Mean Time?
83. Joe put on a sell limit order for the GBPUSD at 1.9205 and he saw on his chart that the price hit limit. He didn't get it, though. Did the forex firm make a mistake?

84. What is slippage?
85. When three or more multiple moving averages compress in a pancake pattern, what does this signify?
86. The default setting on MACD is 12, 26, 9. What do these numbers represent?
87. John came up with his own moving average crossover of 95 and five simple moving averages. He decided to back test it over three years and the result came out quite positive. What is wrong with his approach?
88. Bob signed up to get a news trading report that provides a few seconds' more release of the embargoed economic data on a news release. Will this make a difference in the trading results?
89. Why is holding a position over a weekend very risky?
90. If the yen suddenly sells off and gets weaker, what is gold likely to do and why?
91. A change in the demand for copper affects which currency the most?
92. The ZEW sentiment indicator represents what kind of sentiment?
93. If the Indian rupee starts floating, what is the major risk to their currency reserves?
94. If China increases its value of the renminbi, what would the impact be on Wal-Mart shares?
95. If the EURJPY reaches historical highs, who would be more pleased, European car manufacturers or Japanese car manufacturers?
96. New Zealand has had the second highest interest rates in the world, at 7.25 percent. If they lowered the rate, what would happen to the yen?
97. Jim is trading at an account that is offering 200-to-1 leverage. He has $1000 in his account. How much can he trade with this 1000 without getting a margin call?
98. If crude oil prices collapsed, which country would benefit the most?
99. Tom went long the EURUSD at 1.305 and the price moved to 1.3015. Where would the break even point be if Tom wanted to put a stop there?
100. If the setting for a renko chart was moved from one pips to two pips, and the action was very choppy, what would be the result on the chart?

APPENDIX

Selected *Futures* Columns

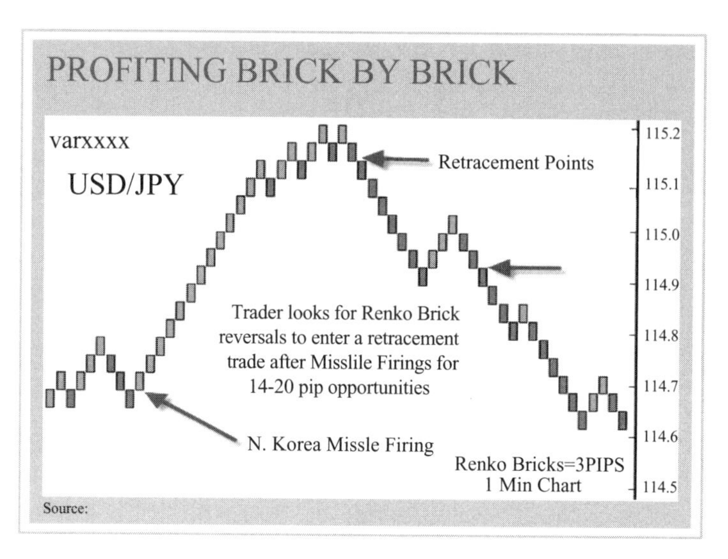
PROFITING BRICK BY BRICK
varxxxx
USD/JPY
Retracement Points
Trader looks for Renko Brick reversals to enter a retracement trade after Misslile Firings for 14-20 pip opportunities
N. Korea Missle Firing
Renko Bricks=3PIPS
1 Min Chart
115.2
115.1
115.0
114.9
114.8
114.7
114.6
114.5
Source:

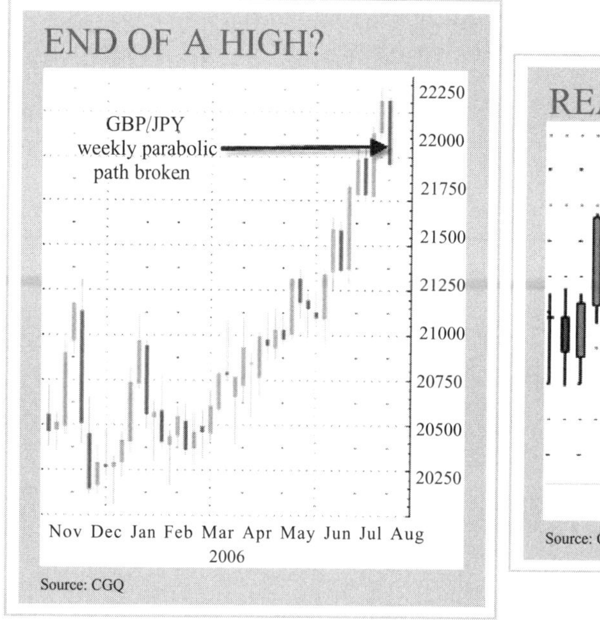
END OF A HIGH?
GBP/JPY weekly parabolic path broken
22250
22000
21750
21500
21250
21000
20750
20500
20250
Nov Dec Jan Feb Mar Apr May Jun Jul Aug
2006
Source: CGQ

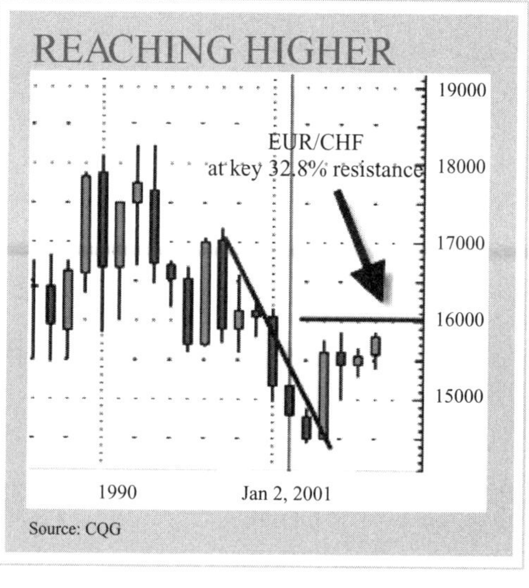
REACHING HIGHER
EUR/CHF at key 32.8% resistance
19000
18000
17000
16000
15000
1990
Jan 2, 2001
Source: CQG

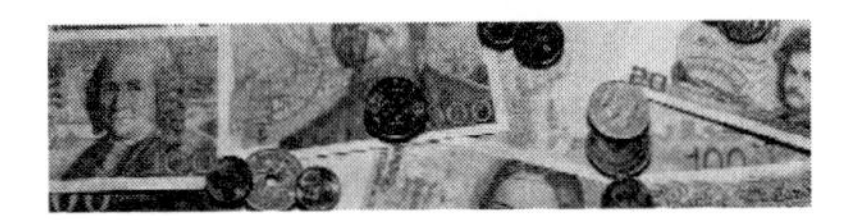

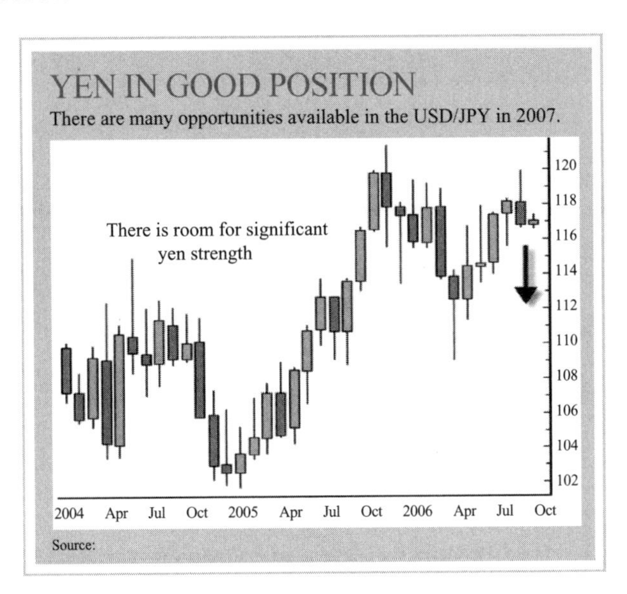
YEN IN GOOD POSITION
There are many opportunities available in the USD/JPY in 2007.
There is room for significant yen strength
120
118
116
114
112
110
108
106
104
102
2004 Apr Jul Oct 2005 Apr Jul Oct 2006 Apr Jul Oct
Source:

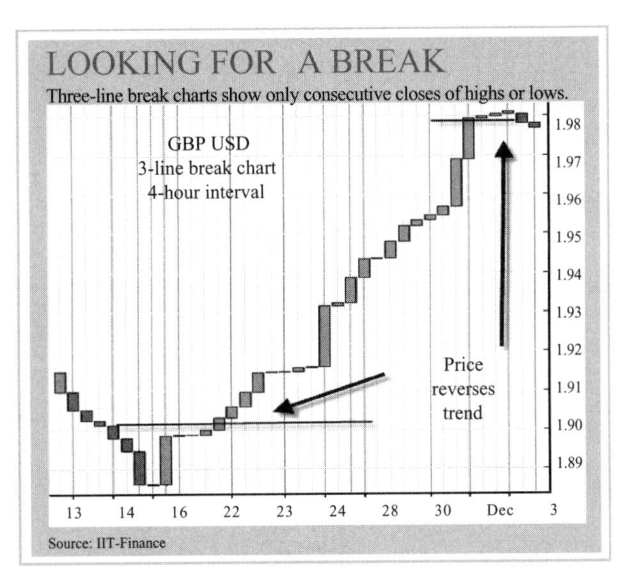
LOOKING FOR A BREAK
Three-line break charts show only consecutive closes of highs or lows.
GBP USD
3-line break chart
4-hour interval
Price reverses trend
1.98
1.97
1.96
1.95
1.94
1.93
1.92
1.91
1.90
1.89
13 14 16 22 23 24 28 30 Dec 3
Source: IIT-Finance

DIVIDING THE DOLLAR

CURRENCY	USDX TRADE WEIGHT	IBOXXFX TRADE WEIGHT
EUR	57.60%	35.70%
YEN	13.60%	19.82%
POUND	11.90%	9.52%
CAD	9.10%	32.17%
SWEDISH KRONA	4.20%	0%
SWISS FRANC	3.60%	2.79%

Source:

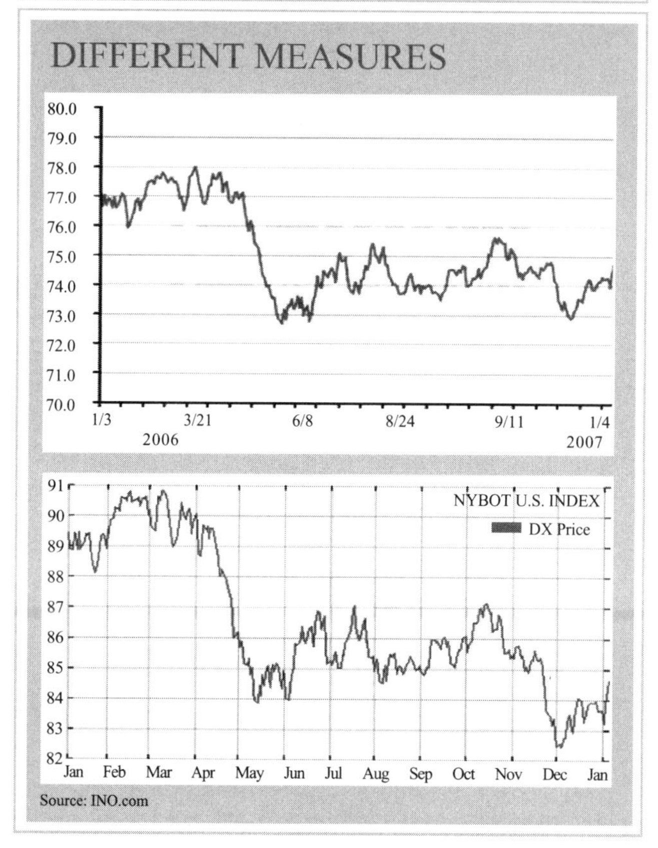

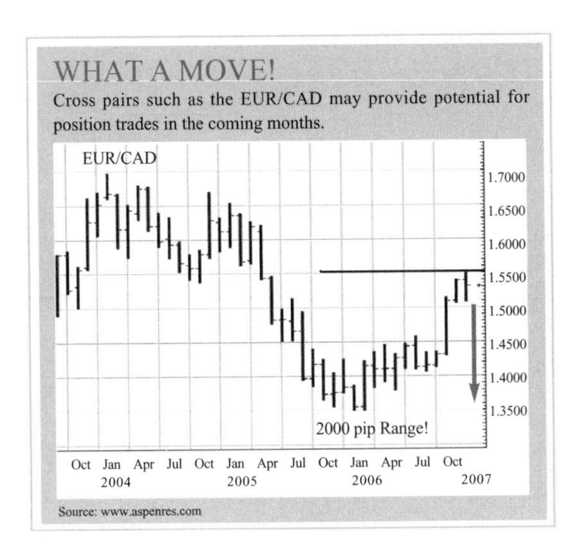
WHAT A MOVE!
Cross pairs such as the EUR/CAD may provide potential for position trades in the coming months.
EUR/CAD
1.7000
1.6500
1.6000
1.5500
1.5000
1.4500
1.4000
1.3500
2000 pip Range!
Oct Jan Apr Jul Oct Jan Apr Jul Oct Jan Apr Jul Oct
2004 2005 2006 2007
Source: www.aspenres.com

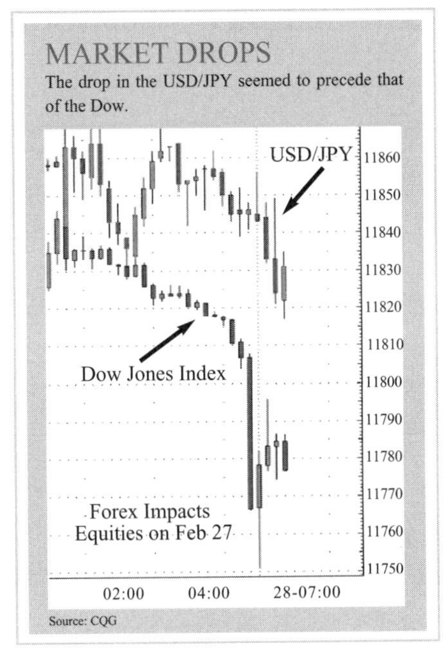
MARKET DROPS
The drop in the USD/JPY seemed to precede that of the Dow.
USD/JPY
11860
11850
11840
11830
11820
11810
11800
11790
11780
11770
11760
11750
Dow Jones Index
Forex Impacts
Equities on Feb 27
02:00 04:00 28-07:00
Source: CQG

Index

F

I

J

K

L

T

U

V

W